UNREGULATED BANKING

Also edited by Forrest Capie and Geoffrey E. Wood and published by St. Martin's:

FINANCIAL CRISES AND THE WORLD BANKING SYSTEM
INTERWAR MONETARY EXPERIENCE

Unregulated Banking

Chaos or Order?

Edited by

Forrest Capie
Professor of Economic History
The City University, London

and

Geoffrey E. Wood
Professor of Economics
The City University, London

Foreword by Gordon Pepper
Director, Midland Montagu Centre for Financial Markets
City University Business School

St. Martin's Press   New York

Scholarly and Reference Division,
St. Martin's Press, Inc., 175 Fifth Avenue,
New York, NY 10010

First published in the United States of America in 1991

Printed in Hong Kong

ISBN 0–312–05317–7

Library of Congress Cataloging-in-Publication Data
Unregulated banking: chaos or order? / edited by Forrest Capie and
Geoffrey E. Wood.
p. cm.
Includes index.
ISBN 0–312–05317–7
1. Banks and banking—Deregulation—History.   I. Capie, Forrest.
II. Wood, Geoffrey Edward.
HG1551.U57   1991
332.1—dc20
90–44988
CIP

Contents

Foreword

If any industry requires regulation it might be thought to be banking. The proposal for unregulated banking is the sort of thing one might expect from the very fringe of free market economics. But there is more to it than that.

In the US regulation of interest rates was one of the original causes of the current financial plight of the savings and loans industry. Further, the US regulations which have stopped banks from spreading risk, by diversifying either into other states or businesses, may have contributed to certain financial problems. Launches of lifeboats to rescue an individual bank have also led to the well-known problem of *moral hazard*. Also, regulators can hinder the private sector from assessing credit risk; if information is not published, the private sector may have no option but to rely on the regulator, and claims for compensation are bound to occur if a regulator slips up. More generally, there is considerable evidence from other industries that regulation ends up protecting producers rather than consumers; industries tend to encapture their regulators.

Whereas there may be doubts about the efficiency of banking regulation in general, surely the lender of last resort function of a central bank is above reproach? Even here it is possible that control of a central bank's own balance sheet might prevent financial bubbles from building up and, therefore, subsequent bursts and crises; such control might avoid the creation of the macro-financial conditions under which a chain reaction cannot be prevented if an individual bank is allowed to fail. But it would still be wise to retain a lender of last resort.

Finally, if competition between currencies is valid for Europe, is there a case for allowing competition within a country? Heresy!

The Midland Montagu Centre for Financial Markets was pleased to have underwritten the Conference. Do read this provocative book. The papers and the discussants' critical comments will stimulate thought.

GORDON PEPPER
Director
Midland Montagu Centre for Financial Markets
City University Business School

Notes on the Contributors

W. A. Allen is head of the Money Markets Operations Division, Bank of England. He was educated at Balliol College, Oxford, and the London School of Economics. He joined the Bank of England in 1972. He has worked in the Economic Intelligence Department, 1972–7, and in the Gold and Foreign Exchange Office, 1977–8, and was seconded to the Bank for International Settlements, Basle, 1978–80. He then returned to the Bank of England, where he worked in the Economics Division, 1980–2 (responsible for monetary policy analysis), and as Senior Manager, Gilt-Edged Division, 1982–6. He became Head of the Money Market Operations Division in 1986.

George J. Benston is the John H. Harland Professor of Finance, Accounting, and Economics in the School of Business, and Professor of Economics in the College of Arts and Sciences, Emory University, and Honourary Visiting Professor at City University (London). Before going to Emory in 1987 he was on the faculties of the University of Rochester (for 21 years), and the University of Chicago, and has been the John M. Olin Distinguished Visiting Fellow at Oxford University and a visiting professor at the London School of Economics, the London Graduate School of Business Studies, Hebrew University and Berkeley. He received his PhD from the University of Chicago, his MBA from New York University, and his BA from Queens College. He has published twenty-nine books, monographs, and articles in academic journals in accounting, forty-nine in finance, six on urban studies and twelve in economics. His latest book is *The Separation of Commercial and Investment Banking: the Glass-Steagall Act Revisited and Reconsidered*.

Michael D. Bordo is Professor of Economics at Rutgers University. He previously taught at the University of South Carolina (1981–9) and Carleton University (1969–81). Professor Bordo has published widely in major journals concerned with monetary economics, economic history and international finance, and has authored or co-authored several books. A Research Associate at the National Bureau of Economic Research since 1982, he also serves on the editorial board of two leading journals in economic history. He has a strong interest in economic policy. He was a visiting scholar at the

Federal Reserve Banks of St Louis and Richmond and served on the research staff for the US Congressional Gold Commission.

Didier Bruneel is Deputy General Manager of the Research Department at the Bank of France and Deputy General Secretary of the Conseil National du Crédit. A graduate of the University of Paris II and of the Institut d'Etudes Politiques de Paris, he taught at the University of Paris I, at the Centre d'Etudes Supérieures de Banque and at the Institut des Techniques de Marches. He is the author of numerous articles and papers on monetary economics.

Forrest Capie is Professor of Economic History and Head of Department of Banking and International Finance at City University, London. Following graduate studies at the London School of Economics, he taught at the Universities of Warwick and Leeds. He has published several books and over fifty articles in the fields of money, banking and international trade.

K. Alec Chrystal is National Westminster Bank Professor at City University Business School. He was previously Professor of Economics at the University of Sheffield, and has also taught at Manchester and Essex Universities, the University of California at Davis and the Civil Service College, London. He was visiting scholar at the Federal Reserve Bank of St Louis, 1983–4, and has published widely in the fields of money, macroeconomics and finance.

Michael Collins is Senior Lecturer in Economic History at the School of Business and Economic Studies, University of Leeds. He is a specialist on British monetary history and has published extensively on the nineteenth century. His recently published book is entitled, *Money and Banking in the UK: A History*, and he is currently working on the role of banks in the provision of industrial loans.

James A. Dorn is Vice-president for Academic Affairs at the Cato Institute, Editor of the *Cato Journal*, and Director of the Cato Institute's annual monetary conference. He is also a Research Fellow of the Institute for Humane Studies at George Mason University and Professor of Economics at Towson State University. He has served on the White House Commission on Presidential Scholars. Recent publications include *The Search for Stable Money* (co-edited with Anna J. Schwartz) and *Dollars, Deficits, and Trade* (co-edited with William A. Niskanen).

Kevin Dowd is a lecturer in economics at the University of Nottingham. He was previously an economic policy analyst on the Ontario Economic Council and a lecturer in economics at the University of Sheffield. Dr Dowd's main research interests are in monetary and macroeconomics, and he has recently published *The State and the Monetary System* (Philip Allan, Oxford, 1989), on free banking.

Charles A. E. Goodhart is the Norman Sosnow Professor of Banking and Finance at the London School of Economics. Before joining the LSE in 1985 he worked at the Bank of England for 17 years as a monetary adviser, becoming a Chief Adviser in 1980. Earlier he had taught at Cambridge and LSE. He has written two books on monetary history; he has just revised his graduate monetary textbook, *Money Information and Uncertainty* (1989), and his institutional study *The Evolution of Central Banks*, was revised and republished (MIT Press) in 1988.

Sir Peter Middleton, GCB, is currently Permanent Secretary to the Treasury. He graduated from Sheffield and Bristol Universities. In 1962 he joined the Treasury as Senior Information Officer; in 1967–9 he was Assistant Director, Centre for Administration Studies; during 1969–72 Private Secretary to the Chancellor of the Exchequer; from 1972 to 1975 Treasury Press Secretary; in 1975 Head of the Monetary Division; and in 1976 Under Secretary. A Member of the Council, Manchester Business School, from 1984 he has been Governor, London Business School and from 1985 of the Ditchley Foundation.

Charles W. Munn is Secretary to the Institute of Bankers in Scotland. He is a graduate of the University of Strathclyde and the University of Glasgow. A former employee of a Scottish bank, he is also a qualified member of the Institute of which he is now Secretary. From 1978 to 1988 he was lecturer and then senior lecturer in the Department of Economic History at the University of Glasgow, where he devised and taught courses on the development of financial institutions and business history. He is the author of two books and several articles on the history of banking and was associate editor of *The Scottish Dictionary of Business Biography*.

Leslie Pressnell has held appointments in economics and economic history in several universities. He is at present a member of the Cabinet Office Historical Section, and is preparing an official history of post-war economic policy, the first volume of which, *The Post-War Financial Settlement*, was published by HMSO in 1987.

Hugh Rockoff is Professor of Economics at Rutgers University in New Brunswick, New Jersey. He is the author of three books and numerous articles in professional journals on banking, monetary, and price history.

Dr Anna J. Schwartz has been a member of the research staff of the National Bureau of Economic Research for many years. She is the co-author with Milton Friedman of the classic study, *A Monetary History of the United States, 1867–1960*, as well as of *Monetary Trends in the United States and the United Kingdom*. She was also a co-author with Arthur D. Gayer and Walt W. Rostow of a study of fluctuations in the British economy in the first half of the nineteenth century. A collection of her articles, *Money in Historical Perspective*, was published by the University of Chicago Press in 1987

Eugene N. White is Associate Professor of Economics at Rutgers University in New Brunswick, New Jersey. In addition, he has taught at New York University and lectured widely in Europe and South America. He is the author of *The Regulation and Reform of the American Banking System, 1900–1929* and has recently edited *The Stock Market Crash in Historical Perspective*. He has also written many articles on nineteenth- and twentieth-century American banking and financial history. His current research is on the monetary and financial history of the French Revolution.

Lawrence H. White is Associate Professor of Economics at the University of Georgia. He is the author of *Free Banking in Britain* (Cambridge University Press, 1984), *Competition and Currency* (New York University Press, 1989), and numerous articles in professional journals and conference volumes. Dr White is presently at work on a book to be entitled *The Theory of Monetary Institutions* (Basil Blackwell).

Geoffrey E. Wood is Professor of Economics at City University, London. A graduate of Aberdeen and Essex Universities, he has taught at the University of Warwick, and been a member of the research departments of the Bank of England and the Federal Reserve Bank of St Louis. He has also written or edited several books, and is the author of over fifty articles on monetary economics.

Introduction

The EC's Second Banking Directive (of 1988) has two aspects. There is a 'home country' rule for bank authorization, while 'conduct of business' rules are determined by the host nation. The distinction between the two types of rule is made very clearly in the report of the House of Commons Trade and Industry Committee (1989):

> Regulatory régimes comprise two main components. First, arrangements to review the 'fitness and properness' of a firm's management; and to ensure that a firm has adequate financial resources – in terms for example, a capital and liquidity – to support the volume and character of the business it is undertaking; and second, a body of principles, guidelines or rules governing the relationship between the firm and its customers and the market (so-called 'conduct of business' rules). The regulatory requirements can distinguish between those who can be expected to look after themselves and the less sophisticated investors who cannot.

That report went on to argue. 'To harmonise all conduct of business rules will be a long process since they are deeply rooted in local law and custom. The UK has therefore taken the view that conduct of business rules of this type should remain the responsibility of the host state, pending an adequate degree of harmonisation.'

Originally a simple 'home country rule', which would permit an EC bank to do anywhere in the EC whatever it was allowed to do in its home country, was proposed. The likely implications of this for the structure of the banking industry in Europe would have been considerable. But would the changes enhance or diminish the stability of that industry? What would the regulatory implications of the changes be? This conference considered the issue of regulation in banking and examined different historical experiences with types and extent of regulation. Understanding these experiences is of great importance in planning future regulation, and changes in regulation, of banking.

In this introductory chapter we first consider why banks are regulated. That leads to an examination of what restrictions bank regulators impose, and then to problems regulators face. First, a definition of regulation is useful. George Stigler has provided a most useful one. It is, 'any policy which alters market outcomes by the exercise of some coercive government power'. Two features of that definition are worthy of note.

It distinguishes clearly between influences on outcomes by coercion and by incentive – tax and subsidy policy may well be intended to 'influence market outcomes', but it is not regulation. Second, and very important, it contains no hint of the *direction* of influence (towards or away from a competitive structure), or of who its beneficiaries might me.

Both features are important. The first narrows the area of discussion most usefully. The second reminds us that there are two sharply contrasting theories of regulation. What is best thought of as the economist's traditional view of regulation has recently been set out very clearly by John Kay and John Vickers (1988). They sum up the traditional view by a simple maxim: 'Competition when possible, regulation where necessary' (p. 287). Regulation, in that view, seeks to identify market failures that prevent an industry from functioning competitively, and to correct these failures.

Regulation can thus be of either structure or of conduct. There can be regulation by some public authority, self-regulation, or regulation within a statutory framework. But whoever does it, and whether it be of structure or of conduct, regulation should on this view be targeted on market failure. That is of course a normative theory of regulation – it tells us what regulation 'ought' to do.

The second approach is identified particularly with George Stigler. He asked, in a pioneering series of studies (e.g. 1962, 1964, 1971), what regulation actually achieves. Who does it benefit and who does it harm? Over a wide range of industries (not, it is worth emphasizing, including banking) he has found that regulation was either totally ineffective or worked to the benefit of existing firms in the industry. It did not eliminate harmful market failures. These results have led to the view that regulation, ostensibly intended to benefit the consumer, is often encouraged by producer groups as a way of restricting competition.

Both views of regulation are worth taking seriously; both yield predictions on the scope of regulatory constraints on the financial sector. Before we turn to discussion of these approaches, however, it is useful to consider just why that sector of the economy is thought to be so special.

WHY BANKS MATTER

It is useful to clarify why there is concern with banks to a much greater degree than with other firms. The basic reason is that the failure of one bank can lead to the failure of another, perhaps the collapse of the whole system, and, via the working of the money multiplier, a collapse in the stock of money. This chain of events comes about because depositors are led to fear that their bank is not safe if they see one bank failing. They therefore fly to cash, and, as banks operate on a fractional reserve system, banks which are solvent, and liquid enough for normal times, are brought down by a surge in the demand for liquid money.

This danger was diagnosed, and the remedy set out, in the nineteenth century. Henry Thornton provided a clear but uninfluential statement of what to do. Subsequently Water Bagehot, by a series of articles in the *Economist*, and subsequently in *Lombard Street*, persuaded the Bank of England to act as 'lender of last resort'. This implies lending cash *on security to the banking system* in the event of a run for cash on the part of the public.

A vivid description of a central bank acting as lender of last resort is provided by Jeremiah Harman, a director of the Bank of England at the time of the panic of 1825:

> We lent it (i.e. gold) by every possible means and in modes we had never adopted before; we took in stock on security, we purchased Exchequer Bills, we not only discounted outright but we made advances on the deposit of bills of exchange to an immense amount, in short, by every possible means consistent with the safety of the Bank, and we were not on some occasions over nice. Seeing the dreadful state in which the public were, we rendered every assistance in our power (quoted in Bagehot, p. 73 of the 1873 edition).

This policy worked then, and has worked subsequently. There is no need for central banks to go further, and engage in supervision and regulation to maintain the stability of the banking system. Such detailed inspection of banks is necessary to prevent moral hazard only if individual institutions are implicitly underwritten by the central bank, and it is a crucial part of the 'Baghehot Rule' that they are not. Why, then, are banks regulated?

REGULATION

The Traditional View

Traditional analysis distinguishes between externalities and market power as sources of divergence from the competitive ideal (see Bator, 1958). More recently, asymmetric information has been added as a third source of market failure. These information problems are the principal rationale for the regulation of financial services. But there are also important externalities in this area. There is one between customers, and another, closely related to the first, between firms.

If a large number of depositors all simultaneously seek to withdraw their funds from a bank, there is a possibility that the bank will have insufficient funds to meet their claims. There is a clear negative externality between depositors – one gains at the expense of another. Indeed, two sources of market failure are endemic to the financial system.

There is almost inevitably asymmetric information between buyers and seller – a bank management knows more about its balance sheet than even the best-informed depositor. Second, there is considerable benefit to the economy as a whole in sustaining confidence in the financial system. The maintenance of confidence in the banking system and the avoidance of bank runs are major benefits to the nation at large. (Any doubts on this are readily dispelled by reading Milton Friedman and Anna Schwartz's account of the consequences of a wave of bank failures in the United States. See Friedman and Schwartz, 1963, ch. 7.)

In terms of encouraging confidence in the system, and promoting its stability, the above argument would seem to point the following conclusions. Structure should be regulated so as to enhance the stability of the key elements of the banking system – these being banks which take deposits from the public and are responsible for maintaining the money supply. Measures of capital adequacy should therefore be developed, and attention devoted to developing measures of the riskiness of *portfolios*, i.e. both assets *and* liabilities. Deposit insurance could be important. There should be rules for capital adequacy because of the existence of externalities. We may wish to encourange competing regulatory domains, for consumers can then choose where to buy these services. There could be self-regulation; reputation is an investment, but self-regulation may be required to produce adequate investment in it because of the externality aspects.

This view sees regulation as a way of eliminating or reducing market failure. The alternative view sees regulation, whatever its intentions, as in fact *producing* market failure – of producing monopoly profits. How is that done? The essence of monopoly is that new entry is difficult – in the (rare) case of natural monopoly, impossible.

The Stiglerian approach

How could a regulatory regime discourage new entry to banking? There are three obvious routes, again concerned with regulation of structure and regulation of conduct. Essentially, all would operate to make entry, except on a large scale, very difficult.

Structure regulation would allow nationwide branching. With nationwide branch networks to compete against, a small entrant to commercial banking would find it difficult to threaten well-established firms. Substantial capital adequacy requirements would exercise a similar deterrent effect. There should be a good measure of self-regulation, for the existing members could make entrance to the club difficult. Thus it appears that self-interest would plainly lead to regulatory proposals similar in outline to those that would be produced by public interest.

THE QUESTIONS

This brief review of the area leads to two main sets of questions. The first is plain. Bank regulation generally takes the form that self-interested monopolists would desire. Lender of last resort action, admitted so far as necessary, does not require supervision and regulation. So why is there supervision and regulation? Does it achieve some ends more widely desired than the protection of monopoly? Does it contribute in some way to the stability of the banking system?

Several of the papers in this volume address these questions by looking at particular episodes. See the papers by Lawrence White, Eugene White, Kevin Dowd, and Hugh Rockoff. George Benston also takes up these questions, and, on the basis of study of a range of US experience, directly asks the question, 'Does regulation produce stability?'

There is also, however, another question concerning the stability of the banking system. The above discussion accepted that a lender of last resort was necessary to prevent financial crises. Several authors have recently argued that it is not; and that, indeed, monetary performance has been worse when a central bank is present than when it is not. Charles Goodhart focuses exclusively on this question; and discussion of it is also contained, with regard to particular episodes, in the papers by Lawrence White and by Eugene White, and by Hugh Rockoff.

Having thus outlined the main lines of discussion in this volume, we turn to a brief outline of the individual papers.

THE PAPERS

In 1984 Lawrence White published his book *Free Banking in Britain*, a book that helped stimulate closer examination of the experience of free banking in Scotland. The traditional view of Scottish banking in this period was that its financial institutions and practices were essentially those of an unregulated free-market monetary system, and White lent support to this in his elegant study. The view did not go unchallenged. Critics offered alternative interpretations, pointing to the fact that important Scottish banks and the Bank of England played quietly controlling roles.

Lawrence White's paper in this volume tackles some of the previous criticisms. It accepts that some of them have been useful in drawing attention to special features of the Scottish case. But White insists that the traditional contrast between the restricted English system and the free Scottish system is warranted. The latter was competitive and efficient. The Bank of England was not a lender of last resort to the Scottish system before 1844, and neither was it a central bank in the sense of providing a reserve base of high-powered money held by the Scottish banks. At the very least from 1810 to 1844, Scottish banking fits the free banking model.

One of the principal areas of contention is the degree of difference between the Scottish and English systems. It may be that it comes down essentially to the limitation imposed on the English system by virtue of the six-partner law. But that may nevertheless be of considerable importance.

Eugene White draws our attention to the somewhat surprising fact that in Revolutionary France there are examples of free banking. In the 1790s the revolutionaries failed to balance the budget and issued assignats. But there was a need for small denomination currency and the need was met by the organization of *caises patriotiques* (patriotic banks) where the assignats could be exchanged for notes of smaller denomination.

These banks flourished in the laissez-faire climate of the revolution, when old regime regulations were eliminated. There were more than 1600 banks of this kind by 1791 with a substantial note issue. They quickly moved from being 100 per cent reserve banks to a fractional reserve system, and they enjoyed almost complete freedom to operate. White exonerates these banks from many of the charges that were laid at their door. There was counterfeiting but only on a small scale, and there was fraud, but again nothing that the reputable banks could not cope with. But most important of all he exonerates them from the charge of being the basis of inflation. Proponents of free banking argue that such a system should help to stabilize the price level. There was galloping inflation in the 1790s in France and the banks were an easy target, but White has shown that the chief cause of inflation was the excessive issue of assignats – the outside money of the system.

An interesting feature of the French experience is that, unlike the Scottish experience, it took place without the discipline of a commodity standard. The implication is that if only the authorities controlled the issue of outside money, the system could indeed be stable, competitive and efficient and deliver price stability.

The English banking system that evolved in the nineteenth century has provided the model for many countries around the world since. It was a three-tiered system, with the Bank of England at the top, and the discount market as a sort of buffer between that and the commercial banking system. The banking system moved from one of many hundreds of small units at the beginning of the century to one of a few dominant large banks, headquartered in London, with hundreds of branches scattered across the country. It was undoubtedly stable, in part as a result of this structure, which allowed a completely diversified portfolio. Behind this stood the Bank of England, which accepted the role of lender of last resort somewhere around the early 1870s.

At the beginning of the nineteenth century there were various pieces of legislation that set the framework for the system to operate within. But there was considerable freedom, and the banking oligopoly that evolved by the end of the nineteenth century took on the appearance of a club that disciplined errant members – a form of self-regulation. It is Dowd's argument that this system did not evolve naturally as the optimal solution to the needs of the nineteenth-century economy, but rather that legislation was important, and it was provided by a state desiring a certain outcome.

Implicit too in Dowd's argument is that the periodic crises that characterized the nineteenth century might have been avoided had a freer system been allowed to develop.

Hugh Rockoff considers America's experience with banking in the nineteenth century, concentrating particularly on the decades immediately preceding the Civil War. This period was chosen because, he observes, it contains in an actual banking system some of the features which are being discussed, and in some cases held up as desirable models, by theorists who are examining and proposing monetary reforms.

His study of this period leads him to consider whether it is desirable to return to 'free banking', i.e. to a completely unregulated system. His conclusion is that the evidence is neither wholly in favour nor wholly against. There were plainly some good features of the banking system in this period. Growth of the monetary base was, in this phase, controlled by a 'semi-automatic mechanism' – the bimetallic standard. This produced growth of the base which was both steadier and slower than has been the US experience with fiat money.

A notable example of this experience, supposedly highly inflationary, was the 1850s' gold rush. High Rockoff observes that this produced monetary base growth scarcely faster than the 1980s in the US. His conclusion from this evidence is that, whatever the details of microeconomic regulation of the banking system, the constraint provided by the monetary base should be regulated by a monetary rule.

A second feature of the period was the absence of a lender of last resort. Here the verdict is less favourable. The crises of 1857 led to a severe recession and a wave of business failures. But against this, systems with extensive bank branching were for all practical purposes unscathed by that episode. Branching certainly ameliorates bank panics; whether it eliminates them cannot, however, be demonstrated. (This conclusion is, of course, in accordance with the UK experience. For discussion of this see Schwartz (1986).) In contrast to the present, banks could (and did) issue currency. Rockoff suggests this proved to be an attractive feature of the system. Of particular importance, it dampened the effects of changes in the note-to-money ratio on the money stock. Like now, the system also protected the unsophisticated. The method, however, was different; part of the money stock was collateralized.

Finally, and very important in view of the restrictive form regulation takes, there was free entry to banking. This, he suggests, certainly facilitated the development of New York as the main financial centre and Chicago and New Orleans as regional centres.

The Lender of Last Resort, whose importance was accepted by Rockoff on the basis of his study of one period, is the focus of Charles Goodhart's paper. He concludes that a lender of last resort is indeed essential. Before setting out the main points of his argument it should be observed that his concept of a lender of last resort is somewhat different from the classical, Bagehotian, one. Bagehot thought the central bank should lend *to the market* during a panic – that is, it should lend on security to whoever brings in the security. Charles Goodhart believes it should bail out individual institutions. This possibly quite major distinction is taken up by his discussants. His paper starts by observing that the traditional case for a lender of last resort may have a major weakness. The case is that because bank deposits are redeemable into monetary base on a first come first served basis, any doubts over the value of the bank's portfolio will lead to a run for cash, as banks hold, and are known to hold, only a small fraction of their assets as cash.

This argument can be circumvented by requiring bank asset portfolios to be continually marked to market, with supervision such that banks are always closed before their own capital is exhausted. This prompt closure would protect depositors. Depositors, meanwhile, aware of this protection, would not panic and there would be an end to bank runs.

His response to this is that banks cannot behave in the way described. They cannot do so because they serve in part to make loans where no market exists – so these assets at least cannot be marked to market. He observes that bundles of such loans are starting to be gathered together and 'securitized', but notes that the scale is still small, and shows signs of remaining so. Banks, he therefore concludes, cannot be made run-proof. Does this matter? He concludes that it does. A wave of bank failures will cause a severe monetary contraction, and induce a debt–deflation spiral. Accordingly, then, waves of bank failures should be prevented.

His review of ways of doing this leads to the conclusion that only a lender of last resort can serve. Clearing houses can help provide stability, but, he argues, only to some extent; and in addition they can and often did act as barriers to entry.

Accordingly central banks are necessary. They act as lender of last resort and, in addition, he argues, can regulate banks so as to prevent the kind of behaviour – running herd-like after apparently profitable opportunities – that can cause banking crises. (He notes they need not have greater wisdom than commercial banks to prevent that but only a different incentive structure.) But their primary function, one restated in his conclusion, is not regulation but provision of lender of last resort facilities. Goodhart's arguments lead him to conclude that central banks are essential for the stability of a banking system.

George Benston's paper complements that by Charles Goodhart, in that it focuses on regulation. It starts by distinguishing two aspects of stability: systemic and the stability of individual banks. The effect of the failure of individual banks on the stability of the financial system is considered first. This leads to the conclusion that the central bank alone can maintain systemic stability. Although individual bank failures may set off runs that result in multiple bank failures, this outcome can be prevented by central bank actions, even when very large banks fail. The role of the Federal Reserve in preventing systemic collapse is then analysed and found wanting.

Payments system risk also is considered. Regulations that restrict branching have given the Fed a monopoly over nationwide cheque clearance, which George Benston concludes has exacerbated the risk.

Regulation affects individual bank stability in four main ways: constraints on diversification, effects on profitability, limiting opportunities for and attitudes of bank owners and managers toward risk taking or avoidance, and monitoring and supervising to prevent fraud and grossly incompetent management. Each of these influences is discussed. The general conclusion is that regulation tends to be destabilizing because diversification is restricted, profitability is reduced, and risk-taking is encouraged (as a consequence primarily of deposit insurance). While supervision may be necessary, it has not generally been adequate.

Finally, alternative explanations for regulation are considered. This part of the analysis lends support to the Stiglerian view of regulation. Benston points out that regulation preceded concern about financial stability by several centuries. What prompted such regulation? He suggests it was a way of capturing seigniorage; it increased bank profits, and thus gave a bigger tax base.

He also reviews some recent arguments, such as the need to encourage economies of scale, and the desirability of providing banking to particular groups and to ensure that there is lending to particular groups or areas. None of these arguments for regulation, he finds, can be supported by evidence. His conclusion is that 'regulation is imposed to redistribute wealth to those with political power'.

OVERVIEW

At the opening of this introduction we raised two main questions. Is there a role for bank regulation? And is a lender of last resort necessary? The answer provided by these papers is clear cut to the first. Regulation seems to bring very few benefits, and is costly. Only a limited defence of it could be presented. The answer to the second question is less clear. Several papers concluded that a lender of last resort was necessary. But it was observed that institutional features, such as nationwide branching, can sharply reduce the frequency with which such lenders may have to act. In addition, it appears that one episode, that studied by Eugene White, found a stable banking system operating well in most difficult circumstances without a lender of last resort.

The papers in this volume plainly have important implications for the future of bank regulation and banking system structure.

References

BAGEHOT, WALTER (1873) *Lombard Street* (London: John Murray).
BATOR, F, (1958) 'The Anatomy of Market Failure', *Quarterly Journal of Economics*.
FRIEDMAN, MILTON, and SCHWARTZ, ANNA J. (1973) *A Monetary History of the United States* (Princeton UP for NBER).
HARMAN, J. Quoted in Bagehot, *op.cit.*
KAY, J. and VICKERS, J. (1988) 'Regulatory Reform in Britain', *Economic Policy*.
SCHWARTZ ANNA J. (1986) 'Real and Pseudo Financial Crisis' in *Financial Crises and the World Banking System*, ed. F. H. Capie and G. E. Wood (London: Macmillan).
STIGLER, G. J. (1962) 'What can Regulators Regulate? The Case of Electricity', *Journal of Law Economics*.

STIGLER, G. J. (1964) 'Public Regulation of the Securities Market, *Journal of Business of the University of Chicago*.

STIGLER, G. J. (1971) 'The Theory of Economic Regulation', *Bell Journal of Economics and Management Science*, Spring.

WHITE, LAWRENCE (1984) *Free Banking in Britain* (Cambridge University Press).

1 Are Central Banks Necessary?[1]

Charles A. E. Goodhart

WHAT IS DIFFERENT ABOUT BANKS?

In the standard approach to the above question, as evidenced, for example, by the papers by Fama (1980) and Tobin (1985), the emphasis has been placed on the special (monetary) features of bank liabilities. Particularly in the American literature, a commercial bank is often regarded as an otherwise standard portfolio manager of a set of securities, with the peculiarity, however, that these security holdings are funded by capital-certain *monetary* liabilities. Consequently, because bank deposits are redeemable into outside high-powered money at par on a first come first served basis, any doubts about the solvency of the commercial bank, i.e. whether the value of its portfolio is sufficient to repay the claims of its depositors, can lead to a run on the bank – a contagious panic. If, however, the value of that portfolio could be ascertained with *certainty* it is arguable that some simple reforms could virtually prevent the likelihood either for such a panic to develop or for an insolvency to ensue, in the course of which the depositors might lose some part of the 'capital certain' value of their deposits.

For example, in a recent 'Statement' by the Shadow Financial Regulatory Committee on 'An Outline of a Program for Deposit Insurance and Regulatory Reform (Statement No. 42; 13 February 1989), the Committee proposed, page 3, that procedures ought to be established to enable market values of bank asset portfolios to be determined at all times, with the value of assets being continuously 'marked to market'. Then, with such market values established, supervisors could work out directly the ratio of existing capital to liabilities; when the value of capital has fallen into a lower range, the bank 'would be subject to increased regulatory supervision and more frequent monitoring of its activities; then, a second level of supervisory concern would follow when the institution's capital ratio fell into an even lower range'. This would involve 'Suspension of dividends, interest payments on subordinated debt and unapproved

1

outflow of funds ... Asset growth would be prohibited to prevent institutions from attempting to "grow" out of their problems'. Finally, the Shadow Financial Regulatory Committee would require mandatory recapitalization and reorganization if capital fell to, say, less than 3% of assets. Accordingly, under this scheme, any bank would be closed before its capital became exhausted, so that the value of depositors' funds would always be protected. There could, of course, still be some problems if the decline in asset value was so steep that it occurred before the bank could be officially closed, but, given a sufficient capital margin at which closure, or reorganization, would be mandatory, this should rarely cause problems; possibly a (public?) insurance scheme could be arranged to protect further against this rare eventuality, remembering that banks would be expected to 'mark to market' at the end of each working day.[2]

The Shadow Financial Regulatory Committee does not envisage many problems in providing a market price for bank assets. It states, 'As a matter of implementation, it is envisioned that market valuation estimates would have three sources; (a) directly observed market prices, (b) prices derived from instruments of comparable tenor, including maturity, credit quality and rate, and (c) estimates based on generally accepted valuation principles'. An alternative approach towards structural 'improvement', in order to stabilize the banking system and to prevent bank runs – and hence, it is often implied, to make a Central Bank unnecessary – is to restrict the set of permissible bank assets, so that their market value *is* always clearly ascertainable, and usually stable. Such suggestions include the proposal that checkable deposits should be backed 100% by a restricted set of safe, liquid assets[3] (reserve assets or short-dated government securities) a proposal advocated both by Tobin and Friedman;[4] and also my own suggestion that mutual funds, holding only marketable assets, with a clearly observable market price, should enter the business of providing payment services on their liabilities. Thus, the problem of bank runs seems to lie largely in the uncertainty surrounding the valuation of bank assets. Given various alternative suggestions for resolving that uncertainty, the likelihood of banking panics could seem to be greatly lessened, possibly eliminated, so that the role of a central bank to stand ready to provide lender of last resort facilities to prevent such crises would become otiose.

Indeed, there are examples of financial intermediaries, both in the public sector, i.e. Giro, POSB, TSB, and in the private sector, e.g. the building societies in recent years, where the constraints and limitations on their asset holdings has meant that their solvency would be unquestioned, so long as they abided by such constraints. Accordingly, even though they have provided a range of payments services, there has been virtually no call for them to be regulated and overseen by a central bank, though there has been a need for regular inspection and monitoring to prevent fraud. So, the argument runs that all that may be needed, to dispose of the services of a central bank, at least for prudential purposes, is to restrict the assets of banks to those that can be given a reliable market value. In so far as the banks wish to continue to invest in assets which cannot be given a precise market value or whose market value is subject to 'excessive' short-run market volatility, then the suggestion is often made that the bank be divided into two separate parts. First, the part issuing monetary deposits, which would be (privately?) insured, would be constrained to hold portfolios of assets with a restricted permissible set of assets involved and could then be closed down, if necessary, following a reduction in capital values, but well in advance of insolvency. The remaining riskier assets would then be segregated into a legally separate financial institution, whose liabilities would, and should, remain uncontrolled, and which could not legally be used in the process of payments.

I believe that it is, indeed, correct that it would be possible to constrain a bank's permissible portfolio set in such a way as to make it unnecessary to maintain any continuing central bank oversight, at least for that constrained part of the bank (though insurance companies, which were insuring deposits, and accounting agencies would still need to check such banks' books against the possibility of fraud). Even so, I do *not* believe that this simple structural change would eliminate the need for a central bank within this field, nor that we could then simply also withdraw central bank support from the *residual risky banking* sector. My contention in this paper is that the special feature of banks that requires central bank support is *not* their joint role as providers of payment services and holders of a portfolio of assets, but rather the particular nature of their asset portfolio.

In the historical period when banking first developed as a profession there were very few organized financial markets; these were restricted to markets in the debt of the central government and also the equity and debt of a few specially chartered companies. Financial markets were then, but also to some large extent remain, incomplete, in the sense that many economic entities which would like to borrow directly on capital markets are unable to do so. What exactly are the factors that allow (financial) markets to be established remains a fascinating part of micro-market analysis. This involves questions, for example, of the extent of dissemination of publicly available knowledge about the borrowing entity that may be necessary before a market can be established, since otherwise the balance between informed and uninformed traders about the particular state of the borrowing entity becomes too unbalanced; also the balance between the size of the set-up costs of establishing a market and the likely volume of trade in that market is important. For our present purposes, however, the essential point is that bank lending provided a substitute source of funds in place of non-existent, or otherwise unavailable, financial markets for the issue of claims upon themselves by those wishing to borrow funds.

To summarize this opening section, then, there is an important question of what, if anything, makes banks so different that they may need, possibly along with other financial intermediaries, special supervision and regulation and support by central banks. This is a subject that has concerned several of us in the Financial Markets Group at the LSE, notably David Miles (1989). Standard American literature has concentrated on the combination of the particular monetary nature of bank liabilities and their role as ordinary portfolio managers. I shall try to argue in the remainder of this paper, rather, that it is the particular nature of bank assets in providing loans in those cases, and to those agents, for which no efficient alternative financial market exists that makes banks different.

INFORMATION ASYMMETRIES

One of the reasons for the non-existence of (financial) markets is that good, accurate, publicly available, information on the prospects for the projects of potential borrowers is often unavailable, or at least strictly limited. This leads to a problem of information asymmetry. The recent analyses by Diamond (1984), and by Gale and Hellwig (1985), have suggested that the appropriate economic response is the establishment of a financial institution (a bank) which would specialize in credit assessment, and would then reduce the extent of risk, and increase economies of scale, by holding a diversified portfolio of loans based on such specialized credit assessment. Moreover, monitoring costs could be limited, and incentives on the borrower to carry out the contract could be maximized, by structuring the form of such bank credit into fixed interest debt form, supported by collateral, and buttressed by bankruptcy penalties.

One issue that has for some time fascinated me is the question of what might be the optimal form of bankruptcy penalty. Putting debtors into prison was obviously self-defeating. Too severe a penalty might restrict risk-taking unduly, while imposing no penalty whatsoever would significantly raise banks' monitoring costs, and might reduce the efficiency of the allocation of loans through the banking system. I have sometimes thought that public humiliation might be a useful form of bankruptcy penalty. The older English custom of placing a transgressor on public display in stocks had, perhaps, some deeper merit. Again, the apparent absence of any additional social stigma in the USA on becoming bankrupt perhaps makes moral hazard a greater risk there than in the UK.

While considering issues relating to the structure of the loan contract, another, and perhaps even more complex, problem concerns the form in which the debt contract is written. It is normally written in nominal terms, but there is no reason, under the analysis as developed by Diamond (1984), that would prevent the debt contract being written in indexed form. Such indexed loans would seem to reduce the real uncertainty facing borrowers. Banks' uncertainty would be increased by indexing their loans, if their deposits were still in nominal form, but, equally, I can see no reason why banks should not issue indexed deposits, i.e. which remain capital-certain in real terms. There is now no legal or other barrier to the development of indexed banking in the UK. Given that there are now available safe assets in indexed form, i.e. the relatively short-dated indexed gilts issued by the UK government, it has remained a mystery to me why no UK institution has sought to enter into the realm of indexed banking. This seems an obvious gap within the set of available financial assets and liabilities. Anyhow, I remain puzzled why indexed banking has not developed, at any rate within this country, in recent years.

Be that as it may, the implications of such information asymmetry, however, are that there is still no well-functioning market for bank assets of the kind that banks very largely provide; after all, in my view it is the basic rationale for banking that they provide loans that are substitutes for non-existing markets. Given, then, the extent of such informational asymmetries, with the borrower knowing more about the likely outcome and form of his project than the lender, there is really no good way for a commercial bank actually to be able to discover the 'true', nor indeed the market, value of much of its loan book. Hence, the accounting procedures in banking, with provisioning, and write-offs, have taken the form that they have. Thus the value of certain loans is written-off only when the project has clearly failed, and a number of specific provisions are made in cases where loans are clearly sub-standard. However, the general provisions are not based on any concept of market valuation, in large part because they cannot be, but instead on historical experience on the likely aggregate probability of default of certain general categories of loans.[5]

Exactly the same problems of information asymmetry, as between the bank and the bank borrower, occurs in the relation between the depositor and his/her bank. Just as the bank cannot discern the likely outcomes of a borrower's project, so a depositor has no real idea whether the asset value of a bank's portfolio is sufficient (under all circumstances) to repay his/her deposits. What is the true value of the bank? What, for example, is Lloyds Bank or Manufacturers Hanover worth? Perhaps a depositor could tell what a bank was worth by looking at its Stock Exchange valuation, but this valuation not only incorporates the often uncertain value of the put option explicitly, or implicitly, provided by the regulatory authorities through deposit insurance, or from the prospect that they will ultimately bail-out a failing institution, but also such Stock Exchange values have provided only limited successful forecasts of continued solvency. In any case many smaller banks have no Stock Exchange quotations, and is it to be suggested that all depositors should every day turn to the City pages of their newspaper to check such Stock Exchange prices?

In any case the depositor is not concerned about the Stock Market value of the bank, but whether the redemption guarantee on his/her deposit will be honoured. Uncertainty on this latter score could well arise while the market value of the bank on the Stock Exchange remains significantly greater than zero. Given information asymmetry, plus the nature of the deposit contract, with redemption on a first come first served basis, it would be perfectly possible, indeed normal, for a run to develop at any time when uncertainty about the redemption guarantee arose, even when the market value of the bank remained strictly positive.

It should, however, be noted that it is *not* necessary for the liabilities of the bank in this respect to be monetary in form, i.e. checkable. Indeed, the withdrawal of funds from banks in difficulties is usually greater in respect of the non-renewal of loans through wholesale markets, i.e. the CD market and the inter-bank market, than in the case of withdrawal of demand deposits. For example, in two recent banking crises – the contagious run on the UK fringe banks, 1973–4, and the run on Continental Illinois – such banks both had, and also lost, very few demand deposits. Instead, the run took the form of withdrawals, and non-renewals, of wholesale deposits.[6]

Another illustration of the argument that it is as much, or more, the nature of financial intermediaries' assets, as of their liabilities, that calls forth the need for central bank type regulation and support, can be seen in the case of mortgage lending institutions. So long as the form of their loans was restricted in a way that ensured their solvency, for example by being limited to first mortgages on residential property which were either in variable rate form, or with a maturity actuarially related to the maturity of their own liabilities,[7] there was no call for central bank, or other regulatory, oversight despite the increasingly monetary nature of such institutions' liabilities. Once, however, their lending profiles were changed, by deregulation, in a manner that potentially threatened solvency, then the possibility of a run arose, and with that the need for some (central bank) support and regulation.

Let me once again summarize the argument. Information asymmetries lead bank lending to have the form of a fixed interest debt contract; the same factors cause bank liabilities to take a similar debt contract format. Uncertainty then about successful redemption, on a first come first served basis (owing to inherent uncertainty about 'true' asset valuation), could lead to runs.

An interesting question at this juncture is whether one might be able to resolve this problem by resorting once again to an 'option clause' contract form, which gives the bank the option to curtail, over some stated period, deposit convertibility, usually in exchange for a higher yield on the deposit meanwhile. Such a possibility has been raised recently by Dowd (1988). Such option clauses were common in Scotland in the eighteenth century. They were subsequently abolished by Act of Parliament. One historical issue that Kevin Dowd has not yet, I believe, pursued (and nor have I) has been the question of what were the historical considerations that led Parliament to abolish such clauses, given that they do have some obvious ability to prevent the development of a panic.

If there were a free choice open to banks whether, or not, to issue liabilities with such an option clause, would there not be adverse self-selection, in the sense that the more secure banks would advertise their position by refraining from including any such clause, whereas banks who felt it necessary to issue such a clause would indicate that they were of lower quality? If so, the additional interest cost of adding on such an option clause would probably be so high as to be a major barrier to their adoption. On the other hand, how would a system operate, if such option clauses, rather than being left to the free choice of banks, were *required* by law to be universally applied? But in such a circumstance, if one bank should exercise the option to limit convertibility, would that not lead to an immediate run on other banks, because of a fear that liquidity would become frozen? The use of option clauses might stop a debt/default spiral developing, but it might still lead to major problems for the continuing functioning of the payments and settlement system.

However, I am not certain how serious the latter, i.e. a breakdown of the payments and settlements system, would be, if that were *not* accompanied by a debt/default spiral. A recent example of the breakdown of the payments system, without any debt/default cycle developing, has been given by the Irish Bank strikes, which lasted for several months. There is an excellent, but not widely known, paper by Murphy (1972) on this subject, which suggested that the dislocation from the breakdown of the banking payments system, in the absence of any debt/deflation spiral crisis, was really of very limited severity. If wealth remains unaffected, then it seems that substitute payments systems can develop quite quickly, as again they did in the crisis in the US in 1907 – see Andrew (1908). So long as the underlying real value of bank deposits remains unaffected, brokers[8] will generally be prepared to discount cheques drawn on banks which were exercising their option clauses. Indeed, I have some sympathy with the option clause proposal, and regard it as an historical and analytical subject worthy of considerable further research, largely because it would seem to me to have some benefit in preventing a debt/deflation cycle developing, whereas its probable failure in preventing the breakdown of the payments system might not be so important. More generally, it is important to distinguish between these two consequences of a bank run, and to assess the social costs of both of these separately.

DEPOSITOR PROTECTION

So far the main consequence of conditions of incomplete (financial) markets, associated with limited and asymmetrically distributed information, which has been stressed, has been the resulting tendency for occasional runs to develop, and I shall revert to that issue further later. First now, however, I want to turn to a more general consequence of limited knowledge, the acquisition of which is expensive. This is a common feature in the provision of most professional services, including financial services and banking, since a large element of what professionals are selling is their specialized expertise. By definition, the customer is at a disadvantage, and is not usually in a good position to ascertain the quality of the services offered with any accuracy. A common response by such professional service industries has been to establish 'clubs' in order to control the conduct of their members, with entry limited to those who have reached a sufficient standard of expertise, often via initial examinations for participants, and rules for continuing good conduct, supported by quasi-legal hearings in the case of transgression, and often a degree of mutual insurance in order to recompense aggrieved customers, but also too often with restrictions on charges, prices, and advertising. This approach has its good points, in providing a guarantee of quality to relatively ignorant customers and hence in reducing their search costs, but also its bad points, generally in the form of an oligopolistic restriction on competition.

Financial services in general, and banking in particular, share many of the same informational problems that lead to the establishment of such clubs. There are, however, further joint services that banks need, in particular in the establishment of a clearing house. One of the incentives in Continental Europe for the establishment of a central bank, in particular the Reichsbank, was not only to unify the currency system, but also to encourage and take the lead in the establishment of clearing houses in the main cities. Certainly in Continental Europe these were often established through the initiative of nascent central banks. Nevertheless clearing houses have been normally established in maturing banking systems, even when no central bank is at hand. A well-known early example in the United States is the Suffolk banking system in Massachusetts. Timberlake (1978 and 1984) has been the leading economic historian of their development and role in the United States. A more recent example of the development of a bankers' club, with an associated clearing house in the absence of a central bank, is to be found in the Hong Kong Association of Bankers (HKAB)[9]. The existence of such a clearing house then adds further to the, already present, incentive for the growth and pyramiding of inter-bank deposits, since any non-clearing banks, as well as non-clearing financial intermediaries, will both want and need to keep deposits with the clearing banks in order to facilitate their own clearings; moreover, such inter-bank deposits will generally also earn interest (as well as functioning as liquid reserve assets), whereas holding specie, or notes, in their own vaults will earn nothing.

Besides deciding who to allow to enter the clearing house system,[10] which itself functions as a form of natural monopoly, somewhat like a railroad line, those in charge of the working of the clearing houses have to decide when, and under what terms, to lend to their members, or to their correspondent members, who find themselves in difficulties with liquidity (and perhaps solvency), problems. While the operation of such clearing systems itself will exert a discipline on the expansion of *individual* member banks, as spelt out nicely in L. H. White (1984) and Selgin (1988), there remains a question whether the system *as a whole* will have a tendency to expand (or contract) unduly, either arising from fluctuations in the availability of outside reserves, or perhaps associated with fluctuations in the reserve ratios maintained by banks; which then may lead on to cycles in nominal incomes. Selgin has some ingenious arguments, notably in chapters 5 and 6, whereby he claims that, under laissez-faire, the volume of bank deposits provided will adjust endogenously into line with that required, allowing stability to be maintained, but, as I have written elsewhere in a review of his book, (1989 in *Economic Affairs*), I do not find his arguments convincing. If there might be fluctuations and cycles in the aggregate provision of bank deposits, though this is a question which I shall address in the next section, there might be a need for those in charge of the clearing house to take measures to try to counter such adverse systemic tendencies.

Anyhow, as a general matter, the operation of professional clubs controlling the conduct, and sitting in quasi-judgement on their fellows, can lead to conflicts of interest, and also to undue and unfair restrictions on entry. Such conflicts of interest similarly arise in banking. Whereas bankers would like to take advantage of the potential benefits arising from substituting inter-bank deposits for (sterile) gold among their reserve assets, which can be achieved by the centralization of specie reserves, such private bankers were concerned with the advantages of size and power that this might give to the central banks, if such central banks were to remain commercial competitors. Again, the enforcement of discipline on the expansion of member banks, which might be carried out by the central banks, which were in charge of operating the clearing house, if such banks were also aggressive competitors, was generally resented by the other member banks. Such resentment formed a large part of the campaign against the renewal of the charter of the two Banks of the United States, and ultimately led to the demise of the Suffolk banking system.

Third, the issue of whether to provide additional support to member banks seeking additional help could lead those in charge of the clearing house (if, indeed, a committee of private bankers could reach a decision quickly or at all), to wonder whether the demise of a competitor – very likely a previously aggressive and risk-taking competitor, or one which was not a valued member of the bankers' club, e.g. because of the characteristics of its owners – would not have certain benefits for themselves. See, for example, the discussion about the refusal of New York banks to rescue the Bank of United States in 1930 in Friedman and Schwartz (1963), pages 308–11.

It is a historical fact that bankers' clubs have developed naturally, in some large part to manage the working of clearing houses. Running such a bankers' club, much like running any other professional club, gives considerable power to those in charge, and can give rise to conflicts of interest among the members. Such power may often be much resented, both among other less powerful banks, and more widely among the electorate. A continuing strand of American politics has been the distrust of the operation of Eastern 'money-trust' bankers, e.g. as represented by the Pujo, or Money Trust Investigation, 1912–13, which, significantly, was taking place at exactly the same time as the Federal Reserve system was being established in the United States. One way of defusing several of the conflicts of interest, and the rivalries and concerns about the use and misuse of such power by competitors, has been to hand over the management of the club, including setting the rules of entry, the rules of good conduct, etc., to an independent, non-competitive, non-profit-maximizing body.

It is extremely difficult for a profit-maximizing entity to turn itself into such a non-profit-maximizing body, since the existing owners have property rights which would thereby be damaged; the history of the Bank of England during the second half of the nineteenth century provides a record of the difficulties of such a procedure. Consequently, many central banks were, and probably had to be, established by the state specifically for the purpose of running the club of bankers.

Nevertheless, the operation of such a bankers' club, setting rules of entry, enforcing good conduct, seeking to maintain quality, organizing mutual insurance, etc., which is indeed common to many other professional clubs, could have been undertaken by a non-competitive body with a far lower profile and much less power than current central banks actually wield. Such a role as professional club manager could have led to an organization, for example, more like the Building Societies Association than the actual Bank of England. There is, I believe, a perceived need among banks for such a club manager, but does the manager also need to have the additional powers of lender of last resort to support banks in difficulties, and also to undertake discretionary aggregate monetary management?

SYSTEMIC PROBLEMS?

The economies achievable in reserve holdings by centralizing these with a central bank (the incentive for which centralization among commercial banks was intensified once they no longer perceived the central bank as a competitor), made that bank simultaneously the main source of commercial banks' reserves, and the sole holder of outside monetary reserves. Thus, the central bank became both the guardian of the convertibility of the national monies into the outside reserve asset, and also the sole source of (net) additional reserves to the banking system, and hence the lender of last resort. On this see Laidler (1988).

Although such a development was perfectly natural, it did establish a power centre, in the form of a Central Bank, which could be somewhat more easily subjugated to the purposes of government than could a myriad of competitive commercial banks. There are those, such as Hayek, who ascribe many of the financial ills of the last century to such a centralization of power, and its misuse either through ignorance (as in the USA 1929–33), or to government to extort a covert inflationary tax, or to time inconsistency problems, or yet other complications. The question of how far central banks have, in practice, been responsible in the past for such ills, or maybe likely to continue to misbehave in future, remains a subject of some considerable debate.

I do not, however, want to enter into that discussion here, in part because the counterfactual discussion of how history might have altered if people and/or institutions had behaved differently is so slippery. Rather, I want to consider two, only slightly less slippery, questions: the first of these is how a banking system without a central bank might function; and the second is how serious are the social costs of a contagious bank crisis.

There is no question but that a banking system *can* operate without a central bank, though some (often considerable) degree of pyramiding of inter-bank deposits with some single, or small group, of central commercial banks is likely to develop, which bank(s) will in turn conduct quasi-central bank functions; for a recent example see the operation of the Hongkong and Shanghai Banking Corporation in Hong Kong. There is also no question but that all inter-bank loans could be left to the free commercial decision of private sector banks, though, as already argued, this may generate potentially severe conflicts of interest, so that the private operation of lender of last resort functions may be insufficient and inefficient. Again, banks need to take co-operative mutual measures to restrain runs and to provide insurance for depositors, and that may be much harder to organize in a committee of commercial bank competitors than by a single, non-competitive, central bank. As earlier indicated, there is also no question but that the natural workings of a clearing house will serve as a discipline and restraint on those individual banks which are growing separately faster than the rest.

There is a school of thought, e.g. Kareken and Wallace (1978), which argues that it is precisely the (implicit) insurance provided by central banks that encourages commercial banks to adopt riskier strategies, and that, without such insurance, market forces would drive each commercial bank to adopt perfectly safe, extremely conservative strategies, which would eliminate the likelihood of failure. Hayek, in his various writings, has claimed that free competition would also lead banks naturally to adopt conservative strategies. While there is obviously some justification in the moral hazard argument about the role of the central bank (hence a reason why central banks try to keep their intentions for supporting private sector banks generally obscure), the claim that the banking system, if left strictly uncontrolled, would behave so conservatively would only be correct in my view, if, either (1) markets were so perfect and information so readily accessible that current market values of bank assets were always clearly and exactly ascertainable, or (2) the penalty for bank bankruptcy was so considerable (perhaps capital punishment?) that no banker dare to invest in a risky portfolio. But either of these two alternatives would negate the primary role, as I have argued, that the banking system undertakes, which is to provide a substitute for incomplete financial markets in conditions of informational asymmetry.

Under such circumstances, the owners, the equity holders of the bank, may be tempted to adopt risky strategies, at the potential expense of the bond and deposit holders, since the latter cannot assess the risks nearly as well as the owners, for much of the information on quality of the loan book is *inherently* private. Thus there *must* remain some possibility of runs occurring in the absence of a central bank.

Indeed, I would go further and argue that the distinction between the general equity holder and the management often provides an incentive structure that leads to a follow-my-leader or herd-type behaviour pattern developing, e.g. among bankers. Keynes emphasized such behaviour, but noted it as an empirical fact rather than analysing its cause. Nevertheless, the following passage is worthy of some repetition.

In his paper 'The Consequences to the Banks of the Collapse of Money Values' he wrote (Keynes (1931), Part 2, p.176: 'A "sound" banker, alas! is not one who foresees danger and avoids it, but one who, when he is ruined, is ruined in a conventional and orthodox way along with his fellows, so that no one can really blame him.' Anyhow, the distinction between management and general equity holders that I would draw here include the following:

(i)   Management will be paid partly, or completely, in the form of a fixed salary, or a bonus related to *current* profits, rather than in the form of a pro-rata share of profits over time.
(ii) Management's period of office is strictly finite, with a pension at the end of that finite period, paid on the basis of final salary, whereas equity owners have potentially infinite lives (e.g. savings institutions, such as insurance companies and pension funds).
(iii) Equity owners can sack management, but cannot themselves be sacked.
(iv) Management has far more information and ability to distinguish luck from good management than do equity owners.

Condition (iv) suggests that equity owners will normally only be able to assess management by its *relative* performance over current periods, except in the case of long-lived management with good past track records, which latter may often be given the benefit of the doubt for current underperformance for some time. The record of GEC in the UK is a good example of the latter. Given the lack of information available to general equity holders, managerial protestations about the current relatively poor profits arising as a result of its getting into a position in order to do much better later on would inevitably be received with some scepticism. In particular, bad management would surely mimic those who truly did see a low current/high future profits strategy as the approach that would lead to the maximization of present market values, if only equity holders could be made aware of the prospects that management itself sees in future. Indeed, management that, with the benefit of objective hindsight, often was 'bad' frequently does truly believe that its strategy would have proven optimal in the long run, if only events had been more favourable.

Because then of conditions (i), (ii) and (iii), management will have an incentive to avoid current relative underperformance, except in those cases where long track records, or other market defences against take-overs or dismissals, provide partial immunity. Now this latter argument can obviously be generalized well beyond banking, but that is not my concern here. Rather, my claim is that the initially successful exploitation of some line of loan business, whether in the form of loans to railroads in the nineteenth century or of lending to selected LDCs at various stages of history, is likely to attract all private bankers to take a part of the action, even when they know that ultimately the expansion is probably unsustainable. If the banker was to stand aside from the current fashion, in the expectation of the ultimate collapse, and thereby might suffer immediately a *relative* profit underperformance, he might be sacked before the equity owners could actually benefit from his long-sighted wisdom. With a sizeable proportion of loan fees available up front, with these indeed often being offered by riskier borrowers to benefit from this very syndrome, and the prospect of rapid movement from job to job of loan officers in banks, the temptation to ride with the current fashion must be considerable. This story is the banking equivalent of the general charge of 'short-termism', which is widely levelled by practitioners and commentators at the operations of financial markets more generally.[11]

Anyhow my own reading of the histories of commercial banking in various western countries in the periods before the advent of an effective central bank is that these were characterized by periods of major loan expansions, often culminating in financial crises, and subsequently followed by periods of conservative retrenchment, with sluggish loan extension and a general recession within the economy. For an example of such an historical account, see Matthews (1954).

Consequently, I would reject those claims that a free-banking system would, if left to itself, adopt steady, safe, conservative policies, and exhibit stable growth. This does not, however, mean that the interposition of a central bank would necessarily improve matters. Mistaken central bank policies, time-inconsistency problems, or inappropriate political manipulation could make things a lot worse. Again, people ask why one might expect central banks to have superior information, foresight, or better economic models than private commercial bankers, which latter, after all, have their own money riding on the outcome of their forecasts, whereas central bank officials do not. Moreover, the direct contact of private banks with their own customers gives them a source of information denied to central banks; per contra, however, central banks probably have a better view of likely future government policies.

My argument here, however, does not reside in there being any superior information, wisdom, or forecasting skills that reside in central banks, though that should be taken as being without prejudice, to use a legal phrase, as to whether, or not, it is the case that such superior skill exists in central banks. (It would be hard to test.) Instead, my point is that central bank officials have a different incentive structure. It is precisely because they are not under pressure to maintain current profits at a level high enough (to satisfy equity owners with limited information), that they should be able to take a longer, and more balanced, view about current banking fashions.

Be that as it may, my next claim is that, even if central banks' more detached, independent role should *not* allow them through regulation and supervision to lessen the incidence of banking fluctuations and crises, their presence, and role, as lenders of last resort should enable them to check and limit any contagious crisis that does arise. And I have earlier argued that a free banking system would *not* be immune to such crises.

It used to be generally accepted that such crises had social costs, externalites, that made their prevention a top priority for policy. Again that argument has recently been challenged, e.g. by Kaufman, (1987). Once again, I would accept that if markets were indeed complete, and/or information was perfect, then the failure of a bank, or even banks, would not matter much because everyone would know what the effective loss ('the haircut', to use US slang) actually was, and that would be that.

Once again, the problems arise from incomplete markets and information asymmetry. Bank failures generally arise from a downwards revaluation, often by nature very large, and appearing as a surprise to commentators and depositors, in the stated value of a bank's loan book. This revaluation then frequently throws doubt on the solvency both of a *class* of borrower, and on a *class* of bank, i.e. those with a large proportion of their loans outstanding to such borrowers. An excellent example of the latter syndrome is provided by the LDC crash in the early 1980s. Virtually all banks cease lending to that *class* of borrower, which borrowers then usually cannot turn to any alternative. Subsequently they become short of liquidity and go bankrupt in large numbers, thereby further threatening the solvency of the set of banks that had lent to them. There is usually a rush towards quality, with banks seeking to shift their assets away from the, now apparently, much riskier loans to (certain private sector or foreign) borrowers towards safe (government) debt. Such credit withdrawal then drives the debt/deflation spiral downwards.

Once again, the standard analysis emphasizes the breakdown in the monetary/payments/settlements system that may, but more frequently does not, accompany a banking/financial crisis as being its main social cost. For examples of crises that had no effect whatsoever on the payments system, consider again the fringe banking crisis in the UK in 1973–4, the Continental Illinois crisis, and the Banco Ambrosiano affair, all of which were important banking disturbances, but none of which had any impact on the payments sytem. Even in those few cases where a banking panic does lead to a disruption of the payments system (the US crisis in 1907 being one of the main examples), this can certainly be serious but is not in my view the main cause of dislocation arising from such crises. Instead, these arise from the credit withdrawal/debt–deflation spiral that ensues. It is my contention that such debt–deflation, credit withdrawal spirals can exist, and can be extremely serious, and that they need a central bank to be in position in order to prevent them. That the USA could have weathered the Continental Illinois crisis, or that the world would have weathered the stock exchange crash of October 1987, or the LDC crisis of 1982, without severe dangers and the potentiality of enormous dislocation had not central banks been in position to play their customary role is very dubious. The contrary claim that the risks adopted by such banks were undertaken solely and entirely as a result of the moral hazard problem generated by the very presence of a central bank ready to provide a degree of insurance, or bail-out support, strikes me from my own experience as extremely implausible. I do not know of a way of disproving such a claim, but for my own part I would regard the dangers of living with a free-banking system as considerably greater than we face at present with our existing central banks.

CONCLUSION

My message in this chapter is simple. The standard case for having a central bank is based on the view that the combination within banks of portfolio management together with the provision of payment services makes them uniquely vulnerable to contagious crises involving adverse social externalities. I believe that this standard case is open to the attack that the permissible asset portfolio of commercial banks could be restricted into a form which limited such vulnerability. My different claim here is rather that it is the unique nature of bank assets, i.e. that they are largely non-marketable, at least not marketed in practice, and therefore that it is virtually impossible to apply any objective market valuation to them, in conditions of information asymmetry and limited information, which puts such financial intermediaries at risk. Indeed, even were the payments system to be separated and segregated to financial intermediaries whose asset portfolios *were* limited to holding assets which were absolutely safe, we would *still* need a central bank to support the residual, risky, 'true', banking institutions, which were undertaking the necessary function of making loans to borrowers who could not otherwise sell their own equity and debt in extant financial markets.

Notes

1. My thanks are due to my discussants, Leslie Pressnell and Geoffrey Wood, for their helpful comments and criticisms; and to George Benston for his persistently acute and stimulating contributions and suggestions. That I continue to make errors is not their fault.
2. Also see Benston and Kaufman (1988) and Benston *et al.* (1989).
3. It is an encouraging sign that discussions of commercial bank supervision and regulation is now concentrating on measures of bank *solvency* with the adequacy of liquid asset holding being considered primarily as

an adjunct to ensuring solvency. In the past much of the discussion in this field concentrated on the need to prevent illiquidity. But, with efficient wholesale markets, other private sector entities will always be prepared to lend money to patently solvent companies. So, absent technical problems, such as computer break-downs, emergent illiquidity in a bank will, almost always, presage fears about potential insolvency problems.

4. Leslie Pressnell has reminded me that the case for separating the payments mechanism from bank lending and investment in risky assets can be traced back to David Ricardo, at least, in the latter's *Proposal for an Economical and Secure Currency*, (1816), and *Plan for a National Bank*, (1824): Thus, for example, Ricardo writes, (1816/1951, p 73), 'Against this inconvenience [of potential failure] the public should be protected by requiring of every country bank to deposit with the government, or with commissioners appointed for that purpose, funded property or other government security, in some proportion to the amount of their issues', and the opening sentences of his 'Plan for the Establishment of a National Bank,' (1824/1951, p. 276) were, 'The Bank of England performs two operations of banking, which are quite distinct, and have no necessary connection with each other: it issues a paper currency as a substitute for a metallic one; and it advances money in the way of loan, to merchants and others. That these two operations of banking have no necessary connection, will appear obvious from this, – that they might be carried on by two separate bodies, without the slightest loss of advantage, either to the country or to the merchants who receive accommodation from such loans'.

    For an account and critique of contemporary proposals along these same lines, see Benston and Kaufman, *op.cit.* (1988), Appendix A, especially pages 71–6.

5. The suggestion is increasingly being made that, whereas the value of a single such loan cannot be accurately established, the value of a 'bundle' of such loans can be reasonably well ascertained from prior experience. Thus such loans may be gathered together and 'securitized'. I have some doubts and reservations about how far such securitization can be taken, given available information and the non-normal probability distribution of outcomes. If my reservations here are misplaced, then I would expect any major trend towards securitization and marking to market of bank assets to be accompanied by a trend towards the transformation of deposits into varying value mutual units.

6. Leslie Pressnell raised the question whether this contrast might arise 'partly because, in a cartelized/oligopolistic system with a non-convertible currency there may be no easy substitute for payments deposits? In contrast, there *are* relatively easy substitutes available for other types of deposit'. I doubt, however, whether this is the source of the differing behaviour, since payment deposit in Bank B should be an excellent substitute for payment deposit in Bank A. It is rather that information, search and transaction costs are comparatively much more severe for small individual depositors than for large corporate depositors.

7. It was the provision of fixed-rate mortages of much longer duration than their liabilities that unhinged the S & Ls when interest rates rose so sharply in the USA in the early 1980s. The subsequent attempts to widen the range of assets/liabilities that S & Ls could hold, via deregulation, then futher enhanced their ability to assume excessive risk on the basis of 100% insured deposits.

8. As might, perhaps, have been expected in the Irish case, it was the pub-keepers who acted in some large part as brokers, and substitute clearing houses. Not only did they have confidence in these circumstances that the banks themselves would resume payment in full in due course, but they also had comparatively good information on the drawers, and endorsers, of checks in the meantime.

9. In this case the Hongkong and Shanghai Banking Corporation (HSBC), together with the Standard Chartered Bank, as the leading commercial banks in the territory, also provided, at least until recently, some quasi central-banking services.

10. Leslie Pressnell has reminded me of the restrictive early history of the London Clearing House. This was formed, and run, by a cartel of private bankers, which kept the joint stock banks out of the clearing house for about 20 years after the JSBs were first legalized in London, until 1854.

11. Most bankers that I have heard comment on this analysis are instinctively sympathetic to it. Most economists are instinctively doubtful about it, and I am aware of some empirical research which does *not* find evidence of such 'herd' behaviour. There is room for more work, both analytical and empirical, on this issue.

References

ANDREW, A. P. (1908) 'Substitutes for Cash in the Panic of 1907', *Quarterly Journal of Economics* (August).

ASPINWALL, R. C., *et al.* (1989) Shadow Fiancial Regulatory Committee, 'An Outline of a Program for Deposit Insurance and Regulatory Reform', Statement No. 41 (mimeo, 13 February).

BENSTON, G. J. and KAUFMAN, G. G. 'Risk and Solvency Regulation of Deposit Institutions: Past Policies and Current Options', Salomon Brothers Center for the Study of Financial Institutions, Monograph Series in Finance and Economics, Monograph 1988-1.

BENSTON, GG. J., R. D. BRUMBAUGH Jr., J. M. GUTTENTAG, R. J. HERRING, G. G. KAUFMAN, R. E. LITAN and K. E. SCOTT (1989) 'Restructuring America's Financial Institutions', pamphlet Washington DC The Brookings Institution.

DIAMOND, D. W. (1984) 'Financial Intermediation and Delegated Monitoring', *Review of Economic Studies*, Vol. 51, No. 3. pp. 393–414.

DOWD, K. (1988) 'Option Clauses and the Stability of a Laisser Faire Monetary System', *Journal of Financial Services Research*, No. 1, pp. 319–33.

FAMA, E. (1980) 'Banking in the Theory of Finance', *Journal of Monetary Economics*, 6, No. 1, pp. 39–57.

FRIEDMAN, M. and SCHWARTZ, A. J. (1963) *A Monetary History of the United States, 1867–1960*, National Bureau of Economic Research (Princeton, NJ Princeton University Press).

GALE, D and M. HELLWIG (1985) 'Incentive-compatible Debt Contracts: The One-Period Problem', *Review of Economic Studies*, Vol. 52, No. 4.

GOODHART, C. A. E. (1989) 'Review of Selgin's, The Theory of Free Banking', *Economic Affairs*. Vol. 9, No. 6.

KAREKEN, J. and WALLACE, N. (1978) 'Deposit Insurance and Bank Regulation: A Partial-Equilibrium Exposition', *The Journal of Business*, Vol. 51, No. 3 (July).

KAUFMAN, G. G. (1987) 'The Truth About Bank Runs', Staff Memoranda, Federal Reserve Bank of Chicago, SM–87–3 (April).

KEYNES, J. M. (1931) 'The Consequences to the Banks of the Collapse of Money Values', in *Essays in Persuasion*, Vol. IX of the *Collected Writing of John Maynard Keynes* (Macmillan for the Royal Economic Society).

LAIDLER, D. E. W. (1988) 'British Monetary Orthodoxy in the 1870s', *Oxford Economic Papers*, Vol. 40, pp. 74–109.

MATTHEWS, R. C. O. (1954) *A Study in Trade-Cycle History: Economic Fluctuations in Great Britain, 1833–1842* (Cambridge: Cambridge University Press).

MILES, D. K. (1989) 'Some Economic Issues in the Regulation of Financial Markets', London School of Economics Financial Markets Group, Special Paper #13 (mimeo, March).

MURPHY, A. E. (1972) 'The Nature of Money – with Particular Reference to the Irish Bank Closure', Trinity College, Dublin (mimeo).

RICARDO, D. (1816/1951) 'Proposals for an Economical and Secure Currency, 1816', in *The Works and Correspondence of David Ricardo*, ed. P. Sraffa, Vol. IV, pp. 43–141. (Cambridge: Cambridge University Press).

RICARDO, D. (1824/1951 'Plan for the Establishment of a National Bank', in *The Works and Correspondence of David Ricardo*, ed. P. Sraffa, Vol. IV, pp. 271–300 (Cambridge: Cambridge University Press.

SELGIN, G. A. (1988) *The Theory of Free Banking* (Totowa, N. J: Rowan and Littlefield).

SHADOW FINANCIAL REGULATORY COMMITTEE (1989); Messrs. Aspinwall, Benston, *et al.* 'An Outline of a Program for Deposit Insurance and Regulatory Reform', Statement No. 41 (mimeo, 13 February).

TIMBERLAKE, R. (1978),, *The Origins of Central Banking in the United States* (Cambridge, Mass: Harvard University Press).

TIMBERLAKE, R. (1984) 'The Central Banking Role of Clearinghouse Associations', *Journal of Money, Credit and Banking*, Vol. 16, No. 1, pp. 1–15.

TOBIN, J. (1985) 'Financial Innovation and Deregulation in Perspective', *Bank of Japan Monetary and Economic Studies*, Vol. 3, No. 2.

WHITE, L. H. (1984) *Free Banking in Britain: Theory, Experience, and Debate, 1800–1845* (Cambridge: Cambridge University Press).

Comment on Chapter 1

Leslie Pressnell

Since the most famous advocate of central banking has obfuscated the debate over bank regulation, a preliminary deck-clearing seems appropriate. In repeatedly declaring but apparently nowhere demonstrating that 'the natural system' would be for commercial banks to keep their own cash reserves, Bagehot implicitly depicts central banking as an artifical contrivance necessitated by the regrettable concentration of Britain's financial activities in Lombard Street.

Bagehot's is poor history, productive of policy puzzles admirably scrutinized by Hugh Rockoff (Rockoff, 1986). In relation to historical problems of bank regulation, Bagehot regrettably illustrates the dictum that good history may do little good, whereas bad history can do much harm.

It was not a Bagehotian black box of Bank of England and other arbitrary influences which led to the centralization of reserves in London, and hence to the alleged necessity for central bank control. Already, when the Bank of England was founded in 1694, Britain's economy revolved around London, through which payments and indebtedness were ultimately cleared. Adjustment to disequilibrium, resulting, for instance, from bad harvests or poor trade, was often facilitated by flexible local charges for London finance, most strikingly in Scotland. Payments within and between areas outside London and with London were broadly on an account basis, using bills of exchange, book entries, and other forms of transfer. Hoarding apart, cash reserves were not wanted for their own costly sake, but to settle adverse local balances of payments with other areas. The significant specie reserves held by eighteenth-century Scottish banks, noted by Bagehot and more recently by Charles Munn and Lawrence White (Bagehot, 1873; Munn, 1981; White, 1984, pp. 43–4) reflected Scotland's chronically weak balance of payments. The financial aspect of Britain's classic industrial revolution was that the greater general strength and improved balance of payments of the non-London economy permitted accumulation of income producing assets in London, including those reserves which Bagehot so misinterpreted.

In short, Bagehot's apparent blind spot over centralized reserves points debate on bank regulation towards a blind alley. Indeed,

Bagehot himself came close to recognizing this when, some two years after the culmination in *Lombard Street* of his prolonged sounding of alarm bells about reserves, he significantly modified his views in his little noticed evidence to a parliamentary committee (Bagehot, 1875, QQ. 8116, 8211–12, 8220). Attention must therefore turn elsewhere in examining the case for central banking.

Bank runs, depositor protection, and portfolio risks: these three attract Charles Goodhart's especial scrutiny, with the last seeming to offer the least refutable case for central bank activity. The following comments deal mainly with the first and third.

Historically, Charles Goodhart's three targets have been ragged excuses for *ad hoc* official intervention which, all too often, was necessitated by perverse governmental influences. Gravely defective operation of the state's near monopoly of coinage – 'near', because foreign or local token coins were grudgingly accepted substitutes – was particularly characteristic of eighteenth-century Britain. In note issues private banks indeed responded in their hundreds, but prolonged legislative prohibition of joint stock status and of limited liability might have been deliberately designed to prohibit adequately capitalized banks, and to frighten investors away from banking.

In respect of depositor protection, the state's limited concern seemed directed as much to the interests of public finance as to the general public's. The trustee savings banks, from the early nineteenth century, were intended but often failed to provide secure deposit facilities; and until quite recently they were restricted largely to public sector assets. Most strikingly, in establishing the Post Office Savings Banks in the 1860s, Gladstone sought a source of public finance that would make the Chancellor of the Exchequer independent of the City, i.e. of financial markets.

By no means least, company legislation in Britain, and the long-held delusive tradition of the supposed virtue of industrial self-financing, had excessively shielded business finance from market scrutiny. The consequence has been the inflation of portfolio risk which Charles Goodhart identifies as underpinning the case for discretionary intervention.

To minimize the possibility of bank runs in a less restricted monetary structure, there may be little mileage left, at least in Britain, for something like the option clause of eighteenth-century Scottish banking. We already have approximations to it. Our quasi-bank building societies operate mixtures of different interest rates and withdrawal constraints. The clearing banks offer a menu of readily available overdrafts, with or without commission, together with current account facilities with or without interest.

From another Celtic fringe of Britain, Charles Goodhart finds reassurance about the possibility that substitute payments systems could emerge fairly painlessly, avoiding a debt–default spiral in the event of a breakdown in the payments system. He deduces this from Murphy's report on the Irish bank strike about 20 years ago, which tells of the Irish continuing to pay each other happily with cheques on temporarily closed banks. Irish experience, however, is notoriously *sui generis*, but in any case Murphy's system depended ultimately on the clearing of cheques with outside money, namely that of the closed banks. Two resulting questions have answers that are far from self-evident. First, could such a system be more than very short-lived, especially if the potential outcome of a strike threatened to be damagingly costly to the banks? Second, given such a threat, might Murphy's system lead to pressure for intervention by the central bank to protect depositors?

In directing major attention to the risks of bank loan portfolios as ultimately necessitating regulatory oversight, Charles Goodhart sustains a persuasive case, despite surrendering traditionally defended ground. Two groups of qualifications nevertheless arise, which may be illustrated from British historical experience.

The first encompasses the lack of, indeed the difficulty of devising, effective sanctions, alike on bad lenders and bad borrowers. So far as bank lenders were concerned, there were almost 20 years of regulatory efforts from 1826. These ranged from relatively simple attempts to strengthen the capital base of banking, by removal of the ban on joint stock banks, to the comprehensive code of 1844 for new joint stock banks. Later, in 1858–62, limited liability was made available to bankers (though unlimited liability remained in respect of note issues). Welcoming this last change, Bagehot fairly commented that 'the system of *un*limited liability is that which fosters the *most* speculative management' (Bagehot, 1862, p. 397).

But those changes were piecemeal, were not mandatory, and resulted in a patchwork of banks operating under a variety of legal dispensations. Many leading bankers, for instance, eschewed limited liability as unprofessional, if not immoral. That attitude was to be temporarily reinforced by the Overend Gurney disaster of 1866, but was ultimately demolished 12 years later, when the City of Glasgow

Bank crash demonstrated that unlimited liability was unsustainable. Long before then, however, the legislative approach to stable banking seemed to have failed, and was tacitly dropped. The 1844 code seemed not to have worked and was virtually scrapped in 1857 (Toft, 1970). In contrast, the three great mid-century crises had so far demonstrated the power of Bank of England intervention that government officials jibbed at further regulation of banking after the 1878 shock. 'Was not the present position satisfactory?' asked a senior Board of Trade official, in which the Bank of England acted 'as a sort of Special Providence entrusted with the duty of looking after the cash and credit of the country' (Welby, 1878).

In respect of borrowers, English banks certainly faced an information problem, compared with Scottish bankers, in lacking the latter's access to details of a man's wealth (White, 1984, pp. 41–2). That *lacuna*, however, was not absolute: banks were likely to keep 'character books' or other records of confidential credit assessments, based routinely on inquiries of other banks and businesses.

Perhaps much more important, however, inhibiting lending and imparting serious risk when bank advances were made, was the gross inadequacy of bankruptcy law, which favoured debtors rather than creditors. For a time, during the French wars of 1793–1815, banks diminished that element of risk by exploiting ancient legal devices originally associated with collection of debts to the Crown, but that escape route was subsequently blocked (Pressnell, 1956, pp. 69–71).

Such wider issues of the broader business environment characterize also the second group of issues arising from Charles Goodhart's stress on banks' portfolio risk as justification of central bank oversight.

It is not necessary to share fully Geoffrey Wood's confidence that even the attenuated role which Charles Goodhart contemplates for central banking can be rendered otiose. Nor is it enough to adduce central bankers' misjudgements, as over Johnson Matthey and Continental Illinois. Rather, an uneasy feeling, that the duties now imposed on central bankers may simply be too much to expect any regulatory body to be able to perform satisfactorily, lingers after reading for instance, the Bank of England's own account of its regulatory responsibilities. (Bank of England, 1988a). Charles Goodhart indeed constructs a strong case for central banking. It is based on a realistic view of serious portfolio risk, when the banking system provides a substitute for incomplete financial markets in conditions of informational asymmetry. This, however, invites a search for significant improvement of financial markets, for ways to make information about bank borrowers less asymmetrical, and hence to trim alike the risks of banking error and of central banking *bêtises*.

On the first aspect, widespread stress in many countries on self-financing by industry involves undesirable avoidance of financial markets in the allocation of resources. In Britain, for instance, the ratio of internally to externally financed investment has normally been something like two to one. Moreover, whereas the external element had traditionally comprised a significant proportion of marketable bonds and debentures, for much of the last half century that element shrank; its recent modest recovery has been over-shadowed by the greater relative importance of massive bank finance (Thomas, 1978, tables on pp. 312–14; Bank of England, 1988b; *Financial Statistics,* May 1989). That reflected the squeezing out of private sector debt instruments by the demands of public sector borrowing in the fixed interest market, as well as unfavourable tax legislation. As the proportion of bank finance increases, so does bank portfolio risk and the strength of arguments for central banking.

On the second aspect, greater resort to the market in private sector debt, which the contemporary shrinkage of public sector debt makes more possible, would doubly reduce informational asymmetry. It would apply market valuation to a larger proportion of private sector financing; such market appraisal would also provide other lenders, such as the banks, with greater opportunities to assess risk. The banks themselves might further reduce their portfolio risk by invest-ing directly in marketable private sector debt instruments. Indeed, Charles Goodhart has noted elsewhere that they were beginning to hold bonds of private utilities by 1914 and, but for World War I 'could slowly have broadened out to encompass a wider range of holdings of industrial debentures' (Goodhart, 1972, p. 135). Re-sumption and quickening of such a trend could not be expected wholly to eliminate risk, but by making its identification less elusive should make regulators' tasks less forbidding. There would be implications, however, beyond adjustment of regulatory mechan-isms: drastic reorientation of company law, tax régimes, bankruptcy legislation, and, by no means least, in the traditional inward-looking attitude to company finance of so many business firms.

The response to the title of Charles Goodhart's paper, 'Are Central Banks necessary?' could then be 'Yes, but not nearly so necessary as we used to think'.

References

BAGEHOT, W. (1862) 'Limited Liability in Banking – I' *The Economist*, 17 May 1862, reprinted in *The Collected Works of Walter Bagehot*, ed. Norman St John–Stevas, London, 1978, Vol. IX.

BAGEHOT, W. (1873) *Lombard Street* (London: John Murray).

BAGEHOT, W. (1875) Evidence to the Select Committee on Banks of Issue, *British Parliamentary Papers* 1875, Vol. IX, reprinted in *Collected Works*, Vol. XI.

BANK OF ENGLAND (1988a) *Report*, 1987–88, 'Banking Act 1987'.

BANK OF ENGLAND (1988b) *Quarterly Bulletin*, February, 'The financial behaviour of industrial and commercial companies, 1970–86'.

FINANCIAL STATISTICS (1989). Her Majesty's Stationery Office, London, for the Central Statistical Office, issue for May 1989.

GOODHART, C. A. E. (1972) *The Business of Banking, 1891–1914* (London: Allen & Unwin).

MUNN, C. W. (1981) *The Scottish Provincial Banking Companies, 1747–1864* (Edinburgh: John Donald).

PRESSNELL, L. S. (1956) *Country Banking in the Industrial Revolution* (Oxford: Clarendon Press).

ROCKOFF, Hugh (1986) 'Walter Bagehot and the Theory of Central Banking', in Capie, F. and Wood, G. E. (eds.), *Financial Crises and the World Banking System* (London: Macmillan).

THOMAS, W. A. (1978) *The Finance of British Industry 1918–1976* (London: Methuen).

TOFT, K. S. (1970) 'A mid-nineteenth century attempt at banking control', *Revue internationale d'histoire de la banque*, Geneva.

WELBY, T. (1878) *Welby Papers*, Vol. 8 (British Library of Political and Economic Science).

WHITE, Lawrence H. (1984) *Free Banking in Britain* (Cambridge: Cambridge University Press).

Comment on Chapter 1

Geoffrey E. Wood

Whether central banks are necessary is a question to which economists and bankers keep returning. It is also one on which their views keep changing. Walter Bagehot (1873) will always be remembered for his advice to the Bank of England on how a central bank should operate. But he thought the system he was prescribing was second best to one of privately issued money. He recommended it only because he considered the English banking system too habituated to living with a central bank to return to the superior monetary system. Subsequently greater enthusiasm was displayed. Central banks were established around the world in the inter-war years. In the course of discussions preliminary to the establishing of one of thesse banks (the Reserve Bank of New Zealand), one of the protagonists noted in his diary:

> I suggested that the first and most foremost thing for New Zealand to do was to determine their attitude, as an economic unit. Were they to be dragged at the tail of Australia or to face their own affairs; in short, did the Government intend to form a central bank?

The enthusiasm is not surprising – the writer was Montague Norman. What is noteworthy is that, in contrast to Bagehot's cautious endorsement of a narrow role, Norman saw a central bank as having an important role (providing sound money) in the economy. Subsequent to that in the conventional view a central bank's role became much wider. In 1957 Richard Sayers wrote, 'The essence of central banking is discretionary control of the banking system . . . A central bank is necessary only when the community decides that a discretionary element is desirable. The central banker is the man who exercises his discretion'.

Charles Goodhart in his paper defends a much narrower version of a central bank than that espoused by Sayers. He does, indeed, return to the kind of central bank recommended by Bagehot. He defends central banks on the grounds not that they are necessary to manage the economy, but that they are necessary to prevent monetary and

29

banking collapse at a time of crisis. He does, however, differ crucially from Bagehot in how he recommends they should behave at such times; this difference is the main focus of these comments.

BANK FAILURES AND THEIR CONSEQUENCES

As Charles Goodhart notes, the failure of a series of banks can have two types of consequence. There can be a collapse in the stock of money, and there can be a breakdown of the national payment and settlements system.[1] He cites some evidence (Andrew (1908), Murphy, (1972)) to suggest that the latter consequence is not overwhelmingly important. This conclusion can be bolstered by analysis.

If there is a central bank with the monopoly right to issue money, then the collapse of the money stock based on that monetary base will disrupt every market in which the money is used, for by law no perfect substitutes can emerge.[2] In contrast, payments and settlements systems are not monopolies maintained by law. If one fails, another can emerge; and the evidence Charles Goodhart cites shows it can do so quickly. It therefore follows that the central bank's primary concern should be with the stock of money; there is no need for it to have any concern with the payments system.

WHAT KIND OF LENDER OF LAST RESORT?

Since the central bank is concerned only with the stock of money, it need not assist an individual bank. *It should not engage in bail-outs.* Rather it should, as Bagehot recommended, lend to the market; that is, it should lend on security to whoever brings in that security at a time of financial distress. It should behave as the Bank of England behaved in the panic of 1825. Jeremiah Harman, a director of the Bank at the time, has left a vivid description of the episode. It is quoted in the Introduction (p. xiv). The policy worked. The panic was allayed, and the failure of one bank did not lead to a financial crisis.

There is no need to bail out insolvent institutions. The lender of last resort should be the classical one, *not* the extended one which Charles Goodhart tries to defend. It should be emphasized also that if central banks behave thus, a wave of bank failures is highly unlikely, and in turn therefore the payments and settlements system is also protected by classical lender of last resort action. Concern for the payments system (for which, as argued above, there is in any event little reason) cannot justify bail-outs.

This leads to a second point. Why should central banks supervise and regulate the banking system? It is clearly not required for their LLR role; they could if they wished even rely on private rating agencies for guidance on the quality of paper presented for discounting. (Such agencies of course are already in prosperous and well-esteemed existence.) There is no support for central bank supervision of the banking system to be derived from its lender of last resort role. And this is fortunate. For there is evidence that central banks are ineffective supervisors – note Johnson Matthey – and the restrictions imposed by supervisors, such as capital adequacy, are either what banks would themselves choose and therefore redundant, or in excess of that and therefore a barrier to entry.

It is also clear that Goodhart's praise for two aspects of central bank behaviour is misconceived. The Federal Reserve was wrong to bail-out Continental Illinois: first, because bale-outs are unnecessary, and, second, because what was affecting that bank was not a flight to cash, but a flight to other banks. The system was not threatened. (Had Continental Illinois failed, there might have been a flight to cash; the Fed was right to go on the alert, but wrong to act.) Moving from the specific to the general, his praise for central banks keeping 'their intentions for supporting private sector banks generally obscure' is misconceived. Central banks should make absolutely clear that they have no such intention.[3]

DO WE NEED A LENDER OF LAST RESORT?

Some scholars have argued recently that a lender of last resort, even in the narrow sense defended above, is unnecessary. Bank runs – to cash – start because of uncertainty about the liquidity of a bank. The failure of one bank leads to a run on others because depositors at these others fear that their banks too will fail. If this fear is unfounded, providing information to show this will end runs. Some writers have in addition argued that holding only marketable assets and continually marking to market will remove uncertainty, and thus end bank runs.

Certain banks of course do this already, but they are rather specialized institutions. Most institutions make at least some loans for which there is no market; indeed, Charles Goodhart cogently argues that banks to some extent exist to make loans for which there is no market. Not all institutions could mark to market, and it would be economically inefficient to restrict their portfolios so that they could. In this conclusion, where he reaches the same result as Friedman and Schwartz (1986), though by a different route, I wholeheartedly concur. There is a role for a classical lender of last resort.[4] This does not, however, mean we should have a lender of last resort. Why this is so is set out in the conclusion, after discussion of two minor points.

DOES DEPOSIT INSURANCE SUBSTITUTE FOR A LENDER OF LAST RESORT?

Deposit insurance evolved partly as a response to the failure of the Federal Reserve to act as a lender of last resort in the Great Depression (See Gilbert and Wood, 1986.) Protecting deposits removes the incentive for depositors to run to their banks for cash. There is thus no threat of a bank run bringing down the banking system. But there is, unfortunately, also no incentive for depositors to pay any heed to how prudent their bank is being. They used to do this; Thomas Huertas (1985), in his work on the history of Citibank, showed how that bank prospered in recessions by being known to hold larger reserves, and to have a more conservative lending policy, than the other New York banks.

In contrast, it is clear that regulators are poor at policing banks. Johnson Matthey has already been cited; the Savings and Loan crisis in the USA is another example.

Deposit insurance creates a considerable moral hazard. Banks can take risks at the taxpayer's expense. One response would be to make insurance premia risk-related. Another, much simpler, would be to restrict deposit insurance to small depositors. This would deal with the concern that many of these had neither the time nor the knowledge to police their bank. Further, and very important, if such depositors were protected, political pressure to engage in bank bail-outs would be diminished. Large depositors meanwhile could be relied on to watch their banks carefully.[5]

To answer the question with which this section opened, deposit insurance *may* serve as a substitute for a lender of last resort. But it should be restricted so that it does not.

SUPERVISE TO PREVENT FOLLY?

Following Keynes, Charles Goodhart argues that bank supervision is necessary to prevent banks rushing herd-like into foolish investment projects. Here he is wrong, and on several grounds. First, as noted above, supervisors are not very good at stopping such behaviour.

Indeed, his characterization of the history of commercial banking in western countries before the advent of effective central banking as comprising 'periods of major loan expansions, often culminating in financial crises, and subsequently followed by periods of conservative retrenchment' fits rather well what has happened since central banking became widespread. Second, even if banks did behave in this way, why does it matter so long as consequences for the money stock are prevented? Third, it is not clear that they really do behave in this way in the absence of supervision.[6] Note, for example, that in the Baring crisis other banks were *not* heavily committed to Argentina – they had *not* rushed herd-like after Barings – and in consequence they were able to help. Herd-like behaviour seems not an intrinsic trait of bankers, but rather the product of a supervisory system where there is a good chance that bankers keep the gains and taxpayers the losses.

CONCLUSIONS

Charles Goodhart's argument for a lender of last resort is persuasive. As banks' balance sheets are at present constituted, bank runs which threaten monetary stability are possible, and having their balance sheets thus constituted is an economically useful function. By developing this argument Charles Goodhart has made an important contribution to both analysis and policy. It must, however, be emphasized that the lender of last resort should be the 'classical' one; it should lend to the market, and not engage in bail-outs of individual banks.

We should observe also that there are substitutes for a lender of last resort. UK building societies have managed well without one. Building societies, like British banks, are often geographically widely dispersed. This of course diversifies their risks and makes them less vulnerable to shocks. (Some building societies are, however, not thus dispersed; they may gain their stability by association with their larger brethren.) Clearing houses can help. Option clauses are useful.[7] (Building societies in effect operate these by restricting daily cash withdrawals to a small amount, usually £300 or £400 per account.) Until recently it was not uncommon for banks' shareholders to have double liability: this was another assurance to depositors, and could be reinstated.

The availability of those substitutes would be irrelevant if lenders of last resort were costless. Unfortunately they are not. The era of managed money we have seen since 1914 has been one of major inflation and major recession, both produced by central bank failure. What we should therefore now consider is how to devise institutional structures which minimize the cost of having a lender of last resort. If we cannot do better than we have done since the beginning of this century in that endeavour, then we might, while fully concurring with Charles Goodhart's argument for a lender of last resort, decide to move to an inferior but less expensive substitute.

Notes

1. The customer relationship may also be affected. As Donald Hodgman (1963) showed, this relationship between banker and customer is sometimes an important contributor to economic efficiency. It is, however, far from inevitable that bank failure destroys the relationship. Many firms, and not a few individuals, have more than one bank. And bank failure need not destroy the relationship; for failure can often mean that the bank continues with much of the same management, but different ownership. This of course preserves also the payment and settlement system. See Benston and Kaufman (1988) for an extended discussion of these points.

2. It should be observed that imperfect substitutes can emerge, and in some cases did. Substitutes for money, known as scrip, were issued throughout the US in 1921–3. One estimate (Willis and Chapman, 1934 p. 15) is that $1 billion of scrip was in use. This of course no more than slightly mitigated the consequences of the failure of the Federal Reserve to act as lender of last resort. The importance of this role is discussed further below. Substitutes for money also appeared in the 1907 panic, as is discussed by Andrew (1908).

3. They should in fact point out from time to time that bank failures are desirable – at least as compared with preventing failures by subsidy from the taxpayers. Otherwise the incentives for dishonesty and carelessness are limited only by the taxpayers' willingness to support them.

4. This may not always be so. Loans that only a few years ago were not are now marketable.

5. George Benston has in conversation provided another example of how

depositors policed banks in the absence of deposit insurance. When he was a junior employee in a bank in Atlanta, and deposit insurance was restricted to small sums, one of his tasks was regularly to telephone large depositors to give them information on the bank's balance sheet, so that they were kept up to date on the soundness of the bank and therefore did not withdraw their deposits.

6.   An additional danger with supervision and regulation is that it may be taken to imply approval and thus diminish depositor prudence still further. This is surely one of the major costs of supervision, particularly if the supervisors feel likewise and undertake bail-outs because of their feelings of responsibility.

7.   Charles Goodhart raises the question of why option clauses disappeared from Scottish banking. According to Horsefield (1941, p. 7, fn. 2) these clauses were 'prohibited in 1765 at the instance of the Bank of Scotland and the Royal Bank of Scotland, because they tended to encourage overissue'.

References

ANDREW, A. P. (1908) 'Substitutes for Cash in the Panic of 1907', *QJE*, August.

BAGEHOT, W. (1873) *Lombard Street* (London: John Murray).

BENSTON, G. J. and KAUFMAN, G. (1988) *Risk and Solvency Regulation of Depository Institutions: Past Policies and Current Options*, Salomon Brothers Center for the Study of Financial Institutions, New York University. Monograph Series in Finance and Economics, Monograph 1988–1.

FRIEDMAN, M. and SCHWARTZ, A. J. (1986) 'Has Government any Role in Money?', *JME*, 17, pp. 37–62.

GILBERT, A. and WOOD, G. E. (1986) 'Coping with Bank Failures: Some lessons from the United States and the United Kingdom', *FR Bank of St Louis Review*, December, pp. 5–14.

HODGMAN, Donald R. (1963) *Commercial Bank Loan and Investment Behaviour*, Bureau of Economic and Business Research (University of Illinois Champaign, Illinois).

HORSEFIELD, J. K. (1941) 'The Duties of a Banker', *Economica*, February.

HUERTAS, T. (1985) *Citibank 1812–1970* (Harvard UP).

MURPHY, A. E. (1972) 'The Nature of Money – with Particular Reference to the Irish Bank Closure', Trinity College, Dublin (Mimeo).

SAYERS, R. S. (1957) *Central Banking after Bagehot* (Oxford: Clarendon Press).

WILLIS, H. PARKER, and CHAPMAN, JOHN M. 1934) *The Banking Situation* (New York: Columbia University Press).

2 Banking without a Central Bank: Scotland before 1844 as a 'Free Banking' system

Lawrence H. White

INTRODUCTION

The traditional view of Scottish banking experience is that the system in operation there before 1844 warranted the label of 'free banking' that it has commonly received. That is, the regulatory regime approximated laissez-faire closely enough that its institutions, practices, and performance were essentially those of an unregulated free-market monetary system. This view was promoted by the nineteenth-century advocates of free banking in Britain, America, France, and elsewhere, who cited Scottish banking as a model to be emulated.[1] It permeates the early histories of Scottish banking, most notably that of Andrew Kerr (1884). In more recent literature, it underlies the summaries of the Scottish experience offered by Vera Smith (1936, ch. 2), Rondo Cameron (1967, ch. 3) and myself (White (1984), ch. 2), and the use of the Scottish experience as counter-evidence to the legal restrictions theory of money (White (1987)).

Several recent critics have challenged this interpretation. Economic historians Checkland (1968), Munn (1985), and Tyson (1985), who are sceptical of any simple picture of a complex historical experience, have pointed to features of the Scottish case seemingly at odds with the free-banking model. They have offered alternative interpretations, according to which the two most important Scottish banks, or the Bank of England, played certain controlling roles. Monetary economists Cowen and Kroszner (1989) and Rothbard (1988), who wish to defend visions of laissez-faire payments systems (the legal restrictions theory of money, and the one-hundred-per-cent gold standard, respectively) that do not coincide with the Scottish model, have argued that the Scottish régime was not laissez-faire. The revisionist arguments of these two groups often overlap, because

37

the second group relies primarily on Checkland (1975) and Munn (1981) for historical details.

The aim of this chapter is to reply to the revisionist criticisms. The revisionists have usefully emphasized certain special features of the Scottish case, and have correctly cautioned against regarding Scotland as a case of pure laissez-faire. Still, their major indictments of the free-banking interpretation do not withstand critical scrutiny. What is at issue is not so much 'basic facts' as their interpretation. I rely here on Checkland (1975) and Munn (1981) as the authoritative chroniclers of events. The issue is, what pattern best fits the facts? I find that the traditional free-banking interpretation fits best.

If this is correct, then the Scottish experience remains relevant to current policy debate. However, although the Scottish example is important, and perhaps (as the traditional interpretation has it) even the most important historical case of relatively unregulated banking, neither the case for nor the case against a free-banking policy depends exclusively on how well the Scottish experience exemplifies free banking.[2]

IS THE TRADITIONAL CONTRAST BETWEEN THE SCOTTISH AND ENGLISH BANKING SYSTEMS FALSE?

As an introduction to the debate between traditional and revisionist views of Scottish banking, it is useful to consider an issue that Sidney Checkland (1968) raised in an essay-review of Rondo Cameron's (1967) work on English and Scottish banking. Cameron (1982) responded belatedly in a *festschrift* for Checkland, but did not criticize his arguments point by point as I shall do here.

Checkland (1968, p. 153) argued that Cameron's contrast between a laissez-faire Scottish system and a legislatively hobbled English system 'is overdone, and rests, in part, on false grounds'. In Checkland's view (pp. 147–8) Scottish banking was not distinctly less regulated than English banking in the early nineteenth century. The British state 'played a minimum role', but a role, in both systems. The state did not attempt mercantilistic control, did not impose 'alien objectives and rules', and did not coerce the banking system in an attempt to foster growth in either contry. Its 'watching brief', Checkland contends, 'was confined to the question of stability'. Thus he concludes (p. 154): 'It is realistic to regard the English and Scottish banking systems as being essentially similar. They share ... that category of banking institutions that were part of spontaneous, atomistic, liberal growth, with its dilemma of stability. The real contrast lies between them and the other systems discussed' in Cameron's book, namely France, Belgium, Germany, Russia, and Japan.

The contrast between Scottish and other systems is indeed greater. But there are important contrasts between England and Scotland before 1844. Cameron (1982, pp. 102–3) quotes from Checkland's own history of Scottish banking to show that 'there were significant differences in the two systems at that time and that the Scottish system was markedly superior'. The contrast between Scotland and England is important because it is more nearly a *ceteris paribus* experiment than other possible international contrasts. In a passage Cameron does not cite, Checkland (1975, p. xviii) notes that its advocates 'wished to see the Scottish system of banking extended to England in the nineteenth [century]'. If these people were not deluded, and Checkland does not suggest that they were, then the English and Scottish banking systems must have differed in important respects.

In saying that the state intervened only for the sake of stability, Checkland neglects the important role of state fiscal concerns – the desire to have a pet bank from which to borrow – in motivating the original grants of privilege to the Bank of England, and presumably in motivating the preservation and extension of those privileges. He also neglects the rent-seeking self-interest of the Bank of England working in the same direction.

Checkland's attempt to argue that England's banking system was practically as 'spontaneous, atomistic, liberal' as Scotland's is clearly strained. He declares (p. 151): 'In England until 1826 there was only one kind of state intervention [in banking], namely the maintenance of the preferred position of the Bank of England'. This neglects the ban on small notes. More importantly, the means chosen for maintaining the Bank's preferred position had profoundly distortive effects. As Checkland recognizes, the chief means were 'the six-partner rule and the employment by the government of the Bank as its fiscal agent'. He tries, unpersuasively in my view, to diminish the importance of both means.

Checkland (p. 151) excuses the fiscal favoritism as justified: 'Though politics and vested interest were certainly present the case was strong for recognising as primary a single institution acting as the financial agent of the state'. It is unclear, however, what this 'strong' case was, or why the state could not have conducted its financial affairs without favoritism. Checkland (p. 150) denies that the Scottish system was freer than the English from distortion due to government finance: 'The Scottish banking system, with its close ties both with the London private bankers and with the Bank of England, together with its holdings of government debt, was no less than the English an instrument of government finance'. But surely there is a difference between the concessionary loans that the Bank of England made to the government in its early days, the *quid pro quo* for which was the six-partner rule, and the Scottish banks' voluntary holding of government debt purchased at the market price. This is Cameron's point. Unless the Scottish chartered banks were compelled to hold government debt as a *quid pro quo* for their charters, which Checkland does not suggest, Scotland without the six-partner rule was indeed freer than England from distortions arising out of government fiscal needs.

This brings us to the question of the impact of the six-partner rule, which restricted other English banks to six or fewer partners (neither could any other bank receive a charter). Checkland (p. 152) dismisses as 'exaggerated' the traditional argument that the rule promoted instability in English banking by preventing the formation of joint stock banks large enough to be adequately capitalized and diversified. I will consider his reasons one by one:

1   Checkland notes that apart from the three chartered banks (and the short-lived Ayr Bank), no large joint stock banks arose in Scotland before 1810. But this tells us that the six-partner rule was more binding after 1810, exactly when the contrast in stability was most remarked upon, not that it was never binding. Furthermore, competition among several chartered banks was a salutary element lacking in England. The six-partner rule prevented any competition with the Bank of England for note-issue business in the London area, and thereby prevented the emergence of a note-exchange system which could discipline the Bank against over-extending its circulation.

2   Checkland argues that the 'relatively greater stability of the Scottish banks' had less to do with the number of partners than with three other distinguishing circumstances: the Edinburgh banks' large holdings of government securities, weekly note-exchanges, and mutual support through inter-bank loans from the two oldest chartered banks. But the first factor hardly seems relevant to the greater stability of the Scottish provincial banks compared to the country banks of England. The absence of a six-partner rule helps to explain why Scotland developed a regular

note-exchange system sooner than England. The plurality of large banks made mutal support possible, and this support could later be safely and hence profitably extended to smaller banks in part because no six-partner rule weakened the other banks.

3   Checkland suggests that the six-partner rule actually promoted stability in two ways. First, with the rule in place, the partners in a bank 'were not endangered by the threat of a joint-stock mammoth invading their territory and destroying them'. Second, joint stock enterprises could be unstable, as seen in the seventeenth century and in the behavior of at least some joint stock banks after 1826. But surely restrictions that shelter undersized banks or other uneconomic enterprises cannot enhance the soundness and stability of the economy, however much they may do for those firms in the short run. That some larger banks made errors is no argument for compulsory smallness.

After 1826, Checkland (p. 151) says, 'the government ended the six-partner rule but began to regulate the English note-issue'. He attributes this regulation to an empirically justified 'fear of a perilous conjunction between those notoriously volatile elements, note-issue and joint-stock promotion'. But the six-partner rule *remained* in place for issuing banks within 65 miles of London, reinforcing the Bank of England's predominance in the financial centre. The drawing of the circle around London seems better explained by concern for the stability of the profits of the government's favorite debt-holder, the Bank of England, than by any proclaimed concerns for the stability of the economy. The Bank's historian Clapham (1945, ii, pp. 87–8, 102–6) documents its directors' lobbying efforts to retain its privileges as the sole bank of the state and the sole issuer in the London area. There likewise seems to be more than 'the influence of the quantity theory of money and the fear of irresponsible note-issuing' that Checkland cites behind the provisions of the 1833 Act giving Bank of England notes quasi-legal-tender status, and behind the provisions of the 1844 Act giving the Bank a more complete monopoly of the note-issue. These essentials of the 1844 Act were proposed to Peel early in 1844 by the Bank of England's Governor and Deputy Governor. Horsely Palmer, Governor of the Bank in the 1830s, had long wanted to monopolize the circulation (Clapham 1945, ii, pp. 113–14, 178–9).

Checkland states that 'After 1826 the Treasury did not really obstruct the spontaneous growth of joint-stock banks'. But the spontaneous growth of joint stock banks was very likely obstructed in an important way by their exclusion from London even after 1826. It certainly was obstructed by the Bank Charter Act of 1844, which froze authorized issues and absolutely barred new banks of issue.

Checkland finds Cameron's criticisms of interventionist British banking legislation unwarranted, apparently because Checkland believes (for unspecified reasons) that a free-banking policy was not really an option. Regarding alternative policy courses, he writes (p. 152):

> There were two possibilities: either the state might have allowed banking to evolve 'freely' (e.g. without control of note-issues or of joint-stock banking organization or of any other aspect, and without creating a special position for certain banks) or the state might have undertaken a much more far-reaching control of banking. Neither was practicable in the Britain of the eighteen-thirties and 'forties.

If free banking was impracticable, then certainly Scotland cannot have practised something close to it.

HOW IMPORTANT WERE THE PRIVILEGES OF THE SCOTTISH CHARTERED BANKS?

The free-banking interpretation of the Scottish system has generally recognized that laissez-faire did not prevail in its purest form. The point at issue is, how important were the deviations from laissez-faire? Several revisionists have argued that the chartered banks in Scotland had privileges that significantly affected the system.

Cowen and Kroszner (1989, pp. 225–7), following Carr, Glied, and Mathewson (1986) and Carr and Mathewson (1988), point to the restriction of limited-liability charters to three particular banks, which made unlimited liability compulsory for other banks, as a barrier to entry.[3] Clearly such a restriction on the contractual risk-sharing arrangements firms may adopt is potentially a barrier to entry. Statements to the effect that Scotland enjoyed 'perfect freedom' (Wilson (1847), p. 30), 'complete freedom from legal restriction' (Wenley (1882), p. 142), or 'complete freedom of entry' (White (1984), pp. 3, 29), are therefore incorrect. But how important was this barrier in practice?

My book (White (1984), pp. 4, 141–2) recognizes that compulsory liability rules are potentially an obstacle to optimal risk-sharing arrangements, but suggests (following Checkland, 1975, p. 480) that the restriction against limited liability banks in Scotland was not binding because 'the unchartered banks of Scotland chose to retain unlimited liability in the 1860s and '70s even after limited liability became available to them' through the Companies Act of 1862. Carr, Glied, and Mathewson (1986) challenge this interpretation of the evidence. They point out that while the 1862 Act allowed limited liability for other bank obligations, it retained unlimited liability for note-issues. They conclude (p. 9): 'Consequently, it is not surprising that no Scottish bank adopted the restricted limited liability privileges of the 1862 Act'. This conclusion seems a *non sequitur*. If unlimited liability was inefficient for Scottish banks, as their theory (Carr and Mathewson (1988) suggests, wouldn't those banks have found a substantial limitation of liability better than no limitation, and therefore have taken advantage of the 1862 Act?

A question of the magnitude arises here. Carr, Glied, and Mathewson (p. 9) say that 'the 1862 Act continued to maintain unlimited liability for a significant share of the liabilities of Scottish banks'. In fact notes were only 7.9 per cent of total liabilities for the Scottish banks in 1865 (Checkland (1975), Table 44, p. 743), or 6.6 per cent of liabilities plus capital (a figure Carr, Glied, and Mathewson themselves cite on p. 10). Whether or not 7.9 per cent is 'a significant share' or not, clearly a limitation of liability for the other 92.1 per cent is not trivial.

A more direct test of the thesis of Carr *et. al.* seems possible but has not yet been carried out. According to Carr, Glied, and Mathewson (1986, p. 5), the inefficiency of banking firms with unlimited liability implies that 'the value of unlimited liability shares are [*sic*] reduced relative to their limited liability counterparts'. It should be possible to test this hypothesis by comparing share prices for the Scottish chartered banks against those for the joint stock banks with unlimited liability. Did the shares of the chartered banks really command a premium *ceteris paribus*? The traditional view implies that any such premium was negligible.

Carr, Glied, and Mathewson (1986, p. 10) believe that the surviving Scottish joint stock banks finally adopted limited liability in 1882 because an 1879 Act offered 'substantially lessened' liability for notes. On my reading, however, the 1879 Act retained greater shareholder liability for notes than the 1862 Act. Historians of the industry have traditionally attributed the adoption of limitied liability not to the change in the law, but to the 1878 failure of the City of Glasgow Bank, which evidently changed the perceptions of shareholders concerning the risks they faced.

We can also assess the bindingness of compulsory unlimited liability before 1844 by contrasting the three limited-liability 'public' banks (the Bank of Scotland, Royal Bank of Scotland, and British Linen Company) with the unlimited banks. Cowen and Kroszner (1989, p. 226) note that the public banks were larger on average, and (following Carr and Mathewson (1988), pp. 776–7) that none of them failed. They plausibly conclude that limited liability made it easier to raise capital and that the corporate form was 'conducive to survival'.

As evidence to the contrary, however, several facts regarding the unlimited-liability banks as of 1845 (White (1984), table 2.2, p. 37) can be noted: (1) the Commercial Bank of Scotland had more branches than any of the public banks, a greater note circulation than two of the three, and more shareholders than one; (2) the National Bank of Scotland had more branches than two of the three public banks, a note circulation only 1 per cent smaller than that of the second largest public bank, and more shareholders than any of the three; (3) the North of Scotland Banking Company and the Edinburgh and Glasgow Bank each had more shareholders than any of the three public banks; and (4) the Union Bank of Scotland had a greater note-circulation than two of the three public banks. All told, the public British Linen Company ranked first, the Bank of Scotland fourth, and the Royal Bank seventh in size of circulation. Banks with unlimited liability apparently did not have great difficulty raising capital on a large scale: five had capitals as large as the Bank of Scotland's £1 million, and eight had capitals as large or larger than the British Linen Company's £500,000. Nor was the survival of unlimited banks obviously impaired once they attained adequate size: none of the five above-mentioned large joint stock banks failed while they had unlimited liability. (Two of the eight with the largest capitals eventually did fail after 1844.)

Still, the banks that made efforts to get legislative charters, and to deny them to other banks, must have wanted them for some reason. Cowen and Kroszner (1989, p. 226, n. 11) correctly point out that 'since resources were expended to fight for and against corporate charters, we can infer that the bankers of the time believed that the privileges associated with charters were valuable'. Cowen and Kroszner cite several possible advantages beyond limited liability, one of which clearly had some value: government customs officers were instructed to accept only the notes of the chartered banks in payment of duties (Checkland (1975), p. 186).

Cowen and Kroszner (1989, p. 226) also claim that 'only they [the public banks] were authorized to "hold and remit" government revenues'. The basis for this claim is unclear, since it is not in the pages of Munn and Checkland that they cite.[4] Checkland (1975, p. 166) in fact relates that the private bank of Sir William Forbes and Company in the late eighteenth century 'had the remittance of the excise duties from Edinburgh to London'. He adds: 'The Royal Bank had long had the remittance of the customs; the British Linen Company that of the revenue of the Post Office[;] the Bank of Scotland had nothing'. Thus a charter was neither necessary nor sufficient to benefit from government patronage.

Cowen and Kroszner cite two other advantages: (1) 'the appearance of official sanction', which Checkland (1968, p. 149) also notes, and (2) escape from 'the uncertain legal identity of unincorporated entities', which existed until a statute clarified their status in 1826. It is not clear how important these really were. But in at least one respect, receivability for duties, the public banks enjoyed politically created rents. The existence of such rents is clearly contrary to strict laissez-faire. Accounts of the Scottish system as free banking have perhaps underemphasized (though they have not ignored) the 'preferred position' of the public banks (Checkland (1975), p. 235) in this respect.

Contrary to Cowen and Kroszner (1989, p. 226), however, the charters did not have the effect of 'reducing competitive pressures (hence relaxing the zero-profit condition)' throughout the free-banking era. The evidence indicates that while the public banks may have enjoyed a more-or-less advantaged position before 1810, they clearly faced effective competition at the relevant margins between 1810 and 1844. Competition between the public banks and the large joint stock banks was vigorous in note-issuing, deposit-taking, lending and discounting, inland exchange, and other aspects of banking.[5] Profit margins for all banks were squeezed as competitive bidding for loans and deposits kept the interest differential down to 1 per cent (Checkland (1975), pp. 384–8), exactly Neil Wallace's (1983) estimate of the competitive spread in the absence of legal restrictions. Contrary to Cowen and Kroszner's hypothesis of a 'relaxed' zero-excess-profit condition, Munn (1982, p. 118) comments that 'the competitive nature of the business' had the result that 'profits were reduced and therefore all earning assets had to be managed with fine attention to detail. There was no room for error or even slackness if dividends were to be maintained'. Attempts were made in the 1830s and '40s to limit interest rates and activity charges through cartel agreements, but such agreements proved unsustainable in the face of strong competitive pressures (Checkland (1975), pp. 449-50; Munn (1982), p. 122).

Munn (1981, p. 93) quotes a statement by the directors of the National Bank of Scotland in 1842: 'The great competition which now exists amongst the numerous banks in Scotland has had the effect . . . of reducing the profits of Banks in operation'. Munn adds, citing Gourvish (1969) and an 1840 Bank of Scotland document:

> [T]he public banks also felt the strain. The Bank of Scotland in particular had its profits squeezed. It attributed the fluctuations and the general decrease in profits between 1814 and 1840 to four causes. The note circulation which had formerly been the major source of profit had decreased due to the increased competition for business and the growing use of cheques. Secondly the yields on government securities had fallen by more than one per cent. Thirdly the par of exchange had been reduced from 50 days to 5 days. Lastly commision on bills and on letters of credit had been reduced while stamp duties on notes had been increased.

The elimination of excess profits in note-issuing, exchange, and bill-discounting, is evidence of the effectiveness of competition among the banks. Cowen and Kroszner fail to inquire after this evidence. It appears that they simply assume, incorrectly, that the infringements of laissez-faire to which they point precluded effective competition. Goodhart's (1988, p. 51) characterization of the Scottish system as 'oligopolistic in form' and his tentative hypothesis that in a system of the Scottish sort 'competitive . . . pressures *may* be less' are similarly misplaced for the 1810–44 period at a minimum.

Checkland's account also sometimes overstates the public banks' advantages. In a chapter on the state of the system as of 1810, Checkland (1975, p. 186) asserts: 'The larger banks, of course, enjoyed self-reinforcing advantages, for because they were the principal sources of lending, they were better able to get their issue out'. He goes on to call this 'the law of cumulative success for larger concerns'. This assertion, however, embodies a complete *non sequitur*. The larger banks lending more notes out equally had more notes returning home each week. It remains to be shown that their efforts to keep notes in circulation enjoyed continually increasing returns to scale. If they had, then the larger banks could have grown ever more dominent. In fact, according to Checkland's own figures (table 8, p. 250; table 14, p. 424; table 15, p. 426) the public banks' share of the circulation declined significantly in the period after 1800, from 54 per cent in 1802 to 46 per cent in 1825, and thence to only 33 per cent in 1850.

DID THE CHARTERED BANKS PLAY A CONTROLLING OR CENTRAL BANKING ROLE IN THE SCOTTISH SYSTEM?

In his review of Cameron, Checkland (1968, pp. 149, 154) suggests that the public banks played a regulatory role in the Scottish banking industry much like the Bank of England played south of the Tweed. In doing so, they acted as stand-ins for the government, which 'wishing to minimize its own participation in banking, thought that it could best do so when 'leadership' (e.g. a sense of responsibility for the working of the system as a whole) was provided by a dominant element within the system'. Thus 'the Edinburgh banks regarded themselves as the custodians of the system', and constituted 'in effect, a state recognised "gild".' Most provocatively, he adds (p. 153) that 'it can be argued that through the chartered banks Scotland's banking was more "controlled" than that of England'. Munn (1985, p. 341) argues along the same lines, citing 'forms of influence from the centre' and the belief by contemporary banker Alexander Blair in 'his role at the Bank of Scotland as policeman of the system'. Tyson (1985) expresses a similar view.

It is noteworthy that Checkland hedges the word 'controlled' with quotation marks. What was the 'controlling' or 'leadership' role of the public banks? Explains Checkland (1968, p. 149): 'They developed a code of banking among themselves, and they sought, not without success, to enforce it upon others'. In particular, they insisted that member banks in the note-exchange system hold a secure secondary reserve in government stock, as well as an adequate primary reserve. This practice, however, was clearly *not* a matter of cartelization or discretionary direction of the banking system. Any note-exchange or clearing-house system requires minimum standards for admission because members are agreeing to accept and to hold until settlement one another's liabilities. This sort of banking industry

'self-policing', as Munn (1985, p. 341) calls it, has nothing intrinsic-
ally to do with some banks having superior legal status to others. It
emerged in United States among legally equal clearing-house members (Timberlake (1984), Gorton (1985), Gorton and Mullineaux
(1987)). The 'gild' of Scottish public banks did not successfully
control interest rates or otherwise prevent inter-bank competition.
The behaviour of the Scottish system, especially from 1810 to 1844,
was shaped by the dictates of competition, not by the desires of the
'leading' banks. Checkland's (1975, p. 205) summary of the situation is consistent with this view:

> The public banks, though they insisted on every possible occasion
> upon their public role, were very limited in their ability to control
> the system ... [I]n a system of free banking, as in Scotland, such
> devices [as they could employ to threaten other banks] could be of
> only limited effectiveness.

Membership in a common clearing system does not itself reflect
cartelization, but instead reflects the natural evolution of a competitive system (Selgin and White (1987)). In opposition to this view,
Munn (1985, p. 341) refers to 'the reign of terror exercised by the
public banks in Edinburgh which forced the other banks to join the
exchange, that is, the exchange did not emerge as if by some invisible
hand but required a very visible hand to bring it about'. It is true that
the public banks played an important role in the development of the
Scottish note-exchange. But the applicability of the metaphor of the
invisible hand does not require that all agents be atomistic and
anonymous, only that their actions produce a pattern which is not
deliberately designed. The emergence of the Scottish note-exchange
system among the provincial banks, before the public banks decided
to join it in 1771 (Munn 1981, pp. 21–5), meets this criterion. The
'reign of terror' to which Munn so colourfully refers (his book of
1981, p. 27, termed it more mildly as 'period of "rough wooing"')
was simply the public banks' self-interested policy of redeeming notes
over the counter when an issuer short-sightedly resisted participating
in the regular exchange. Non-participation was short-sighted because, as Munn (1981, p. 28) indicates, mutal acceptance and regular
exchange increased the demand to hold a bank's notes and thus
increased its sustainable circulation, even though it shortened the
average circulation period of its notes.

   Munn (1985, p. 341) mentions as an additional form of 'influence from the centre' the willingness of the Royal Bank of Scotland to 'act as a lender of last resort to the provincial banking companies'. It is not clear what sort of 'influence' the Royal Bank attached to its loans, though it naturally insisted on certain evidence of soundness in its borrowers. Inter-bank lending has no intrinsic connection with hierarchical relations among banks, as today's Fed Funds market in the United States shows.

DID DEPENDENCE ON LONDON MAKE SCOTTISH BANKING A MERE SATELLITE SYSTEM?

Several critics have argued that the Scottish system's status as a mere 'satellite to the London centre' (Goodhart (1987), p. 131) under-mines the free-banking interpretation of Scottish experience. There are two sets of claims here. The first is that the Scottish banks customarily 'pyramided' their credit on that of the Bank of England, or that the Scottish money supply was geared to the quantity of Bank of England liabilities. The second is that the Scottish system de-pended on the London money market for occasional liquidity needs or, even more damaging to the free-banking interpretation, de-pended on the Bank of England as a lender of last resort.

The question of pyramiding

Sechrest (1988, p. 247) advances the first claim: 'the Scottish system was *de facto* a central bank system in which individual private banks pyramided their note issues upon the reserves of the three chartered banks, which, in turn, pyramided their issues upon the reserves of the ultimate source of liquidity for the entire British Isles: the Bank of England'. Rothbard (1988, p. 231) similarly asserts that the Scottish banks 'pyramided credit on top of the Bank of England'.

To say that one bank 'pyramids credit' on top of another is to say that the first holds fractional reserves in the form of the second's liabilities. (The credit structure then forms an 'inverted pyramid' in which each dollar of the second bank's liabilities 'supports' several dollars of the first bank's.) This is indeed what Sechrest tries to demonstrate. Sechrest (p. 250) quotes[6] Checkland's (1975, p. 186) statement that 'it became the custom of other banks, both the private bankers . . . and provincial banking companies, to hold part of their cash in the notes of the public banks, rather than hold cumbersome gold' and takes this to indicate (p. 253) that 'much of the reserves of the nonpublic banks were held in the form of public bank notes'. He then adds, quoting Fetter (1965, p. 34): 'Similarly, "the three chartered banks of Scotland kept their reserves largely in deposits with the Bank of England"'.

If this demonstration were successful, it would indeed upset the traditional picture of Scottish banking as a system in which 'each bank held onto its own specie reserves' (White (1984), p. 43). On closer examination, however, it does not stand up. Although there were some exceptions in the earlier days of the system, other Scottish banks did not generally pyramid on the public banks, and especially did not do so during the heyday of the system. Nor did the Scottish public banks customarily pyramid on the Bank of England, except possibly during the Restriction period.

Checkland says that certain other banks held 'part' of their reserves in the form of public bank notes – not 'much', as Sechrest would have it. Was it a negligible part or a significant part? Balance-sheet figures sufficient to answer this question unfortunately are not provided by Checkland, or by Munn (1981, pp. 239–84), who presents provincial bank balance sheets that lump all reserve items together as 'cash'. Munn (1981, pp. 139–40) does offer a summary discussion of the question, however, which Sechrest appears to have overlooked. Munn notes that 'the most liquid of the assets of the banking companies took three forms – namely balances with correspondents in London and Edinburgh, the notes of other banks, and specie'. After discussing the first item, Munn says the following about the holding of other banks' notes:

> The mixed notes which often figure in the balance sheets were the notes of other banks and banking companies which had been taken in the course of business. These were unimportant as a reserve asset because they were exchanged at least once per week after the formation of the note exchange in 1771. The amount which appeared in the balance sheet would largely depend on whether the exchange took place before or after the balance was struck. Nevertheless, in times of pressure the amount of mixed notes taken between exchanges might prove to be a useful temporary relief from a liquidity crisis.

This provides a very different picture from Checkland's statement or Sechrest's interpretation of it. The provincial banking companies evidently did *not* customarily hold on to public bank notes as a part of their reserves. It makes little sense, moreover, to suppose that they would. Public bank notes would be no less costly to hold than specie in terms of forgone interest. It is difficult to believe (contra Checkland) that the degree to which gold is more 'cumbersome' than notes mattered much for the form in which reserves were held.

In the early days of Scottish banking, provincial banking companies whose notes had geographically limited circulation may have held small inventories of public bank notes for the sake of certain customers (those travelling to Edinburgh, say) who preferred to make withdrawals in that form. But it is unlikely that such holdings formed a significant part of reserves, and Munn does not mention them. Travellers could have instead used drafts on correspondent banks. Other customers would just as willingly have taken the provincial banks' own notes as public bank notes.

The case of the non-issuing private banks is different. It makes perfect sense for such banks to have held reserves of public (or other widely acceptable) bank notes to satisfy customers who preferred to make withdrawals in the form of notes rather than specie. These banks did then 'pyramid credit' on top of the banks whose notes they held. Their role in the industry was small, however, and vanished before the end of the free-banking era.

Checkland's statement concerns Scottish banking practices as of 1810, before the entry of the larger joint stock banks, which displaced the Edinburgh private banks and the provincial banking companies to which he refers. The joint stock banks evidently did not hold public bank notes as reserves, and there is no reason to suppose that they would have. Thus Scottish banking at the most developed stage of the free-banking era did not exhibit pyramiding of other banks' note issues on the reserves of the public banks.

Fetter's (1965, p. 34) statement that the Scottish public banks held Bank of England deposits appears during his discussion of the Restriction period (1797–1821). During that period Scotland, like England, was on a Bank-of-England-note standard rather than a gold standard. Given that Scottish notes were ultimately convertible only into Bank of England notes, pyramiding on Bank of England liabilities might be expected. According to Fetter there was direct pyramiding. Fetter also says that during the Restriction period 'Scottish private banks held most of their reserves in notes and deposits of the chartered banks of Scotland'. (This may be the source of Sechrest's statement that 'much' of the reserves of non-public banks were normally so held.) This would also make some sense during a period in which gold redeemability was suspended and an alternative redemption medium was needed to maintain par acceptance among the Scottish banks. I have been unable, however, to find evidence in Checkland (1975) supporting or contradicting either of Fetter's statements. Fetter does not supply the evidence for them.

Other evidence indicates that the Scottish banks did not hold significant Bank of England deposits either during the Restriction or during other periods. In discussing the forms of liquidity held by the Scottish banks as of 1810, Checkland (1975, p. 194) writes:

> It had become necessary to provide a secondary reserve, after specie, against a sustained run. The Scottish banks had discovered by the 1760s, if not earlier, that in times of trouble they needed assets that were readily realisable in London. They had tried various devices: seeking credits with the Bank of England, or in Holland. But they learned from the late 1770s that nothing served so well as a hold of good securities, of a kind that could be realised in London without serious loss. These were of three kinds: government obligations (including Exchequer Bills), Bank of England stock and East India Company stock. If these were sold, creating a credit with a London correspondent, then a bill could be drawn upon London, which could be tendered to note holders and depositors as very nearly the equivalent of specie.

This statement will concern us again later for the light it sheds on the extent of Scottish reliance on the London money market for occasional liquidity needs. But for the present it serves to indicate that deposits with the Bank of England or other London banks were not held by Scottish banks as reserves in any quantity worth mentioning.[7]

Elsewhere, Checkland (1975, p. 445, 453) relates views of Horsely Palmer of the Bank of England, and of Alexander Blair of the Bank of Scotland, which also indicate that Scottish banks did not hold Bank of England deposits as reserves. Their views do suggest, on the other hand, that Scottish banks held BOE *notes* as reserves. The size of these note-holdings is unclear, but in light of the above discussion it was probably not significant. The likely rationales for reserve holdings of BOE notes (the convenience of customers travelling or remitting funds to England) suggest very small inventories. Checkland's information on the Bank of Scotland's and the Royal Bank of Scotland's balance sheets (1975, tables 39, 41–2, pp. 740–2) unfortunately does not distinguish between BOE notes and notes of other Scottish banks accumulated between exchanges.

If Scottish banks did not hold Bank of England liabilities, or deposits at London banks (which in turn held Bank of England liabilities) as reserves, then the Scottish money stock was not specifically geared to the quality of Bank of England liabilities. In the long run, Scotland's money stock was determined by the quantity of money demanded at the given purchasing power of the monetary unit. The purchasing power of the monetary unit was in turn determined by global supply and demand for gold. Cowen and Kroszner (1989, pp. 228–9) suggest that Scotland played the role of a 'small' country to England's 'big' country in 'a two-country model' of international finance. But surely Britain as whole was an open economy during the period of an international specie standard.

In the short run, the Bank of England could disturb the quantity of money in England significantly enough to cause cyclical effects on the price level, interest rates, and real activity, with spill-over effects on the Scottish economy. Far from being inconsistent with the free-banking view of Scotland, this view of the Bank of England's powers was first developed by the Free Banking School in the 1820–44 period. (The School argued in defence of Scottish free banking that cyclical disturbances in Scotland had been imported and had not originated with the Scottish banks.) The existence of spill-over effects from London to Scotland would imply that the English and Scottish economies were integrated, as the traditional view of Scottish banking has always recognized. It would not imply, contrary to Cowen and Kroszner (1989, p. 11) that 'BOE policies effectively controlled the Scottish ... banking system', or that 'the Scottish system must be considered as a part of the overall British banking system under the aegis of the BOE'. A finding of spill-over effects of BOE actions on the United States economy, about which American writers at the time complained, would not lead one to deny the distinctness of the English and US banking systems.

The question of a lender of last resort

Was the Bank of England a lender of last resort for the Scottish banking system? Sechrest (1988, p. 252) argues that a reading of Checkland (1975) and Fetter (1965) 'certainly seems to establish the Bank of England as the lender of last resort for the whole British isles rather than just for England'. Cowen and Kroszner (1989, p. 227) claim that 'the readiness of the BOE to act as a lender of last resort for the Scottish system provided a source of insurance'. They suggest that the Bank, acting as a lender of last resort, extended support at subsidy rates that distorted the banking system: 'The support of the BOE effectively socialized the costs of stability and redemption problems'.

To act as a lender of last resort, as Humphrey and Keleher (1984, pp. 227–8) define the role, is to act as a 'backstop or guarantor . . . of a fractional-reserve banking system' or to take on 'the responsibility of guaranteeing the liquidity of the entire economy'. If this definition is accepted, the Bank of England clearly was *not* a lender of last resort for Scotland before 1844. In a few cases the Bank provided loans to Scottish banks. But in other cases (most importantly the crises of 1825–6 and 1836–7) it refused to lend. In the case of the Ayr Bank in 1772, which Sechrest (1988, p. 252) curiously cites as an example of last-resort lending, the Bank of England set such stiff terms that the Ayr Bank declined its 'support' (Checkland 1975, p. 131). Cowen and Kroszner, along with Sechrest, give as an example of last-resort lending a long-term credit the Royal Bank negotiated with the Bank of England in 1830. But Checkland (1975, p. 444) adds that 'in October 1836 . . . the Bank, as part of a general credit contraction, required the Royal Bank of Scotland to pay off its advance'. This withdrawal of credit in a time of stringency was not only much to the consternation of the Royal Bank's general manager, but contrary to the behaviour of a lender of last resort.

Sechrest (1988, p. 252) cites a third supposed example of last-resort lending: 'In the crisis of 1793, a total of £404,000 was granted to several Scottish banks'. Cowen and Kroszner (1989, pp. 227–8) cite the same episode. Closer reading of the sources both cite (Checkland (1975), pp. 219–20; Andreades (1924), p. 188), however, shows that the loans in question were granted not by the Bank of England, but by the government, and were granted not to the banks, but to Scottish business firms. Officials of the Scottish banks had gone to London to plead for general relief measures for Scotland, not for Bank of England loans to the banks. Cowen and Kroszner seriously misrepresent this episode when they describe it as an example of how 'the [Scottish] public banks depended upon the BOE directly in crisis times'. None of the three examples stands up as evidence of a last-resort lending policy by the Bank of England.

Fetter (1965, p. 267) makes a relevant distinction between 'supporting the market *ex post*, as compared with giving assistance *ex ante* that credit would be available at some price'. The second is an essential part of the lender of last resort role of guaranteeing liquidity. Before 1844 (and apparently until the Baring Crisis of 1890) the Bank of England played only the first role, and did not do even that consistently. Fetter elaborates:

> Historically, in a given situation the Bank might have advanced £5 million, but the result – and the expectations for the future – would be quite different if this were rationed credit, given as an *ex gratia* act by the Bank in a crisis, than if it had been known in advance that credit would be available at a uniform rate to all who wished it. To support the market in time of crisis is not necessarily to act as a lender of last resort in the Bagehot sense, as the action of the Bank in 1793, 1825, 1835, and 1847 had shown.

One might question whether the loans the Bank extended were given as *ex gratia* acts, or whether the Bank was instead simply acting to maximize its profits. Contrary to Cowen and Kroszner, there is little reason to believe that the Bank of England extended inter-bank credit at subsidy rates that 'socialized' costs.

Because the Bank of England did not assure its willingness to lend, or even act consistently with such an assurance, it was not a lender of last resort (in the standard sense) to the Scottish system before 1844. This is not just a terminological point. The substantive point is that the Scottish banks did not rely *ex ante* on advances from the Bank of England as a backstop source of liquidity. Cowen and Kroszner (1989, p. 227) acknowledge that 'there was no explicit obligation for the BOE to act as a central bank for the Scottish system'. Neither was there any implicit policy of acting in such a manner. Thus Cowen and Kroszner (pp. 228–9) are incorrect in calling the Bank of England a "shadow" central bank' for the Edinburgh banks, and in saying that the Scottish banks faced 'incentives to . . . come under the wing of the Bank of England'.

In fact the Bank of England explicitly rejected the idea that it had lender-of-last-resort obligations. Fetter (1965, pp. 118-20) describes the Bank's unwillingness to extend credit during the crisis of 1826. In correspondence accompanying the Bank of England's withdrawal in 1836 of its advance to the Royal Bank of Scotland (quoted by Checkland (1975), p. 447), Horsely Palmer of the Bank of England wrote to the Royal Bank that

> he deemed it expedient to reduce the Bank's advances to other Banks of issue, thereby making them dependent in such times upon

their own respective resources. . . . Every Bank of issue should be prepared to support its own circulation by its own reserve . . . without requiring any issues from the Bank of England.

The question of 'dependence' on the London market

Did the Scottish banks rely on the London financial market to meet occasional liquidity needs? In one sense they clearly did. The Scottish banks held 'secondary reserves' in the form of 'good securities, of a kind that could be realised in London without serious loss' (Checkland (1975), p. 194). The ability to sell these assets quickly and at low cost for claims on London banks, which the Scottish banks could in many cases use as a redemption medium, permitted the Scottish banks to meet their liquidity needs with less specie in the vault. As Goodhart (1988, p. 51) notes, it is 'clear that Scottish banks felt able to economize in some part on individual [specie] reserve holdings by being able to draw on London when necessary'.

Contrary to Goodhart (1987, p. 131), however, this does not make it 'questionable whether the Scottish case is a good example of "free banking"'. In any free-banking system banks economize on their specie holdings, *inter alia*, by holding liquid securities as secondary reserves. In the Scottish case the market in which these securities could be sold happened to be outside their banking orbit. Why does that matter?

The market was outside their orbit because London was indeed Britain's financial centre, and because the Scottish banks were legally excluded from opening branch offices in London. This exclusion *was* an infringement of their freedom. It compelled them to use London correspondents rather than participating in London banking themselves. Thus the Scottish banks did face a legal restriction here. But this is presumably not what is at issue when 'dependence' on the London financial market is cited. Had they opened London branch offices, the Scottish banks would presumably have made similar use of the London market.

What is at issue is the significance of the Scottish banks' use of the London financial market as a source of liquidity. Goodhart (1987, p. 131) makes the following argument:

> The Scottish banks relied on London, and ultimately on the Bank [of England], as a financial centre . . . The Scottish banking system could be regarded as a satellite to the London Centre . . . I do not

believe that the performance of such satellite systems really gives much indication of how a free banking system would work in a closed economy, or when its centre was shut.

Several issues are raised in this passage, which I will consider in turn.

1 The Scottish banks did rely on the London centre in the short-run sense that at any given moment they held securities that they counted on being able to sell there. A surprise suspension of the gold standard in London clearly would affect them, as it did in 1797. But they did not rely on London in the long-run sense that Scottish access to the London market was essential to the way the Scottish banks economized on specie holdings. Alexander Blair (1926, p. 51), then general manager of the British Linen Company, testified that the Scottish banks might draw gold from Hamburg if it were not available in London. Checkland (1975, p. 194) indicates that they could also draw on Holland to meet occasional liquidity needs.

2 The ability of Scottish banks to borrow reserved money from foreign financial centres is consistent with, and indeed implicit in, the free-banking interpretation of Scottish banking according to a model of a small open economy whose base money (specie) is money throughout the world economy. My book explicitly argues for the applicability of such a model to Scotland (White (1984), p. 11). It does not claim that the Scottish experience provides *direct* evidence on 'how a free banking system would work in a closed economy'. Sechrest (1988, p. 252) incorrectly infers that I 'apparently' believe that Scotland had 'monetary autonomy' in the strong sense proposed by Checkland (1975, pp. 447–8) as an unrealistic foil.

3 The nub of Goodhart's argument for rejecting Scotland as a good example of free banking is the suggestion that in relying on the London market, the Scottish banks ultimately relied on the Bank of England as a central bank in that market. He quotes Checkland's (1975, p. 432) statement that for the Scottish banks 'the principal and ultimate source of liquidity lay in London, and, in particular, in the Bank of England'. It is true that the Bank of England was the principal source of specie in London. To draw gold from London, the Scotish banks acquired and redeemed Bank of England liabilities. Concentration of London's specie reserves in the Bank of England may have distorted the market

for specie somewhat. But it probably did not loosen constraints on the acquisition of specie, compared with those the Scottish banks would have faced had there been a plurality of issuing banks serving as specie sources in London. It is not true, as we have seen, that the Bank guaranteed to make reserves available to the market in times of stringency. Inter-bank loans, such as the Bank of England occasionally made, might have been at least as readily available on similar terms from competitive London issuing banks. An inter-bank loan market surely would have existed even without a privileged bank in the financial centre, and might well have been *more* active.

In the crisis of 1839 the Bank of England turned to the Bank of France for an emergency extension of credit, to meet severe liquidity needs that had brought the BOE close to suspending payments. The Bank also arranged for sizable credits in Hamburg (Fetter (1965), p. 175). Yet no one would say that the London banking system customarily 'depended' on the Bank of France, or the Hamburg market, as a lender of last resort. Still less would anyone say that the London banking system was a 'satellite' to the Paris centre.

To borrow the words Sechrest (1988, p. 252) uses in anticipating such an argument, I have tried to establish here that 'recourse to the London money market does not necessarily imply recourse to a central bank'. Sechrest asserts that those who would make such an argument 'need to refute Checkland's statement that the Bank of England directly controlled both interest rates and the supply of credit in London'.[8] This assertion is confused. That the Bank of England had the power (in the short run) to alter the total supply of credit at the margin, and thereby to disturb interest rates, does not mean that any firm drawing on the total pool of funds in London was explicitly or implicitly borrowing from the Bank of England.

CONCLUSION

This chapter has reviewed the principal arguments against considering Scotland before 1844 a good example of free banking. Needless to say, not *all* criticisms of the free-banking view of the Scottish case have been considered.[9] The conclusions may be summarized as follows. The traditional contrast between the freer Scottish system and the more restricted English system is warranted.

The privileges of the chartered Scottish banks may have generated some small rents worth protecting, but they did not impede competition in intermediation or in the provision of inside money. The chartered banks may have played a special leadership role before 1810, but did not control, direct, or cartelize the Scottish banking industry. The Bank of England was not a lender of last resort to the Scottish system before 1844. Nor was it a central bank in the sense of providing a reserve base of high-powered money for the Scottish banks, except perhaps during the Restriction period. The Scottish banks used the London financial market to meet occasional liquidity needs, but this did not imply reliance on the good graces of the Bank of England.

At least from 1810 to 1844, then, the traditional free-banking model is valid for understanding the Scottish banking system. Correspondingly, the Scottish experience provides useful – and favourable – evidence on the performance of a competitive banking system without a central bank.

Notes

I am grateful to Kurt Schuler for comments, research assistance, and editorial suggestions. I thank Charles Munn and Alec Chrystal for their delivered comments, and I am sorry not to have had them in writing as I revised this paper.

1. See Vera Smith (1936), White (1984), chs 3–3), Nataf (1984), and White and Selgin (1990).
2. Charles Goodhart (1987, p. 131) is correct to point out, as against my statement that the Scottish case 'provides unique evidence on the workability of monetary freedom', that there have been many other relevant historical experiences. Something like fifty countries have had plural note-issue (see Conant (1927); Schuler (1989)).
3. In the nineteenth century Henry C. Carey (1840) raised this point as an objection to the Scottish banking system.
4. Cowen and Kroszner cite *inter alia* Checkland (1975, p. 150), a page not relevant to the question. Perhaps they meant to cite Checkland (1968, p. 149), which contains the statement that 'A charter was a useful prelude to gaining a share in the holding and remitting of government revenues, a source of trading funds of great value'.
5. Generalizations about the Scottish system thus need to be carefully dated. Munn (1985, p. 342) contrasts my statements (White (1984), p. 34) concerning features of the Scottish system 'in its heyday' with the

features of system as of 1826. I should have made it clearer that I was referring to the system as of 1844. Munn (1982) discusses the structural changes in Scottish banking between 1810 and 1844.

6.   Sechrest actually misquotes Checkland slightly, but the details are not important to his argument.

7.   Elsewhere, Checkland (1975, p. 385) does speak of Scottish banks holding 'London reserves often yielding no interest' against their personal credit-line ('cash-account') commitments. This suggests inter-bank deposits, but he does not provide details.

8.   Here Sechrest cites a page of Checkland (1975, p. 447) that speaks of 'the increasingly dominant role of the Bank of England as final arbiter of British credit availability'.

9.   In particular, I have not addressed the arguments (1) that Scottish banking was not significantly less failure-prone than English banking; and (2) that Scottish notes were not in practice redeemable on demand. For one rebuttal to these claims see Dowd (1989, pp. 198–207). The first can be rebutted with the testimony of credible contemporary observers. The second is more troubling. It rests in part on statements by the late Sidney Checkland (1975, pp. 185–6), who unfortunately cannot tell us what evidence lies behind them. Nor have I here addressed (3) the argument of Cowen and Kroszner (1989) that the Act of 1765 banning the option clause profoundly distorted the evolution of Scottish payments institutions. But see White (1989; 1990) for discussion.

References

ANDREADES, ANDREAS MICHAEL (1924) *A History of the Bank of England*, trans. C. Meredith, 2nd edn. (London: P. S. King).

BLAIR, ALEXANDER (1826) Testimony in the *Report from the Select Committee Appointed to Inquire into the State of the Circulation of Promissory Notes under the Value of £5 in Scotland and Ireland . . .* British Sessional Papers, House of Commons, Vol. 3 (New York: Readex Microprint).

CAMERON, RONDO (1967) *Banking in the Early Stages of Industrialization* (New York: Oxford University Press).

CAMERON, RONDO (1982) 'Banking and Industrialisation in Britain in the Nineteenth Century', in *Business, Banking and Urban History*, ed. Anthony Slaven and Derek H. Aldcroft (Edingburgh: John Donald).

CAREY, HENRY C. (1840) *Answers to Questions What Constitutes Currency? What are the Causes of Unsteadiness of the Currency? and what is the Remedy?* (Philadelphia: Lea & Blanchard).

CARR, JACK; GLIED, SHERRY; and MATHEWSON, FRANK (1986) 'Unlimited Liability and Free Banking in Scotland', unpublished ms, University of Toronto (August).

CARR, JACK L., and MATHEWSON, G. FRANK (1988) 'Unlimited Liability as a Barrier to Entry', *Journal of Political Economy*, 96 (August) pp. 766–84.

CHECKLAND S. G. (1968) 'Banking History and Economic Development: Seven Systems', *Scottish Journal of Political Economy*, 15 (June), pp. 144–66.

CHECKLAND, S. G. (1975) *Scottish Banking: A History, 1695–1973* (Glasgow: Collins).

CLAPHAM, John (1945) *The Bank of England*, 2 vols (New York: Macmillan).

CONANT, CHARLES A. (1927) *A History of Modern Banks of Issue*, 6th ed. (Fairfield: Augustus M. Kelley), 1969 reprint.

COWEN, TYLER, and KROSZNER, RANDY (1989) 'Scottish Banking before 1844: A Model for Laissez-Faire?' Unpublished ms, University of California, Irvine (October). Forthcoming in the *Journal of Money, Credit, and Banking*.

DOWD, KEVIN (1989) *The State and the Monetary System*, (Oxford: Philip Allan).

FETTER, FRANK WHITSON (1978) *Development of British Monetary Orthodoxy* (Fairfield: Augustus M. Kelley). Reprint of 1965 ed.

GOODHART, CHARLES (1987) Review of White (1984), *Economica*, 54 (February), pp. 129–31.

GOODHART, CHARLES (1988) *The Evolution of Central Banks*, (Cambridge Mass: MIT Press).

GORTON, GARY (1985) 'Clearinghouses and the Origins of Central Banking in the United States', *Journal of Economic History*, 42 (June), pp. 277–84.

GORTON, GARY, and MULLINEAUX, DONALD J. (1987) 'The Joint Production of Confidence: Endogenous Regulation and Nineteenth Century Commercial-Bank Clearinghouses', *Journal of Money, Credit, and Banking*, (November), pp. 457–68.

GOURVISH, T. R. (1969) 'The Bank of Scotland, 1830–45', *Scottish Journal of Political Economy*, 16 (November), pp. 288–305.

HUMPHREY, THOMAS H., and KELEHER, ROBERT E. (1984) 'The Lender of Last Resort: A Historical Perspective', *Cato Journal*, 4 (Spring/ Summer), pp. 275–318.

KERR, ANDREW W. (1884) *History of Banking in Scotland* (Glasgow: David Bryce).

MUNN, CHARLES W. (1981) *The Scottish Provincial Banking Companies, 1747–1864* (Edinburgh: John Donald).

MUNN, CHARLES W. (1982) 'The Development of Joint-Stock Banking in Scotland, 1810–1845', in *Business, Banking and Urban History*, ed. Anthony Slaven and Derek H. Aldcroft (Edinburgh: John Donald).

MUNN, CHARLES W. (1985) Review of White (1984), *Business History*, 27 (November) pp. 341–2.

NATAF, PHILIPPE (1984) 'Competitive Banking and the Cycle [in French Economic Thought] (1850–1868)', unpublished ms, University of Paris (May).

ROTHBARD, MURRAY N. (1988) 'The Myth of Free Banking in Scotland', *Review of Austrian Economics*, 2, pp. 229–45.

SCHULER, KURT (1989) 'The World History of Free Banking', unpublished ms, University of Georgia (May).

SECHREST, LARRY J. (1988) 'White's Free Banking Thesis: A Case of Mistaken Identity', *Review of Austrian Economics*, 2, pp. 247–57.

SELGIN, GEORGE A., and WHITE, LAWRENCE H. (1987) 'The Evolution of a Free Banking System', *Economic Inquiry*, 25 (July) pp. 439–57.

SMITH, VERA C. (1936) *The Rationale of Central Banking* (London: P. S. King).

TIMBERLAKE, RICHARD H. (1984) 'The Central Banking Role of Clearinghouse Associations', *Journal of Money, Credit, and Banking*, 16 (February), pp. 1–15.

TYSON R. E. (1985) Review of White (1984), *Economic History Review*, 2nd series, 38 (May), p. 310.

WALLACE, NEIL (1983) 'A Legal Restrictions Theory of the Demand for "Money" and the Role of Monetary Policy', *Federal Reserve Bank* of *Minneapolis Quarterly Review* (Winter), pp. 1–7.

WENLEY, JAMES A. (1882) 'On the History and Development of Banking in Scotland', *Journal of the Institute of Bankers*, 3, pp. 119–45.

WHITE, LAWRENCE H. (1984) *Free Banking in Britain* (Cambridge: Cambridge University Press).

WHITE, LAWRENCE H. (1987) 'Accounting for Non-interest-bearing Currency: A Critique of the Legal Restrictions Theory of Money', *Journal of Money, Credit, and Banking*, 19 (November), pp. 448–56.

WHITE, LAWRENCE H. (1989) 'What Kinds of Monetary Institutions Would a Free Market Deliver?', *Cato Journal*, 9, (Fall) pp.367–91.

WHITE, LAWRENCE H. (1990) 'Scottish Banking and the Legal Restrictions Theory: A Closer Look', *Journal of Money, Credit, and Banking*, 21 (November), in press.

WHITE, LAWRENCE H., and SELGIN, GEORGE A. (1990) 'Laissez-Faire Monetary Thought in Jacksonian America', in *Perspectives on the History of Economic Thought*, vol. 4, ed. Donald E. Moggridge (London: Edward Elgar).

WILSON, JAMES (1847) *Capital, Currency, and Banking* (London: The Economist).

Comment on Chapter 2

Charles W. Munn

As the free-banking debate re-emerged in recent years, I rather hoped that it would go away again, at least in the form espoused by White. I felt then, and still feel, that insufficient research has been done to prove some of the points which have been claimed by some of the participants on both sides of the debate; and to transform an insufficiently researched eighteenth- and nineteenth-century historical topic into a policy prescription for the late twentieth century seems to me to be a highly questionable procedure. Indeed there is another aspect of this debate which worries me, and that is the eagerness of some of the participants many of them economists, to get into print without even reading some of the basic historical work which has been done – let alone doing any of the historical work themselves. Some seem to have got into this debate by reading Checkland[1] and nothing else. In some of the contributions I look in vain for a mention of Max Gaskin, Norio Tamaki or even myself,[2] and older historians such as William Graham and Charles Boase[3] suffer even greater neglect. In White's paper I am described as a 'revisionist', – as is Checkland. Just what is it that we are 'revising'? Mainly it is the work of A. W. Kerr, one of my predecessors in office as Secretary of the Institute of Bankers in Scotland. Yet in the introduction to his pioneering book on the history of Scottish banking, first published in 1884, Kerr writes: 'No similar work having, so far as the writer is aware, been ever before published, allowance will, perhaps, be made for incompleteness and other faults, arising from the difficulty of obtaining information'.[4]

Kerr had little access to archival information and much of what existed then has been lost, but Checkland, Gaskin, Tamaki and I have had access to what remains. It is a considerable volume of material. Checkland worked for 10 years and I for 18 years on Scottish banking records (I have also done some work on Irish and English bank archives). White acknowledges that this makes us 'the authoritative chroniclers of events', but somehow he has come to the conclusion that our judgement about these events is either 'invalid, or doubtful, or of little importance'. I find this opinion a little disconcerting.

I find it even harder to forgive his practice of lumping all revisionists together and attributing what one says to all, as when he says: 'They have offered an alternative interpretation according to which the two most important Scottish banks and the Bank of England played certain controlling roles'.

I personally never attributed any controlling role to the Bank of England, as the archives of provincial and joint stock banks which I have examined hardly ever mention the Bank of England, and if they did, it was never in the context of borrowing money. Nor did I attribute a *controlling* role to the Bank of Scotland and Royal Bank of Scotland. Theirs was more a supervisory function. They had no legal basis for direct power to control the other banks in their lending, deposit-taking, note-issuing or branch extension policies. They did, however, see themselves as policemen of the system and, more importantly, would have liked to have even more power over the system than they were able to wield.

Occasionally they got closer to this kind of power. This is an area in which more research could be done. Somewhat interestingly, however, the episodes in the 1830s when the public banks excluded the Western Bank of Scotland from the note exchange, because they felt that its policy was imprudent and likely to destabilize the system, is usually omitted from the writings of the new free-banking school. The event is mentioned in Checkland and in one of the articles which I have written. It is even in A. W. Kerr, who was writing over 100 years ago and of whose work Checkland and I are supposed to be revisionists.[5] It seems to me to indicate a fairly serious example of control from the centre, although without any basis in law. Interestingly enough, Kerr also cites another example of this type of activity – also ignored by the free bankers. Speaking of the early years of the nineteenth century Kerr writes: 'This rapid expansion of banking naturally occasioned anxiety to the Edinburgh banks, who, in order to check it, intimated that they would not receive the notes of any new country banks that might be established'.[6] Their action had the desired effect of slowing the number of new banks which were formed.

There may well be other examples of this type of thing happening but again there is scope for more research. There is also the interesting question here of why the public banks acted in this way. Was it self-interest, a genuine desire to protect the banking system from destablizing influences, or a question of government policy, with the public banks acting as government agents?

Another chapter in my first book describes the correspondent banking relationships which Scottish banks had with banks in Edinburgh and London. This seems to have been ignored by those who have chosen to become involved in this debate. All the Scottish banks had a correspondent in London. What did they do? They ran accounts. The Scottish banks were able to send bills for collection and draw bills on their London correspondents, either maintaining funds there for the purpose or running up an overdraft with their correspondent. This relationship also worked in reverse, with London bankers drawing bills on their Scottish correspondents. The amount of information which I was able to uncover on the precise nature of this relationship was quite small and rather inconclusive, but it appears that these accounts were mostly kept in credit. I wait in vain, however, for someone to argue that the London money markets depended on these balances from the provinces for their liquidity and survival. The argument is always in terms of the periphery's dependence on the centre and never the other way about. Clearly there is a dimension here which has not been explored by those engaged in this debate.

I find myself more in tune with White's paper when he talks about the differences between Scotland and England. I believe that there were ways in which the Scottish system of banking was superior to the English. The historian of English country banks, Professor L. S. Pressnell, maintained that legislation which limited the size of these banks had the result of 'depriving the country of a banking system commensurate with a period of rapid economic growth'.[7] Even when the hyperbole and rhetoric are stripped away from Joplin and the other writers of the early nineteenth century, enough remains to show that the Scottish system was more stable and more responsive to its customers' needs. It was probably also less profitable than the English system, an indication perhaps of its more competitive nature. I am surprised that White does not make more of the differences between Checkland and myself on this point. Checkland and I had a number of very enjoyable discussions about this. We differed I believe because he was looking at the debate from the viewpoint of Edinburgh and London while I was looking at it largely from a Glasgow standpoint. Glasgow was the industrial capital of Scotland in the nineteenth century.

White raises the question of how important were the privileges of the so-called 'chartered banks', and argues that they were not very important. I agree. The formation of a large number of unlimited liability joint stock banks in the 1810–44 period is testimony to this.

These were not strictly unincorporated bodies as White implies. In Scots law a partnership was a separate legal person and the joint stock banks were just large partnerships.

Bankers outside Edinburgh could wield some power of their own. From the 1770s the public banks fixed the exchange on London. This is indicative of the power they were able to use, but when they were seriously challenged in the 1820s by a small bank from Aberdeen,[8] their ability to charge quite a high rate for the exchange crumbled. There seems little doubt that in the 1820s and 1830s the public banks struggled to retain their power and influence, especially in the face of competition from the new generation of joint stock banks, some of which grew quickly to rival the public banks in size. There are, however, a number of cases where they tried to continue to be highly influential, as when the Usury Laws were reduced in the 1830s. The Bank of Scotland, in the guise of its Treasurer, Alexander Blair, headed the negotiations for an agreed response among the Scottish banks but without much success. This was clearly self-interest at work, as the Bank of Scotland was extremely worried about its profits.[9] The evidence suggests a very competitive environment. In this I agree with White.

I also agree with him on the point about the joint-stock and provincial banks not holding bank notes issued by the public banks. I agree with him because he quotes me – accurately.

In conclusion let me summarize. I find substantial agreement with White in what he says about the distinctiveness of the Scottish system compared to England, and about the relative unimportance of the charters and acts of the public banks. I find that the public banks had more influence than White and others gave credit for, although their power was without statutory or other legal basis. On the question of the role of the Bank of England I certainly found that the provincial and joint stock banks had no recourse there for funds and they seldom borrowed from the public banks in Edinburgh. On this area in particular I would like to see some more work done.

I feel that this debate tends to force history into a strait-jacket of economic theory which, like all strait-jackets, is very uncomfortable to wear. I think that White recognizes this when he says 'neither the case for nor the case against a free-banking policy depends exclusively on how well the Scottish experience exemplifies free banking'. This is White's Option Clause.

In addition to having its own fairly distinctive banking, educational and ecclesiastical system Scotland has its own legal system. Under that system there are three possible verdicts. Guilty, not guilty and not proven. The case for free banking in Scotland is I believe 'not proven'. Having said that, and having read some of the material which attempts to argue against free banking in Scotland, my opinion is that the case against is not yet ready to be brought to court.

Notes

1. S. G. Checkland (1975) *Scottish Banking: A History 1695–1973* (Glasgow: Collins).
2. M. Gaskin (1955) *Note Issue in Scottish Banking 1844–1953*, Liverpool University MA Thesis. N. Tamaki, *The Life Cycle of the Union Bank of Scotland, 1830–1954* 1983. C. W. Munn (1981) *The Scottish Provincial Banking Companies 1747–1864* (Edinburgh: John Donald): (1982) *Banking in Scotland*, (Edinburgh: Institute of Bankers in Scotland); (1988) *Clydesdale Bank: The First 150 Years* (Glasgow: Collins); (1975) 'Origins of The Scottish Note Exchange', *Three Banks Review*; (1980) 'The Dundee Banking Company: the Early Years', *Three Banks Review*; 'The Development of Joint-Stock Banking in Scotland 1810–1845', in A. Slaven and D. H. Aldcroft (eds.), (1982) *Business, Banking and Urban History* (Edinburgh: John Donald); 'The Coming of Joint-Stock Banking in Scotland and Ireland', in T. M. Devine and D. Dickson, (eds.) (1983) *Ireland and Scotland 1600–1850* (Edinburgh: John Donald); 'Bank Finance for Industry: Scotland in the 19th Century', in P. Roebuck and R. Mitchison (eds.) 1988 *The Comparative Economic and Social Development of Ireland and Scotland* (Edinburgh: John Donald); 'The Emergence of Joint-Stock Banking in the British Isles: a Comparative Approach', in R. P. T. Davenport-Hines and G. Jones (1988) *The End of Insularity: Essays in Comparative Business History* (London).
3. W. Graham (1911) *The £1 Note in the History of Banking in Great Britain*, 2nd ed. (Edinburgh) C. W. Boase (1867) *A Century of Banking in Dundee*, 2nd ed.
4. A. W. Kerr (1884) *A History of Banking in Scotland*, Second ed (Edinburgh: Grant).
5. Checkland, *op. cit.*, pp. 328–9; Munn, (1982) *op. cit.*, pp. 123–4; and Kerr *op. cit.*, p. 189.
6. Kerr *op. cit.*, p. 132.
7. L. S. Pressnell (1956) *Country Banking in the Industrial Revolution* (Oxford: Clarendon Press), p. 6.
8. The firm was John Maberly and Co. See Munn (1981) *op. cit.*, pp. 75–8.
9. T. R. Gourvish (1969) The Bank of Scotland 1830–45', *Scottish Journal of Political Economy*, 16 (November).

Comment on Chapter 2

K. Alec Chrystal

It is curious how economists who wish to make a point for which they can find no supporting evidence in their own countries will search worldwide and back through time for episodes which can be quoted to confirm their views. In some cases, it may be positively desirable to choose your example from overseas, because the point you are making may be offensive to some groups. One example I stumbled across was of the case of the Giffen good, which appears in every introductory textbook. Every English textbook I have ever read quotes potatoes in Ireland in the nineteenth century. However, I have been reliably informed that one standard English text has a special Irish edition. The only difference between the English and the Irish editions appears to be that the example of the Giffen good used in the Irish edition was bread in England in the nineteenth century.

I now turn to the American version of Scottish banking history. I should make it clear right away that until recently I knew so little about the subject that I thought the 'free banking' debate was about whether banks should pay interest on current accounts. My reference to the Giffen good above, however, was more than just a joke to divert attention away from my ignorance of the subject. It was a caution on the potential dangers of seeing in specific episodes what you want to see, whether the reality of the situation justifies the interpretation put upon it or not. It is a particular danger when a group of scholars with a strong belief in the power of free markets, such as exists in the United States, tends to talk largely to each other and therefore accepts uncritically the validity of evidence which may be much less unambiguous. My co-discussant is much better placed than I to assess that failing and so I merely raise it as an obvious danger.

I found Lawrence White's account extremely scholarly, but very hard for someone like myself who is new to this area to comment on. It is really a reply to those who had raised doubts about Professor White's earlier study of the free-banking episode. In that respect it takes a considerable amount of background knowledge for granted. To understand what that background is, and in order to help myself try to identify what the key issues are, I turned to Professor White's excellent book *Free Banking in Britain: Theory, experience, and debate 1800–1845* (Cambridge University Press, 1984). This I can heartily recommend to anyone sufficiently interested in the topic to be reading these comments.

The key question seems to be this. Does government have any well-founded reason to play a role in producing money or in regulating private firms that produce money?

Professor White's aim in this line of work is explicitly stated by him as to show that 'the Scottish experience continues to provide useful and favorable evidence on the feasibility of banking without a central bank'. That the system which existed was feasible is certainly established, but two further questions follow. First, is the establishment of feasibility sufficient to establish optimality? Second, was it really as 'free' as is claimed? The second of these I can only leave as a question but the issue of optimality requires more discussion.

In his book Professor White says that free banking comprises two conceptually distinct elements: the unregulated issue of transferable bank liabilities and the unmanipulated supply of basic cash. Most modern commentators would agree that the banking industry should be competitive. However, it is less clear that the total absence of regulation guarantees a competitive outcome. Indeed, there must be some framework of law, and it is arguable to what extent even such a framework establishes government interference.

An even bigger question surrounds the other characteristic of free banking – the unmanipulated supply of cash. It may be that the viability of the Scottish type free-banking system was heavily dependent upon the unquestioned convertibility of bank paper into gold. Evidence from such times clearly does not necessarily prove relevant to judgements about the viability of free banking in the absence of such a commodity standard. It is just such cases that are most interesting and controversial. Is a system in which banks are free to issue competing currencies better than one in which the central bank has the monopoly of currency issue? The Scottish experience is not very much help because the currency standard was not in doubt. It is a question which has relevance to contemporary Europe, since the answer must condition moves towards a new European monetary system. Should there be a central creation of a single money or should existing monies (and perhaps new ones) compete for dominance?

Before concluding let me make a slight deviation in the form of a question to the scholars of free banking. Is it necessary to look at historical episodes which may or may not illustrate free banking? Does not the contemporary Eurocurrency market provide us with an unregulated example of free banking? However, does it not also provide an example of how such a system can over-issue, the result being a bail-out by the central banks and global regulation the price of that bail-out?

Finally, let me say that, while I am sceptical that Professor White has established that free banking would provide the best monetary system under all circumstances, it is, nonetheless, quite clear that he is making an important contribution to increasing our understanding of alternative monetary systems. For that we should all be grateful.

3 Lessons from the American Experience with Free Banking

Hugh Rockoff

NEW INTEREST IN OLD INSTITUTIONS

Two decades ago the early history of American banking was dismissed as an object of study for someone concerned about current monetary problems, except perhaps as an object lesson about what can go wrong if the government does not apply a stern regulatory hand to the banking system. An article that appeared in *Banker's Magazine* in 1971 entitled 'The Early Ways and Crazy Days of Banking' (Lasdon (1971)), accurately reflected contemporary thinking. Since that time, as recently noted by Milton Friedman and Anna J. Schwartz (1986), a number of factors have produced a renewal of interest in radical forms of banking regulation, and this period is now the object of intense research in academic circles.

The most important force for change has been, of course, the continuing failure of existing institutions to produce anything like price and output stability. Interest in monetary reform tends to rise and fall with the rate of inflation. But there have been a number of intellectual currents (themselves partly reflecting economic conditions) that have contributed to the new interest in nineteenth-century Americn banking. One is the startling suggestion by Fredrich Hayek (1976) that the path to monetary stability was simply to open up banking, and the provision of the monetary base, to the same competitive forces that operate effectively in other sectors of the economy. Hayek sketched a counterfactual history of how competitive monetary institutions might evolve once controls were lifted. This speculation naturally encouraged attempts to find out whether actual systems when at least partly free of regulatory constraints had evolved along the lines Hayek predicted.

A second development has been the 'rational expectations revolution'. It emphasized the importance of underlying monetary institutions in contrast with current monetary policy, since it is the basic institutions that ultimately determine expectations about future monetary and fiscal policies. Growing out of the rational expectations revolution has been a distinct approach, the Minnesota School, that stresses the 'legal restrictions' placed on the issue of fiat money, and the way in which those restrictions influence the relationships among money, prices, and real output. Finally, there is the development of what Tyler Cowen and Randal Krozner (1987) have called the New Monetary Economics. Motivated in part by recent developments in finance, as well as the other currents noted above, this literature, like Hayek's speculates about how the economy would behave under radically different monetary arrangements.

All these developments are strong motives for academics who want to test these ideas to turn to the history books to find monetary systems that contain some of the features being discussed by the theorists. In many ways there is no better period to examine than American banking in the nineteenth century and particularly in the 25 years that preceded the American Civil War.

THE FREE-BANKING ERA

America did not begin its life as an independent nation with a strong presumption toward laissez-faire in banking. The Constitution did not say anything directly about banking. It provided simply that states could not issue bills of credit (paper money) and that the right to coin and regulate currency (presumably the coinage) was reserved to the federal government. Alexander Hamilton, the first Secretary of the Treasury, proposed in 1790 that the US create a state bank modelled in certain ways on the Bank of England.

The following year the Congress chartered the First Bank of the US to last for a period of 20 years. When its charter came up for renewal, there was opposition from a variety of sources, including the concern that the Constitution did not authorize a bank and it was not renewed. The experience of federal financial difficulties in the War of 1812, and the intervening evolution of constitutional doctrines, helped produce a new bank, the Second Bank of the US, in 1816. But this bank too ran into considerable opposition when it came up for renewal. This was the famous Bank War between the pro-bank forces led by the president of the Second bank, Nicholas Biddle, and the anti-bank forces led by President Andrew Jackson. The upshot of the war was that the government's deposits were removed and the bank's federal charter was not renewed. Although it survived for a time under a Pennsylvannia charter, the Second Bank ceased to be a major force in financial markets after 1836.

Under the Independent Treasury plan inaugurated in 1845 the divorce of the federal government from banking was taken a step further. Under this legislation the federal government was required to receive and pay out only specie (gold and silver), and to keep surplus funds as specie in its own vaults. Although practical neccesity, and certain exceptions introduced in the law, made this divorce between the banking system and the Treasury less complete than it appears in a simple description, it is nevertheless true that one would be hard pressed to find a period that matched the two decades before the Civil War in terms of the degree of freedom permitted to private banks.

The problem of regulating banking, then, was left during this period entirely in the hands of the states. Ideas on banking were numerous and vigorously pressed, and the states adopted a wide range of regulatory systems. Some followed the lead established in the Independent Treasury and tried to prohibit all banks, or all new banks, and force people to deal in specie. But increasingly the most popular form of legislation was the so-called free-banking law. This legislation, first adopted by Michigan and New York in the late 1830s, and then by a large number of states in the 1850s, had two main provisions.

1   Entry into banking was open to all as long as certain minimum requirements with respect to capital and other matters were complied with. Under the older system of chartered banking (still the dominant mode in many states), each bank required a separate charter from the state legislature.
2   Bank notes intended to circulate from hand to hand as money had to be redeemable in specie and backed by government bonds (typically issued by the state where the bank was located). These bonds were deposited with a state official who was empowered to sell the bonds and redeem all the notes of a bank if one note was protested for non-payment.[2]

Obviously, as one can see from this brief description, banking during this period was restricted in many ways: it was a far cry from pure laissez-faire. To emphasize this point it may be worth listing some of these restrictions:

1   In states with free-banking laws bank notes had to be backed by
    government bonds.
2   Most states had usury laws. In some states, moreover, the
    maximum that could be charged by banks was lower than the
    maximum that applied to other lenders.[3]
3   The basic monetary unit was the dollar as defined and minted by
    the US government.

Nevertheless, as our early discussion made clear, there were also
many respects in which the banking system was unusually free of
federal regulation. How well did this system work? Should we turn
the clock back to the free-banking era? To give a tentative answer to
these questions I will examine the experience of these years for the
light they throw on four potential reforms of the monetary system
that have drawn considerable interest in recent years:

1   Should the current system for providing the monetary base be
    replaced with a gold standard or some other commodity-based
    standard?
2   Should the current system, in which the Federal Reserve poten-
    tially acts as a lender of last resort, be replaced with an alternative
    system in which protection against bank runs is supplied by some
    decentralized market mechanism?
3   Should banks be allowed to issue notes that circulate from hand to
    hand as money?
4   Should free entry be permitted into banking?

CONTROL OF THE MONETARY BASE

The free-banking system did not provide, it is important to emphasize, a test of Hayek's speculation that banks freed of all governmental restraints would begin to produce some new form of monetary
base. Hayek (at his most radical) imagined banks issuing their own
monetary units. Citibank might issue Citimoney, perhaps redeemable
in some basket of commodities, but not necessarily in a basket of
commodities defined by the US government. On the contrary, free
banking, like all American systems during the nineteenth century
(except for the period of the War of 1812 and the period of the Civil
War), was based on an ultimate metallic monetary base – during this
period a bimetallic standard of gold and silver. The free-banking era

can tell us something about how those systems work, but not about how free banking might produce a private unit of account.

The free-banking era witnessed one of the most important disturbances of the metallic-based systems of the nineteenth century: the inflation produced by the great discoveries of gold in California in 1848 and subsequently in Eastern Australia and elsewhere. The gold discoveries show that even under a commodity standard severe shocks to the monetary system can occur. In the actual circumstances that shock appears to have been cushioned in the US by a rapid growth in the demand for money. This is illustrated in Table 3.1,

Table 3.1   Money, prices, and related variables, 1847–59

Year	(1) Money[a]	(2) Monetary base[a]	(3) Wholesale price index[b]	(4) Consumer price index[b]	(5) GNP deflator[b]	(6) Real GNP[c]
1847	267	109	104	99	87	2.666
1848	259	118	80	95	87	2.460
1849	316	149	79	92	85	2.664
1850	360	176	93	94	89	2.872
1851	409	191	90	92	87	2.977
1852	451	217	94	93	91	2.976
1853	505	220	99	93	96	3.179
1854	509	231	114	101	102	3.281
1855	535	230	124	104	105	3.479
1856	575	241	111	102	109	3.488
1857	477	248	137	105	105	3.941
1858	547	244	102	99	104	3.550
1859	565	233	107	100	98	4.029

[a]Millions of dollars
[b]1860 = 100
[c]Billions of 1860 dollars

Source: Column (1) – Milton Friedman and Anna J. Schwartz (1970) *Monetary Statistics of the United States: Estimates, Sources, Methods* (New York: Columbia University Press), Table 13, columns 5, 12 and 17, p. 222–5. Column (2) – *Monetary Statistics*, Table 13, columns 4 and 5, pp. 222–4. Column (3) – Walter Buckingham Smith and Arthur Harrison Cole (1935) *Fluctuations in American Business, 1790–1860* (Cambridge, Mass.: Harvard University Press), p. 167. Column (4) – Paul A. David and Peter Solar (1977) 'A Bicentenary Contribution to the History of the Cost of Living in America', in *Research in Economic History*, ed. Paul Uselding, Vol. 2 (Greenwich, Conn: JAI Press Inc.), p. 16. Columns (5) and (6) – Thomas Senior Berry (1988) *Production and Population Since 1879 Revised GNP Series in Constant Dollars*, (Richmond VA: The Bostwick Press), pp. 21, 19.

which shows the monetary base, the stock of money, three measures of prices, and real GNP from 1847 to 1859.

The effect on both the monetary base and the stock of money were dramtic by antebellum standards.[4] Between 1848 and 1856 the monetary base was multiplied by a factor of 2.04 and the stock of money was multiplied by a factor of 2.22.[5] Today, of course, many countries experience monetary growth of this magnitude as a matter of course. Increases of nearly this magnitude in the US have come to be seen in the 1980s as a tight money policy. It is a measure of the success of the metallic standards of the nineteenth century that increases in the quantity of the monetary metal resulting from the discovery of unbelievably rich mines resulted in a growth rate of the monetary base considered rather conservative in recent years.

This increase in the stock of money produced, as the quantity theory of money predicts, an increase in nominal income and prices. Indeed, the cyclical expansion, which the NBER dates from 1848 to 1854, is the longest on record from 1834 (when the table I am following begins) until World War II. The coincidence of this long and inflationary expansion with a large increase in the stock of money cannot be attributed to channels of causation running from the rise in income to the stock of money, since the increase in the monetary base resulted from chance discoveries of major goldfields in California and eastern Australia. This episode is a good example of a natural experiment well-structured to test the quantity theory of money.

The surprising thing is that a monetary shock of this magnitude apparently produced a mild increase in the price level. One of the available wholesale price indexes does increase by a factor of about 1.39 between 1848 and 1856, corresponding to an annual growth rate of 4.09 per cent per year. But the GNP deflator shown in column 4 was multiplied by a factor of only 1.25, an annual growth of 2.82 per cent. A modern estimate of the consumer price index shown in column 3 of Table 1 reveals hardly any effect at all until 1854. Between 1848 and 1856 the consumer price index increased by a factor of only 1.07.[6]

International adjustments played some role in inhibiting price increases. The flow of gold into bimetallic France during this period produced an outflow of silver to India and the Far East, the so-called golden parachute; and, as predicted by the Humean-Price-Specie-Flow Mechanism, the balance of international payments turned against the US. By one measure (Berry 1988, p. 26) the net export position of the US changed from a surplus of $7 million in 1848 to a maximum deficit of $45 million in 1853; the deficit then declined to $14 million in 1856. But international competition cannot explain why real money balances in the United States rose dramatically, and remained high despite a long period of adjustment.

If price increases had been held down in the rest of the world, by whatever mechanism, and the demand for money had been stable in the US, the US would have run even larger balance of payments deficits, and lost even more of the new gold. Instead the US made very large additions to its stock of real cash balances; or, to put it differently, international price competition cannot explain why monetary velocity in the US fell at the rate of 2.79 per cent per year from 1848 to 1856.

Velocity in the twentieth century tended to rise in cyclical expansions. In the nineteenth century, however, because of the long secular decline, velocity tended to fall somewhat even in expansions.[7] This phenomenon has been examined in depth by Michael Bordo and Lars Jonung (1987). They attribute the long-run decline in velocity, a phenomenon they observe in a number of countries, to the spread of the money economy and the development of commercial banking. The fall in velocity during the gold rush boom, however, appears to have been larger than can be accounted for solely by secular trends. For example, from 1833 (the beginning of Macesich's monetary series) until 1859 velocity fell – 0.81 per cent per year. From 1820 (the beginning of Temin's money stock estimates) until 1859 velocity using this measure of money fell – 0.89 per cent per year. The acceleration of the decline in velocity during the gold rush boom might, however, be due to an acceleration of the forces behind the long-run decline in velocity, a possibility I will return to below.

FREE BANKING AND THE GOLD RUSH

This paradox, a large monetary shock combined with a mild inflation, has been neglected by monetary historians. There isn't sufficient space here for a full investigation, but it is appropriate to ask whether the advent of free banking had anything to do with the mildness of the inflation generated by the gold discoveries. The reason for focusing on this issue is that much of the current interest in free banking stems, I believe, from the hope that free banking can contribute to macroeconomic stability. Of course, even if the only benefit from free banking was improved financial services (lower loan ratess, higher interest on deposits, service with a smile, and so on) the gain would be worth pursuing. But it is the connection with monetary policy that makes competition in banking potentially more interesting than competition in other important industries.

Before examining the relation between free banking and the expansion in detail, we want to know how much can be explained by the traditional arguments in the demand for money function: interest rates and real income. Table 3.2 shows several interest rate series. There is some evidence of a downward trend. But it seems unlikely that declines of the magnitude shown here could account for such large accumulations of cash balances. The federal government bond rate, for example, falls about 160 basis points between 1848 and 1856, a fall of 23 per cent, while real cash balances rise 54 per cent, so the demand for money would have to have been unusually sensitive to interest rates to produce decreases in velocity of this magnitude. The commercial paper rate does show a large decrease between 1848 and

Table 3.2   Interest rates, 1847–59

Year	(1) Federal Gov. bonds	(2) Commercial paper	(3) Boston (all banks)	(4) New York City (12 banks)	(5) Philadelphia (12 banks)
1847	5.77	9.59	3.48	5.65	n.a.
1848	5.71	15.10	3.99	5.41	n.a.
1849	5.16	10.25	8.12	4.92	n.a.
1850	4.58	8.04	5.30	5.81	4.01
1851	4.47	9.66	4.94	5.59	7.85
1852	4.39	6.33	2.87	4.28	1.51
1853	4.02	10.25	6.20	4.05	4.97
1854	4.14	10.37	4.07	4.89	4.75
1855	4.18	8.92	2.80	4.20	4.75
1856	4.11	8.83	4.90	4.40	4.10
1857	4.30	11.56	4.73	3.99	3.24
1858	4.32	4.81	4.30	3.67	5.57
1859	4.72	6.14	4.68	4.18	3.26

Sources: Columns (1) and (2) – Sidney Homer (1963) *A History of Interest Rates* (New Brunswick NJ: Rutgers University Press), pp. 287, 318–19. Columns (3), (4) and (5) – Hugh Rockoff (1988) 'The Short-Term Capital Market Before the Civil War: An Exploratory Inquiry', unpublished working paper, pp. 12, 19 and 22. These were computed by dividing dividends plus change in surplus by total earning assets. Realized yields can be low in a period of financial stringency even though lending rates are high, hence the discrepancies in 1857.

1856, but the volatility of this series makes it unlikely that this was representative of short-term rates. The rates derived from bank balance sheets and earnings given in columns 4 and 5, do not show a clear trend.

Real per capita income grew .82 per cent per year from 1848 to 1856. This implies, when one works it through, that an income elasticity of 4.37 would be required to account for the decline in velocity, ignoring the contribution of interest rates and other variables. But over the whole period 1820 to 1859 an income elasticity of 1.70 could account for the decline in velocity. The results of these 'back of the envelope' calculations are confirmed when demand for money functions are estimated. Examples are presented below in conjunction with tests of other explanations for the paradox.

One way increased competition might have contributed to stability was by forcing banks to provide better services for depositors and noteholders, thus increasing the demand for money. One piece of evidence for increased competition is the increase in the number of banks. In Massachusetts the number of banks increased from 112 in 1848 to 172 in 1856; In New York State the increase was 171 to 338; in Pennsylvania the increase was from 47 to 71; in Ohio the increase was from 48 to 65.[8] All these increases, and those in many other states, were large by historical standards, although the antebellum period in general was a period of rapid growth in the number of banks. Bordo and Jonung (1987, pp. 81–2, and *passim*) cite growth in the number of bank offices per capita as an institutional change leading to a decline in velocity. So a prima facie case can be made that the introduction of free banking cushioned the impact of the gold discoveries. In an earlier draft of this chapter I put considerable weight on this argument. But critics of the argument have convinced me that the case is somewhat weaker than I believed.

First of all free-banking laws, *per se*, cannot explain the vast increase in the number of banks, because only a fraction of all states adopted them and some states that did adopt them incorporated costly requirements that discouraged entry. For example, of the four states cited above, only two, New York and Ohio, had free-banking laws, and in Ohio formation of the free banks was suspended for part of the period. This point is related to one made recently by Kenneth Ng (1988). Ng shows that in most cases (the exception was New York) the passage of a free-banking law did not lead to faster growth of bank assets in the free-banking state than the national or regional average.

But it may be that to look at the free-banking law as the only vehicle for providing increased competition in banking is to take too mechanical a view of the process. Commercial freedom, indeed political freedom, was in the air. Some states responded by passing a free-banking law. Nineteen free-banking laws were passed in the antebellum period, twelve in the period 1848 to 1856.[9] But the legislatures in other states may have responded by simply becoming more willing to charter additional banks, thus giving more weight to the up-and-coming class of potential entrepreneurs rather than to established interests. Richard Sylla (1985) argues that bank entry in New England was essentially free, although it relied mostly on legislative charters.[10]

The potential political interactions here are complex. Greater willingness to charter banks in some cases may have been a way of undermining pressures for a formal free-banking law. In other cases, the intent of free banking could be undermined by including various restrictions in the free-banking law.

George Green's (1972, pp. 130–5) discussion of the origins and structure of Louisiana's free-banking law shows just how complex the political context could be. The State Constitution of 1845 and the general incorporation law of 1848 prohibited the chartering of new banks, reflecting democratic hard money sentiments. But attitudes changed quickly, spurred in part perhaps by the high profits said to be earned by the New Orleans banks, protected as they were by an absolute prohibition on competition. A constitutional convention in 1852 permitted the legislature to charter banks one by one or enact a free-banking law. In 1853, a free-banking law was passed, but it contained a requirement of a one-third reserve against deposits. This requirement followed an older Louisiana tradition rather than the free-banking model of the North. Given the restrictiveness of the actual legislation, it is not surprising that bank assets in Louisianna did not grow faster than in surrounding states. But the reversal of the state of opinion between 1845 and 1852 is a sign of how strong political pressures for easing bank entry requirements had become.

Even if we can see our way around the probelm raised by Ng, there are still a number of problems facing the argument that increased competition in banking explains the fall in velocity:

1   A greater number of banks would reduce the time required to get to the bank, but this 'shoe-leather' cost, while it might explain the increase in balances held in the frontier areas, does not seem

sufficient, intutitively, to explain the equally great rise in real balances in the eastern financial centres.'

2 Another possibility is that explicit payment of interest on deposit accounts may have increased. But at least in Massachusetts, one of the few states for which we have data, the ratio of interest-bearing deposits to total deposits actually fell during this period, continuing a long-term trend.

3 Finally, the number of banks is not significant in regressions explaining the demand for money, when other variables such as interest rates and real income are included.

How then can we explain the broad correspondence between the increase in the number of banks and the increase in real money balances? A line of causation may have run from the growth in real cash balances to the growth in the number of banks. With the demand for banking services on the rise, legislatures may have been swamped with applications for new charters. Some legislatures may have met this problem by adopting free-banking laws while others simply responded to the challenge by rapidly chartering new banks. Just as a rise in the demand for wheat would produce a rise in the number of farms, the rise in the demand for real balances would produce a rise in the number of banks. This point can be confirmed econometrically. Lagged values of real money balances are more highly correlated with the current number of banks than are lagged banks with current real money balances.

Finally, it appears that there are other potential explanations for the mildness of the inflation. One possibility that I have explored in a preliminary way turns on the rapid increase in asset prices triggered by the gold rush. Rising asset prices can be expected to increase the demand for money in several ways, two of which seem relevant here: (1) rising asset prices represent an increase in wealth; and (2) rising asset prices are normally accompanied by an increased volume of transactions on financial markets.[11] It seems beyond question that there was a substantial boom on asset markets, and that it was nationwide. In the East, particularly in New York, the speculative spirit was manifested in financial markets. In the West, land prices rose: in the South, the price of slaves. Unfortunately, there is no comprehensive index of asset prices or quantities that would permit a decisive test of this explanation. Table 3.3, however, presents two representative regressions based on an index of stock prices.

Another possibility is that monetization of the economy increased

Table 3.3   Estimates of the demand for money, 1820–58

Dependent Variable: Logarithm of real per capita money balances[a]

Independ. Variables	1821–58 Coeff.	1821–58 Absolute t	1834–58 Coeff.	1834–58 Absolute t
Constant	−3.18	3.04	−2.74	1.57
Long interest rate[b]	.02	.03	—	—
Short interest rate[b]	—	—	−.13	2.14
Real per capita income[d]	.97	3.36	.63	1.49
Specie–money ratio[e]	−.08	2.05	−.11	1.77
Real stock prices[f]	.17	1.84	.17	1.96
Gold rush[g]	.14	2.24	.09	1.25
Lagged money	.43	2.88	.68	3.48
Adj. R^2		.90		.83
S.E. Regression		.10		.09

[a]Natural logarithm of per capita money balances divided by the GNP deflator. See Table 3.1 for sources.

[b]Natural logarithm of the New England Municipal Bond Rate from Homer (1963, pp. 286–7).

[c]Natural logarithm of the commercial paper rate from Homer (1963, pp. 318–319).

[d]Natural logarithm of per capita GNP in 1860 dollars. See Table 3.1 for sources.

[e]Natural logarithm of the ratio of currency in the form of specie to money, from Temin (1969, pp. 71, 159).

[f]Natural logarithm of an index of stock prices divided by the GNP deflator. Three stock price series from Smith and Cole (1935) were linked. The June value of their index of Bank and Insurance Stock Prices from 1820 to 1833 (p. 174), the June value of their Index of Railroad Stock prices from 1834 to 1845 (p. 183), and their index of Railroad Stock prices from 1845 to 1858 (p. 184). The average ratio of the series in the available overlapping years was used to link them.

[g]A dummy variable that takes the value 1 in the years 1850–6.

during this period. It has been said, for example, that in Indiana production by farmers of goods for the home (as opposed to the market) fell by one half during the 1850s (Esarey (1947), p. 100). This is one of the factors stressed by Bordo and Jonung (1987), and a variable to account for this factor is also included in Table 3.3

The dependent variable in each case is the natural logarithm of real per capita money balances. Each equation contains six explanatory variables (all taken in logarithms) besides a constant term:

1 An interest rate. A long term bond rate is used in the first equation, the commercial paper rate (available for only the shorter period) in the second.
2 Real per capita income.
3 The ratio of money held as specie to the total money supply. This variable, suggested by the work of Bordo and Jonung (1987), was included to account for the gradual monetization of the economy. Their argument is that as people become more sophisticated in the use of money, they switch from currency to deposits, and hold larger real balances. In our context this implies a negative coefficient.
4 Real stock prices. In the second equation these are railroad stock prices divided by the GNP deflator. To get a long-term index I linked in an index of bank and insurance stocks for the pre-1834 period. This is not as farfetched as it might at first appear, since in each period the index then reflects the dominant stocks in a narrow market. But a more representative index would be useful. Some of the potential problems in using this data are discussed in Schwert (1989).
5 A dummy variable (gold rush) that takes the value one in the years 1850 through 1856. The purpose of this variable is to test whether these years still appear special after other factors are taken into account.
6 The lagged value of the dependent variable. This variable, a common one in demand for money studies, allows for the gradual adjustment of desired to actual real balances.

Most of the variables were signed as predicted and were statistically significant. This was generally true in a wide range of similar regressions designed to test alternative specifications. There is some evidence of serial correlation in the residuals, but at least the Cochrane–Orcut adjustment left the results similar, if anything a bit stronger. In particular, the specie–money ratio designed to capture the increasing monetization of the economy had the expected negative sign confirming the results obtained by Bordo and Jonung (1987) for a large sample of countries. And the stock market variable had the expected positive sign confirming a result obtained by Friedman (1988) with much more recent data. But despite taking these factors into account, the gold rush variable is still significant. Real money balances, in other words, still appear unusually high in these years.

But I read these regressions as saying that variables other than the introduction of free banking may be able to account for the rise in real balances in the gold rush expansion. In particular the gold rush dummy falls in size and significance in the second equation, when a better proxy for short-term interest rates is available, although the sample is then extremely small. With better measures of the rise in asset prices, and a better way of allowing for the slow adjustment to the increase in money supplies produced by the gold rush, the residual to be explained by free banking might prove even smaller.

Finally, it should be emphasized that the free banking explanation for the mildness of the inflation depends not on the existence of competition, but rather on the *introduction* of competition offsetting the increase in the monetary base. Had deregulation of the system occurred earlier so that the effects had worked out of the system by 1848, the gold rush boom on this argument might have had more repercusions on prices or the balance of payments.

To sum up, although the introduction of free banking occurred during a period in which a major monetary shock was absorbed with apparent ease, this may have been fortuitous. The evidence suggests that at most free banking deserves only a limited share of the credit.

A COMPARISON OF 1848–56 WITH 1981–8

Whatever the roles future research ultimately assigns to deregulation of banking, monetization of the economy, asset price changes, and so on in the explanation of the decline in velocity, it seems useful here to compare the gold rush boom with another period in which people have examined similar factors in an effort to explain the ability of the economy to absorb unusually large increases in the stock of money: the current prolonged expansion in the US. This comparison is made in Table 3.4.

The growth of nominal GNP was rapid in both expansions, but it was divided slightly differently between real and nominal changes. Inflation was about nine-tenths of 1 per cent higher and real GNP growth about 1.4 per cent lower in the modern period. The increase in the stock of money was faster in the earier episode (more so if we compare the antebellum money stock with modern M2), and, partly on that account, the decline in velocity was greater. If we move from the GNP deflator to less comprehensive indexes, we see an interest-

Table 3.4   A comparison of the period 1848–56 with
1981–8 (Annualized growth rates)

Variable	1848–56	1981–8
Money (M2)	9.97	7.41
(M1)	—	8.14
GNP deflator	2.82	3.69
Real GNP	4.36	2.96
Velocity (M2)	−2.78	−.76
(M1)	—	−1.49
Consumer prices	.89	3.73
Producer prices (ag.)	4.74	1.36
Producer prices (ind.)	4.99	1.26

Sources: 1848–56 – Table 3.1, and for producer prices,
Smith and Cole (1935, p. 168). 1981–8 – *US Economic
Report of the President, 1989*, pp. 385, 312, 310, 308, 373
and 382; 1988 figures were the June observation when
monthly data was given or the average of the second and
third quarters.

ing reversal. In the earlier period consumer prices appear to have
risen less than producer prices; in the modern period consumer prices
rose faster than producer prices. The explanation in both periods may
lie in the rate of inflation in international markets, since producer
prices tend to follow this trend more closely than more comprehensive indexes.

Perhaps the main lesson of this comparison is that over periods as
short as one-half of a business cycle, the relations among money,
prices and real income are subject to considerable variation. The gold
rush did produce an increase in prices and real output. But it did not
produce as much inflation, or as severe a balance of payments deficit,
as might have been expected. But this appears to have been a
somewhat fortuitous, due (perhaps) to the acceleration of the long-
term process of monetization or to the revaluation of assets triggered
by the economic expansion. Free banking, *per se*, probably deserves
only a small part of the credit for the relatively favourable outcome of
a potentially inflationary money shock.[12]

In a similar way, the current expansion does not appear to have
produced as much inflation as might have been anticipated, particularly by an analyst inclined to focus on M1. These deviations from
trend should be regarded as spurs to further research rather than
reasons for abandoning monetary analysis.

A BIMETALLIC STANDARD

The monetary standard during the free-banking era was not a monometallic gold standard, but rather a bimetallic standard. The mint stood ready to coin silver into legal tender dollars. But first, since the mint ratios set in 1834 were favourable to gold, and, second, because of the vast increase in the production of gold, there was very little silver money actually in circulation in the 1840s and 1850s. Many midwestern bankers, it was said, had never seen silver coins, except for those brought in by German immigrants. Nevertheless, the *potential* availability of a second monetary metal was an important safeguard of price level stability. It is the existence of this safeguard that makes it appropriate to refer to the antebellum system as a bimetallic system.

To illustrate this point suppose (1) that the US had been on a monometallic gold standard in the 1850s instead of a bimetallic standard and (2) that gold had not been found in California and Australia. Could the existing supply of gold have maintained a stable price level, or would the economy have been forced to undergo the sort of deflation, with all of its disruptive political and social consequences, that occurred in the US from 1873 to 1896 (when insufficient supplies of gold were forthcoming)?

If real income and velocity had changed from 1848 to 1856 at the rates they actually changed (4.36 per cent and 2.79 per cent), then an increase in the stock money of 7.15 per cent per year would have been necessary to maintain price level stability. While money growth exceeded this rate in the expansion that followed the depression of the early 1830s, over the longer run it did not. Macesich's money series begins in 1833. From 1833 to 1848 the stock of money rose only 3.55 per cent per year. To see what a continuation of this rate would have meant, apply it to the growth in the demand for money of 7.15 per cent per year that actually prevailed over the period 1848 to 1856. The difference implies a deflation of 3.60 per cent per year. In other words, had the economy truly been on a gold only standard and had no new sources of gold been discovered, the resulting deflation would have been fairly severe. By way of contrast, from 1879, when the US returned to the gold standard, and 1896, when opposition to the gold standard peaked in the US, with the nomination of free silver candidate Wiliam Jennings Bryan for president by the Democrats, the decline in the GNP deflator was about 1.5 per cent per year and the decline in the consumer price index was about 1.1 per cent per year.

Obviously, these calculations do not allow for the myriad of factors that would have impinged on the relationship between money and prices under the twin hypothetical assumptions of a monometallic gold standard and no new gold discoveries. To the extent, for example, that the fall in velocity during the period 1848 to 1856 was caused by the revaluation of assets produced by the monetary expansion, the example overstates the decline in prices that would have occurred under the twin assumptions of a monometallic gold standard and no gold rush. But the calculations do illustrate that there was a potential for a disturbing deflation.

Now replace assumption (1) with the actual antebellum arrangement. Under the bimetallic system deflationary pressures generated by stagnant gold supplies would have encouraged producers of silver and owners of existing stocks of silver to bring their silver to the mint (since there was unlimited demand for silver at the mint price) and increased supplies of silver base money would have mitigated the fall in prices.

Against this undeniable benefit of a bimetallic system it is often argued that the alternating replacements of one metal by another are a major cost of a bimetallic system. The point is sometimes made by saying that a 'true' bimetallic standard (according to this definition one in which both metals circulate side by side) is unlikely to exist for very long, and that the most likely outcome is an alternation of gold and silver standards. But this argument places too much weight, I believe, on the day to day functioning of the system and too little on the macroeconomic properties of the system. True, gold coins may be somewhat lighter, and to some people more attractive, so that a rapid replacement of gold by silver would cause some transactional and psychological costs. (The replacement of silver by gold is usually welcomed.) But it is hard to see how costs derived from these preferences could be the source of major economic costs from society's point of view. During World War II in the US (to take an extreme case) copper cents were replaced by steel cents in one year, and for several years the nickel was removed from the 'nickel' (the American 5 cent piece). These were matters of interest primarily to numistmatists.

There is no guarantee, of course, that a bimetallic standard will produce a smoother increase in the monetary base than a gold only or silver only standard. But the logic of not putting all one's eggs in one basket, and the American experience from 1873 to 1896, suggest that a bimetallic standard is to be preferred to a monometallic standard if a choice must be made between the two.

THE NEED FOR A LENDER OF LAST RESORT

There was no lender of last resort during the free-banking era. Indeed, the US had no clear lender of last resort during the period from the fall of the Second Bank of the US until the Federal Reserve was established in 1913. One could make the case, however, that the response of the system to the crisis of 1857 (the major crisis in the period) is particularly informative. By the latter part of the postbellum period, the large New York banks had attained such a major position within the financial system that one could argue that at times, particularly under the leadership of J. P. Morgan, they sometimes acted as lenders of last resort. During the free-banking era, moreover, banking legislation varied so much from state to state (since there was no national banking system) that this episode can shed considerable light on the type of system most likely to survive a banking panic in the absence of a lender of last resort.

It was in many respects a classic crisis. Although there had been difficulties in 1854, the crisis of 1857 seems to have come as almost a complete shock to the market. The spark was the failure of the Ohio Life Insurance and Trust Company. Based in Ohio, this bank had a reputation for soundness, but its New York agent had speculated heavily in railroad bonds. Here is how Hugh McCulloch, president of the Bank of the State of Indiana, remembered the crisis.

It came without premonition; it was a financial sirocco which at once dried up the springs of confidence and faith. Those who had money held it with the grip of misers. Trust ceased; confidence between men, confidence in everything but money, and hard money at that, disappeared. Men who were worth millions could not raise the few thousands that were needed to save them from discredit. Distrust, as general as it was causeless, pervaded the country (McCulloch (1889), p. 133).

Given the violence of the crisis, it is not surprising that a suspension of specie payments took hold in New York and quickly spread through the rest of the country. A few banks and banking systems, however, managed to hold out against the general suspension. In New York the Chemical Bank, alone, continued to redeem its notes. Among banking systems, only the Bank of the State of Indiana, the State Bank of Ohio, the banks of Kentucky, New

Orleans, and Charleston (as far as I have been able to learn) continued to redeem in specie.

The systems of free banking in New York, or chartered banking in New England, were not able to survive the crisis unscathed. The interesting thing here is that three of the western systems escaped suspension, despite the origin of the panic in the failure of the Ohio Life Insurance and Trust Company, and the general reputation of the West for free and easy banking. What these three groups of banks had in common was that they were, to an extent, branch banking systems. They were not branches in the modern sense, but rather more like federations of banks. Each branch was in many ways an independent bank, but there was a board to oversee the operation of the banks, and each branch was in some degree responsible for the liabilities of the other branches.

Bray Hammond (1957, p. 712) argues that it was the small number of banks in these states that allowed them to 'act in concert' and avoid the crisis. But he does not define exactly what actions they took in concert that banks in the East could not. It is unclear, for example, whether there was any actual transfer of specie among branches in the three western systems during the crisis. Hugh McCulloch's (1889, pp. 134–5) description of his monitoring of the demands on the branches of the Bank of the State of Indiana in the crisis suggests that no actual transfers were made, although he had this eventuality in mind. More likely, it was the potential reinforcements from other branches (both in the short and long runs) that reassured note-holders and so modified the demands on the bank. The participation of the state government in the Ohio and Kentucky systems may also have reassured depositors and note-holders.

It should be noted, however, that there were some special circumstances at work here. The Bank of the State of Indiana had commenced operations in the January of 1857, and the crisis hit in August.[13] So the Bank may not have been fully loaned up.[14] It was also true that the Bank of the State of Indiana was legally bound to give up its charter if it suspended payments. Under ordinary circumstances it might have expected legislative relief from this provision in the event of a nationwide financial crisis. But the political circumstances in Indiana were such that the Bank of the State could not count on this possibility. In other words, in other states suspending redemption was a way of preserving the long-run value of a bank charter, but not in Indiana.

In addition, McCulloch denigrates the performance of the Kentucky banks on the grounds that many of the notes were issued by branches that were not easily accessible, and of the State Bank of Ohio on the grounds that the Onio note brokers considered the branches of the State Bank to be so weakened by the failure of the Ohio Life and Insurance Company that the brokers did not bother to make a run on them (McCulloch, 1889, pp. 133–4). Although, McCulloch's desire to cast the performance of his own bank in the most favourable light is obvious, it is nevertheless true that he was well informed and generally reliable. Clearly, it would be useful to know more about how and why the western systems escaped the general panic.

There was an example of co-operation in New Orleans when one of the chartered banks (as distinct from the free banks) was bailed out by the other chartered banks at the governor's request. But Green (1972, p. 162) concludes that the major factor might be simply that the crisis hit at a moment when the banks were unusually strong. The high (one third) legal reserve ratio against deposits for the free banks and the one-third ratio against notes and deposits for the chartered banks may also have played a role. According to Hammond (1957, p. 716), New Orleans led the nation with a 52.46 per cent reserve ratio against notes and deposits.

The experience of the western branch systems in 1857, despite the reservations, helps to strengthen a point made by Friedman and Schwartz (1963, pp. 352, 457–8), following work by George Morrison, and recently expanded upon by Eugene White (1984, pp. 131–2), based on a comparison of the US and Canada during the Great Depression. Canada, with a small number of banks but many branches, suffered no failures during the Depression; but the US, with many small independent banks, suffered thousands. It would seem to follow that permitting branch banking may be an effective way of reducing the chance of a financial panic.[15]

These experiences do not say, however, that branching systems will be better in all circumstances. For example, one could imagine in our current politcal climate that a large financial centre bank could be forced by political pressures to keep uneconomic branches in the hinterlands open, thus weakening the bank as a whole, and increasing the probability of a major failure.

Morover, while it is true that the experience during the crisis of 1857 suggests that there were banking structures likely to be resistant to panic, it is hard to make the case that a widespread branching could reduce the probability of a panic to zero. There still appears to be some irreducible minimum of risk inherent in a fractional reserve banking system. A central bank acting as lender of last resort may be the only politically feasible institutional arrangement for eliminating this risk.[16] It is useful, however, to turn the question around and ask whether we should build into the banking system additional mechanisms such as branch banking for minmizing the risk of and damage from financial crises. The answer is clearly yes. A central bank may fail to act as lender of last resort (as the Federal Reserve system did in the 1930s) for a variety of reasons. Under a specie standard, for example, a central bank might be paralysed by a lack of specie, or by the fear that a reduction of its specie reserves would add to the panic.

A BANK-ISSUED CURRENCY

In the free-banking era private banks rather than the government issued the hand to hand currency. There were, it must be admitted, numerous complaints that the lack of a uniform currency was an inconvenience for the public. Instead of accepting a dollar in almost perfect certainty that it is legal tender, as we do, people in those days had to accept a risk that the money they took might turn out bad. In practice, things were not as disorganized as a reading of some descriptions of the period suggests. Normally, merchants and their customers dealt with notes issued by local banks they knew well. When dealing with unfamiliar notes, a merchant might have to use a bank-note reporter – a publication that listed the value of notes – or a counterfeit detector. But the process for him was not that different from a modern merchant checking a credit card number, or worrying about the value of a cheque being offered.

But were there advantages to a bank-issued currency to offset the lack of uniformity? One advantage when notes were issued on general bank assets (as in New England) was that the seigniorage from note issue would be invested by private bankers, perhaps more wisely, than when it was spent by the government. The free-banking law, however, by requiring banks to back notes with government bonds, returned part of the seignorage to the government in the form of higher bond prices.

A more technical advantage of a bank-issued currency is that banks can then accommodate changes in the public's desired ratio of currency to deposits without there having to be a change in the stock of money. Under the present system an increase in the desired ratio of currency to deposits will lead to a withdrawal of currency from the banking system, and a decrease in the stock of money, since currency is high-powered money.

This point can be put more formally as follows.[17]

Let

S_p = specie (gold and silver coins) held by the public
S_b = specie held by banks
N_p = notes held by the public
N_b = notes held by the banks
D = deposits held by the public
M = the stock of money
B = the monetary base
s = the ratio of specie to money desired by the public
n = the ratio of notes to money desired by the public
r_n = the reserve ratio of the banks against notes
r_d = the reserve ratio of the banks against deposits

The stock of money can then be defined as

(1) $M = S_p + N_p + D$

and the monetary base as

(2) $B = S_p + S_b$

Equation (2) has been specialized for the free-banking era. Notes are assumed to be issued by banks; only specie is treated as part of the monetary base.

With a little bit of manipulation we can set up the following identity:

(3) $M = B\{1/(n(r_n - r_d) + r_d(1-s) + s)\}$

This equation can be viewed as a money supply function, showing how the money supply varies depending on the monetary base (which varies with the output of the mines and the balance of payments), the preferences of the public for notes and specie, and the preferences of the banks for reserves. The key point here is the term $n(r_n - r_d)$. Variations in the proportion of their total money balances the public wishes to hold in the form of notes (holding constant the proportion they desire to hold as specie) affect the stock of money only to the extent there is a difference between the reserve ratios against notes and deposits. If the two reserve ratios are equal, changes in the desired proportion of notes have no effect on the stock of money.

It is important to remember, however, that this is not protection against runs on banks during a financial crisis. In that case what people would want is not notes, but hard money. If the ratio s rises in equation (3), then the stock of money falls.[18]

We can contrast this system with one in which notes are high-powered money issued by the government. Redefine the monetary base as

$$(2') \ B = S_p + S_b + N_b + N_p$$

If we also redefine the reserve ratios of the banks to include notes, we have the following equation for the stock of money:

$$(3') \ M = B\{1/(n(1 - r_d) + r_d(1-s) + s)\}$$

The only difference in the two money supply equations is in the $n(1 - r_d)$ term. Now, since notes are base money, increases in the note-to-money ratio have a depressing affect on the stock of money.

But how large were these effects in practice? If we take the time derivative of equation (3'), allowing money and the note issue to vary while holding other variables constant, omit the subscript on r, and rearrange terms we get

$$(4) \ M' = -n'\{n(1-r)/[n(1-r) + r(1-s) + s]\}$$

where the apostrophe after a variable refers to the time rate of change (growth rate) of the variable. Equation (4) is an upper bound estimate of the fluctuations in the money stock avoided because notes were issued by banks.

Over the years 1847 to 1859 the standard deviation of year to year percentage changes in the note-to-money ratio was 7.54 per cent. The standard deviation of year to year percentage change in the full term $-n'\{n(1-r)/[n(1-r) + r(1-s) + s]\}$ was 2.43 per cent – perhaps not a major gain, but not negligible either. This figure might be contrasted with the standard deviation of the year to year percentage change in the stock of money of 9.64 per cent. So, on this crude calculation, fluctuations in the stock of money were reduced by perhaps 20 per cent from what they would have been. As equation (4) makes clear, this advantage of free-banking shrinks as n, the proportion of notes in the money stock, shrinks. Today, with this ratio less than 7 per cent, this effect is not of great moment.

Perhaps the most compelling reason for allowing banks to issue currency is that it would encourage innovation in the supply of currency. One reason for the acceptance of a government monopoly of the note issue is the implicit assumption that innovatiion is not possible. The government, obviously, can print pieces of paper as easily as banks can. Given the printing technology available at a point in time, it would seem that any differences in the cost of production or technical quality between a bank-issued currency and a government-issued currency would be small. But given the fast pace of innovation in communications in general, the assumption that innovation in the issue of currency is unlikely may no longer be correct. Bank debit cards are but one example of the type of innovation that would be more likely in a private regime.

WILDCAT BANKING

Wildcat banking was the most romantic aspect of the American experience with free banking, and also the least understood. What was a wildcat bank? Perhaps the best way of explaining is by quoting an account of an encounter with a wildcat bank:

> The story is told of the hunt by an Adams Co. [an express company] agent for the Bank of Morocco. With a thousand dollars in Morocco bills, the man traveled through half of Indiana without discovering anyone who had heard of the bank. Late one afternoon he came upon two isolated log cabins on a backwoods road. One was a blacksmith's shop; the other was the Smith's house. The smith admitted that he was the proprietor of the Bank of Morocco, that the Bank itself was his potato barrel. He paid off the notes with gold concealed in the barrel, but begged the agent to keep the location of the bank a company secret. If the whereabouts of the Bank of Morocco became known, he pleaded, a general presentation of its outstanding notes would ruin him (Schultz and Craine (1937), p. 248.

There are two aspects of this story worth noting:

1   This was something that happened under Indiana's free-banking law. Bad banking, of course, could happen under chartered banking as well. But it was likely to be of a different form, cronyism would play a role, and the banker who got a charter would more likely be an established businessman and politician than the local blacksmith.
2   It was a frontier phenomenon. The chance of this happening in a

more developed region with better means of communication, and more sophisticated bankers and note-holders, was small.

But given the bond security function, how could this happen at all? The crucial variable was the number of notes a potential banker could issue for a given dollar in bonds deposited. There are two cases to consider. (1) The nominal value of notes that could be issued exceeds the value of the bonds deposited. In this very simple case there is an obvious incentive to set up a wildcat bank. All one has to do is deposit some bonds, issue the notes and pocket the difference. There is no reason the process has to stop after one round. Suppose a banker could issue $100 on the basis of $90 in notes. Then the wildcatter could deposit $90 worth of bonds, issue $100 worth of notes, use those notes to purchase $90 worth of bonds and $10 worth of gold, deposit an additional $90 worth of bonds, issue $100 more in notes and so on and on. Hopefully, he would be out of town when someone finally came to redeem the notes.[19]

Now, of course, there are a number of problems with this game. First of all, banking regulations normally made the value of bonds to be deposited far exceed the value of notes issued. In a few cases, however, it appears that state authorities did accept securities less in value than the notes issued, for a variety of reasons generally having to do with the insistence by the state that its bonds be valued at par. A second problem was getting someone to take the notes at par or at least at a sufficiently small discount to make the game worthwhile. This was no mean feat. People were naturally suspicious of unfamiliar private notes. Reportedly some of the Indiana wildcats employed river-boat gamblers on the Mississippi to 'launder' their notes. But even with techniques such as this, it seems likely that much of the wildcat money never entered circulation, or did so only at very high discounts.

Although this model has been thought of as the standard case, there is a second case. (2) The value of the bonds deposited exceeds the value of notes issued by a very small margin. Here the trick is to use the notes to leverage the purchase of a large mass of bonds, and to profit from the interest. In this case the bank must remain in operation long enough for the wildcatter to receive the interest payment.

THE EXTENT OF WILDCAT BANKING

Most studies of wildcat banking, including my own (1971, 1974), have emphasized that it was a rare phenomenon. However, recent studies, by Arthur Rolnick and Warren Weber (1983, 1984, 1988) and one by Andrew J. Economopoulos (1988) have, I believe, gone overboard in their attempt to show that wildcat banking was not a problem.

Rolnick and Weber (1984) attempted to show that even in states that suffered from very high rates of bank failure, this could not have been due to wildcat banking. They contrasted a theory that most failures were caused by wildcat banking (a theory they attributed to me) with a theory that the failures were caused by a decline in the value of assets held by banks produced by shocks independent of the banking system; and they offered evidence which they claimed showed that it was the decline in asset values that produced high rates of bank failures rather than wildcat banking.

Although I appreciate being credited with a theory worthy of being tested in an article in the *Journal of Monetary Economics*, I did not, in fact, actually attempt to explain the failure rate under free banking by reference to wildcat banking. I did try to analyse the phenomenon of wildcat banking in the limited circumstances in which it occurred. But it is clear that many free banks failed for the usual reasons: bad management, bad times and financial crises, and so on. A physician can spend a great deal of time studying cirrhosis of the liver without believing that this disease is important in explaining a major part of the death rate.

But there is a more fundamental issue here. Trying to compare a theory that bank failures are caused by falling asset prices with a theory that they were caused by wildcat banking is unsatisfactory because it compares different levels of analysis. Although the notion that falling asset prices cause bank failures is not strictly a tautology, it is hard to imagine a case of massive bank failures in which falling asset prices did not play a role. The interesting questions centre on why asset prices fell when they did, and what role administrative practices, legal restrictions, regulatory agency behaviour, and so on played in the process.

A reference to the Great Depression in the US, a more familiar case to most economic historians, may clarify the point I am trying to make. We could, of course, develop a theory that bank failures in the early 1930s were caused by falling asset prices of banks, and this theory could be tested by correlating the value of assets held by banks with the number of failures. Although I haven't performed the calculation, my assumption is that such a theory would successfully 'explain' the high rate of bank failure observed in the early 1930s. We could also develop a theory that bank failures were caused by the unwillingness of the Federal Reserve to act as lender of last resort or of legislation that prohibited branch banking. Obviously it wouldn't make sense to try to contrast the latter theories with the falling asset theory. The latter two theories are attempts to go behind the immediate failure and falling asset mix to get at the underlying causes. All these 'theories' have a role to play in explaining the banking situation of the early 1930s.

Similarly, without denying that falling asset prices are going to be a part of any process of massive free bank failures, we can certainly agree on a number of ways in which wildcat banking laid the groundwork for the mix of falling asset prices and bank failures examined by Rolnick and Weber:

1   Wildcat banking in certain cases explains why there were banks there to fail in the first place. In Indiana in 1853 numerous banks failed. Even if we accept Rolnick and Weber's point that the failures were caused by some calamity affecting the value of assets held by the banks, we must still see that the high failure rate depended on the large number of banks having been set up in previous years. If the smith in Indiana, referred to above, had not planted the Bank of Morocco in his potato barrel, it would not have failed when some independent shock hit the market for government bonds.

2   The restriction of free banks to a limited set of bonds for backing notes, and the tendency of wildcat bankers to do nothing but issue notes, meant that the resulting banking system would have a limited portfolio and would be extremely vulnerable to any factor affecting the price of the particular asset held by the wildcat banks. Other sorts of banks, banks that issued deposits as well as notes and that invested in local loans and discounts, might have been able to weather a shock that was confined to the class of securities backing the notes.

3   Banks do not have to go out of business simply because their assets (if sold off) are temporarily worth less than their liabilities. If a bank has sufficient liquid assets to meet withdrawals, it may stay in business for years with the market value of assets less than the liabilities. All that is required is that depositors, noteholders, and shareholders are confident that the bank has an adequate cash flow to meet temporary withdrawals and that it has some prospect

of regaining profitability in the long run. If the shock affecting its assets is expected to be temporary, there is no reason to go out of business. There may have been times in the past decade when some of the largest banks in New York had insolvent balance sheets because of heavy loans to Latin America. But that does not mean that it was accounting tricks that kept them in business. Depositors and shareholders assumed that in the long run these institutions would return to prosperity.

Another way of putting this point is to say that banks normally have some assets which are not usually shown on the books and which disappear when the bank is liquidated: its 'reputation', long-term relationships with customers, the working relationships built up over the years among its top managers, or other institution-specific forms of capital. If these assets were properly valued, it would be seen that total assets exceed total liabilities and that there is a good reason for the market to pay a positive price for the shares of the bank even though shareholders would receive nothing if the bank was liquidated. It is these unmeasured assets that made the shares of large New York City banks valuable investments even when their balance sheets were crowded with questionable loans to third world countries. The wildcat banks, on the other hand, were merely shell corporations created for the purpose of holding bonds and issuing notes. They had no institution-specific capital, so there was no reason for creditors to permit them to stay in business when the market value of their assets was less than their liabilities. The explanation proposed by Rolnick and Weber, then, is not a truism that applies to all banks at all times. It applies to wildcat banks precisely because they were dubious operations to begin with.

The nature of the free-banking law and wildcat banking can help explain why the shock to asset prices caused so many banks to throw in the towel in periods when bond prices were low and note redemptions were high. Part of the problem was that, as we noted above, if a single note was protested, then the state banking authority was required to redeem all the notes of the bank. But to this must be added the problem that simply issuing notes was the *raison d'etre* of the wildcat banks. Since, to go back to our example, the bank of Morocco had no other purpose than circulating notes (it was not, for example, collecting deposits or making local loans), there was no reason for it to stay in business once the notes began to come back.

4   So far, I have been following Rolnick and Weber in assuming that the fall in asset prices is completely independent of anything going on in the banking system – a completely independent shock. This, of course, will not normally be the case. As banks are closed and their assets are sold, asset prices will fall. This in turn will weaken the balance sheets of the remaining banks. Rather than there being a simple line of causation running from asset prices to bank failures, there is very likely to be an interactive process at work. Indeed, one could even imagine cases where a collapse of the banking system was anticipated, and reflected in asset prices before failures began in earnest.

My point here is not to oppose Rolnick and Weber's story (exogenous shock – falling asset prices – bank failures) with the exact opposite (wildcat banking – bank failures – falling bank asset prices). Although I do think that their failure to identify the nature of the shocks that affected asset prices weakens their argument, it seems most likely that the relationship between the collapse of some of the bond-based free-banking systems and the value of the assets they held was a two-way street. Falling asset prices weakened the banks, and the dumping of bonds by failing banks weakened the market for bonds.

In a more recent paper Rolnick and Weber (1988) examine the case of Minnesota. This is one that I identified, following traditional accounts, as a case of wildcat banking. On the basis of newspaper accounts (which show that there were plenty of warnings that the banks might be forced to suspend specie payments) Rolnick and Weber reached the conclusion that what existed in Minnesota was not wildcat banking, but rather a well-functioning market for small denomination mutual fund securities. The idea is that once the bank failed, the notes were worth whatever their bond backing was worth. People saw through the whole process and bought the notes at a sufficient initial discount to earn a competitive return when the notes were paid off. But while there is considerable evidence that people were wary of the notes and discounted them, it is a long leap from that evidence to the notion that these were small denomination mutual fund securities.

To some extent it is a matter of semantics. Rolnick and Weber find banks that were located away from Minneapolis to forestall redemption. They find banks that only held bonds and did no local lending. They find banks that were referred to as 'bantlings' in the local press.

I would call them wildcat banks; Rolnick and Weber want to call them mutual funds issuing small denomination securities. But Rolnick and Weber's terminology leads one to think that there was a general market for these securities in the antebellum period. Never, as far as I know, did anyone ever try to issue a note which said 'This is not a bank note and it is not redeemable in gold. This is a claim to state government bonds and its value will vary depending on the market value of the securities held at the time of redemption'. To my knowledge there was no law preventing the issue of such securities – laws could be changed in any case – so it seems likely that there was no demand.

Rolnick and Weber have one example in the paper of how these notes actually circulated.

> M. E. Ames, a St. Paul attorney, reported his experience on April 11 and 16, 1859. He said he had received $200 of Owatonna notes from a 'respectable Banker of this City'. (Ames did not say, however, what he paid for these notes, so that it cannot be assumed that he purchased them at par.) Trying, then, to purchase $125 of exchange on New York (New York bank notes), he said he could not find a bank that would make such a trade 'at any price.' Since New York exchange was roughly selling at par, the implication is that Owatonna money was selling for less than 63 cents on the dollar. [Ames eventually took his notes to Pease who, as Ames knew was the Owatonna broker. With some difficulty, Ames persuaded Pease to buy the notes for St. Paul city scrip, but could get neither New York exchange or gold out of Pease.][20]

This could be described as the behaviour of the happy purchaser of small denomination mutual fund securities, but it sounds more like the disgruntled buyer of a used car who finds out that Honest Al has set back the odometer even more than the buyer thought.

The paper by Economopoulos, following Rolnick and Weber, tries to use Illinois to test whether free-bank failures were caused by wildcat banking or falling asset prices.

Economopoulos manages to reduce the number of wildcat banks in his sample by using an extremely rigid and narrow definition of wildcat banking. First, consider his definition of the expected lifespan of a typical wildcat bank. Economopoulos takes one year as the maximum potential life of a wildcat and concludes that any bank that survives longer lacks a major defining characteristic. He gets his figure of one year from Rockoff (1975, p. 8), an unfortunate circumstance that somewhat reduces my ability to criticize his choice. But there I was asking how a banker could expect to make a profit if the bank could expect to last, say, one year. I was not estimating the actual lifespan of such banks. The weasel word 'say' was inserted, moreover, precisely to avoid having to commit myself to a precise numerical figure. Studies such as Economopoulos's can help to give a more precise numerical content to the idea of the expected lifespan of a wildcat bank. Clearly many of his banks lasted longer than a year, and might have lasted much longer had the Civil War not undermined the value of their southern bond security. How long they might have survived is an open question.

Economopoulos reaches the conclusion that the Illinois banks were not set up in inaccessible areas because only ten banks in his sample violated an express requirement of the law that they be located in towns of more than 200 inhabitants. He concludes that a majority were set up in highly populated locations. But it seems more than passing strange that out of ninety-three banks set up in Illinois in this period, not one was set up in Chicago, the commercial and transportation centre of the midwest and, it is said, the fastest growing city in the world. On the other hand, the town of New Haven Illinois, a metropolis of 200 souls, merited three banks.

But even if wildcat banking was more widespread than some of these recent papers suggest, it was still clearly a rare phenomenon, and was preventable, by requiring a substantial backing for notes in bonds measured at market prices.

SHOULD WE TURN THE CLOCK BACK TO THE FREE-BANKING ERA?

The answer, of course, is that we could not do so even if we wanted to. But more than that, it is clear that the free-banking era does not represent some ideal monetary system. There were problems: a major disturbance to the stock of high-powered money, a financial crisis of major proportions, and wildcat banking on the frontier. Nevertheless, the free-banking system embodied a number of desirable features, or attempted to do so, which are well worth adopting today, even though the precise institutional arrangements would have to be different. First, the control of the monetary base was left to a semi-automatic mechanism. In this case it was the bimetallic standard. Today, my preference would be for some form of monetary rule, or perhaps, as Friedman (1984) has recently suggested, or a freeze on the monetary base. But if a choice had to be made between the current system and a metallic commodity standard, then there is much to be said for a metallic standard, primarily because it sets an upper limit on the monetary base, while a fiat system does not. As we have seen above, even the gold rush boom of the 1850s produced little more monetary growth than we have observed in the supposedly stable 1980s; and if a choice had to be made between the antebellum bimetallic system and the postbellum gold standard, then my preference would be for a bimetallic standard, since it would minimize the chance of severe deflations.

Second, the free-banking system tried to get by without a lender of last resort. The record here is not altogether encouraging for those economists who argue that a lender of the last resort is not needed. There was a major crisis in 1857 that left a sharp recession and many business failures in its wake. But some of the systems escaped the general suspension of specie payments. Of particular interest are the branch systems of Indiana and Ohio, which were able to maintain general payments. This adds a bit of support to the idea that banking panics in the nineteenth century could have been ameliorated had branch banking been permitted.

Third, banks were permitted to issue hand to hand currency. This led, I would argue, to a more satisfactory allocation of the seigniorage, and to a damping down of the affect of changes in the note-to-money ratio on the stock of money.

Fourth, protection was provided for unsophisticated users of the banking system (noteholders) through the bond security system. It is hard to imagine a system today that did not incorporate some protection for the unsophisicated. Collateralizing that part of the money stock likely to be used by the poor and undereducated was a straightforward way of tackling the problem. A similar arrangement today, one providing a high level of protection for small depositors, while allowing most others to bear the risks and earn the returns of unregulated deposits, is well worth considering.

Fifth, there was free entry into banking. It would be hard to make the case that free entry was crucial to the emergence of New York as the nations's primary financial centre, or to Chicago and New Orelans as regional centres. Undoubtedly their dominant positions in the inter-regional movements of agricultural commodities and other products were the key. Nevertheless, at the margin the ease with which new banks could be started must have helped.

The US in the 1840s and 1850s was a politically troubled society; a great Civil War lay close at hand. But it possessed a rapidly growing economy. The frontier was being settled rapidly and immigrants were flooding into the country. By 1860 the US was the second leading industrial power in the world. All this was carried out with a banking system designed to minimize the role of government, maximize equality of economic opportunity, and protect the legitimate interests of unsophisticated users of the banking system. We can still learn something from an appreciation of such a banking system.

Notes

1. I owe a large debt to Michael Bordo, George Benston, James Dorn, Anna J. Schwartz, and Eugene White for comments on an earlier draft. James Dorn and Anna J. Schwartz, in particular, prepared extensive comments which they delivered at the conference from which I have greatly benefited. I am indebted also to the NBER for continuing support, but this chapter does not represent any views the NBER may have on this subject. I have no one but myself to blame for the remaining errors.

2. Although all free-banking laws contained these two basic features, they differed in many particulars (for example, the type and amount of bonds required to back a note). Some of these differences are important for explaining the diversity of experience under the free-banking laws.

3. High Rockoff (1988) 'Origins of the Usury Provision of the National Banking Act', unpublished working paper.

4. The money supply figures shown in the text are the sum of Friedman and Schwartz's (1970, pp. 222–5) estimates of specie held by the public, bank notes held by the public, and adjusted deposits. This is the same as estimates by George Macesich (Friedman and Schwartz, 1970, p. 231–2) in each year except 1850, when there is a modest 5 per cent difference. There are also money supply estimates made by Peter Temin (Friedman and Schwartz, 1970, p. 231–2) on a slightly different basis, but for broad comparisons the differences are not important.

5. The NBER chronology shows an economic expansion lasting 5 years from 1848 to 1853 (Moore (1980) p. 152). There was a recession from 1853 to 1855, followed by an expansion from 1855 to 1856. In the text I have generally given rates of change from the trough in 1848 to the peak in 1856 for two reasons: (1) the recession appears to have been mild, and does

not show up in the real income data, and (2) taking rates of growth to the second cyclical peak allows for a lagged affect of money on prices.

6.   As my critics have pointed out, the data may be unreliable. There has been a good deal of work done on wholesale price indexes in the antebellum period, but the resulting numbers undoubtedly have a wide margin of error. Broader measures such as the consumer price index probably have a wider margin of error. A perusal of the prices of individual commodities naturally shows a wide range of changes, with a tendency for prices of internationally traded commodities to increase faster than prices of domestically traded goods. The price of wheat, for example, rose 5.02 per cent per year from 1848 to 1856 and the price of bricks 1.55 per cent per year. The conclusions in the text, then, must be considered tentative until more reliable data become available.

7.   See the graphs in Milton Friedman and Anna J. Schwartz (1969, pp. 129–9)

8.   US Comptroller of the Currency. *Annual Report, 1876*, pp. XCVIII, CII, CIV, CXVI.

9.   High Rockoff (1975, p. 3). This total includes two separate laws passed in Michigan.

10. An exception is the attempt by the New England country banks to obtain a charter for a bank in Boston to compete with the Suffolk, the bank that redeemed country bank notes. This effort was frustrated until a charter was finally obtained for the Bank of Mutual Redemption in 1857.

11. See Friedman (1988) for a full analysis.

12. To the extent that the crisis of 1857 can be linked to the expansion (I am not convinced that it can be) the favourable impression created by looking primarily at the period 1848 to 1856 is misleading.

13. The Bank of the State of Indiana was an entirely private successor to the State Bank of Indiana, a similar, but partially state-owned institution then in the process of being wound up. The State Bank of Indiana in 1840 had surmounted a general suspension affecting the South and West. Specie payments were not made uniformly, but most demands were arranged in some fashion (Harding, 1895, p. 18).

14. The Bank of the State of Indiana took over the business of the State Bank of Indiana. But the managers of the State Bank had not foreseen that there would be a successor and had begun to wind up its affairs.

15. Friedman and Schwartz (1963, p. 353), however, argue that, as paradoxical as it may seem, high rates of bank failure (given the decline in the stock of money) may actually have been better for the US, because it encouraged people to spend money rather than hoard it.

16. See Goodhart (1988) for a development of this point, using a wide range of historical evidence.

17. Friedman and Schwartz (1963, Appendix B, pp. 776–98) present a general discussion of this approach. The same point has been made in somewhat different terms by White (1984, pp. 9–14), and Selgin (1987, p. 114).

18. There are some reasons why the public might want to convert from

deposits to notes in a crisis. For example, noteholders were preferred creditors in some cases, so depositors might want to convert in order to get a higher place in the bankruptcy line. In the free-banking states the bond-backing for notes, and the fact that the bonds were held by state authorities, made notes more attractive in a panic. These factors may explain the increase in noteholding during the crisis of 1857.

19.   The wildcat banker could not simply sell his bonds when the volume of note redemptions exceeded his specie reserve. Remember that the bonds were in the hands of the state banking authority. They would be returned only when the notes were returned, and the notes could be gathered up only by repurchasing them from the public. On particular occasions, of course, the bank might see a favourable chance for arbitrage, purchasing its own notes at a discount and using them to redeem its bonds.

20.   Rolnick and Weber (1988), p. 9. The material in brackets is on p. 69 in footnote 10.

References

BORDO, MICHAEL, and JONUNG, LARS (1987) *The Long-run Behavior of the Velocity of Circulation: The International Evidence* (Cambridge (UK) and New York: Cambridge University Press).

BERRY, THOMAS SENIOR (1988) *Revised Annual Estimates of American Gross National Product, Preliminary Annual Estimates of Four Major Components of Demand, 1789–1889* (Richmond VA: The Bostwick Press).

COWEN, TYLER, and KROSZNER, RANDALL (1987) The Development of the New Monetary Economics', *Journal of Political Economy*, 95 (June), pp. 567–90.

ECONOMOPOULOS, ANDREW J. (1988) 'Illinois Free banking Experience', *Journal of Money, Credit and Banking*, 20 (May), pp. 249–64.

ESAREY, LOGAN (1947) *The Indiana Home* (Crawfordsville, Indiana: R. E. Banta).

FRIEDMAN, MILTON (1960) *A Program for Monetary Stability* (New York: Fordham University Press).

FRIEDMAN, MILTON (1984) 'Monetary Policy for the 1980s', *To Promote Prosperity: US Domestic Policy in the Mid-1980s*, ed. J. H. Moore, (Stanford, CA: Hoover Institution Press), pp. 40–54.

FRIEDMAN, MILTON (1985) 'The Case for Overhauling the Federal Reserve', *Challenge*, 28 (July–August), pp. 4–12.

FRIEDMAN, MILTON (1988) 'Money and the Stock Market, *Journal of Political Economy*, 96 (April), pp. 211–45.

FRIEDMAN, MILTON and SCHWARTZ ANNA J. (1963) *A Monetary History of the United States, 1867–1960* (Princeton: Princeton University Press).

FRIEDMAN, MILTON, and SCHWARTZ, ANNA J. (1969) 'The Demand for Money: Some Theoretical and Empirical Results', *The Optimum*

Quantity of Money and Other Essays, Milton Friedman (Chicago: Aldine Publishing Company), pp. 111–55.

FRIEDMAN, MILTON, and SCHWARTZ, ANNA J. (1970) *Monetary Statistics of the United States: Estimates, Sources, Methods* (New York: Columbia University Press.

FRIEDMAN, and SCHWARTZ, ANNA J. (1986) 'Has Government Any Role in Money?', *Journal of Monetary Economics* (January), pp. 37–62.

GOODHART, C. A. E. (1988) *The Evolution of Central Banks* (Cambridge Mass.: MIT Press).

GREEN, GEORGE D. (1972) *Finance and Economic Development in the Old South: Louisiana Banking, 1804–1861* (Stanford: Standford University Press).

HAMMOND, BRAY (1957) *Banks and Politics in America: from the Revolution to the Civil War* (Princeton: Princeton University Press).

HARDING, WILLIAM F. (1895) 'The State Bank of Indiana', *Journal of Political Economy*, 3 (December), pp. 1–36.

HAYEK, F. A. (1976) *Denationalization of Money* (London: Institute of Economic Affairs).

HOMER, SIDNEY (1963) *A History of Interest Rates* (New Brunswick NJ: Rutgers University Press).

KAHN, JAMES A. (1985) 'Another Look at Free Banking in the United States', *American Economic Review*, 75 (September), pp. 881–5.

KING, ROBERT G. (1983) 'On the Economics of Private Money', *Journal of Monetary Economics*, 12 (July), pp. 127–58.

LASDON, OSCAR (1971) 'The Early Ways and Crazy Days of Banking', *Banker's Magazine* CLIV (Spring), pp. 49–58.

McCULLOCH, HUGH (1889) *Men and Measures of Half a Century* (New York: Charles Scribner's Sons).

MOORE, GEOFFREY H. (1980) 'Business Cycles, Panics and Depressions', in Glenn Porter, ed. *Encyclopedia of American Economic History: Studies of the Principal Movements and Ideas* (New York: Charles Scribner's Sons).

NG, KENNETH (1988) 'Free Banking Laws and Barriers to Entry in Banking, 1838–1860', *Journal of Economic History*, 48 (December), pp. 877–89.

ROCKOFF, HUGH (1971) 'Money, Prices, and Banks in the Jacksonian Era', in ed. Robert William Fogel and Stanley L. Engerman, *The Reinterpretation of American Economic History*, (New York: Harper & Row), pp. 443–53.

ROCKOFF, HUGH (1974) 'The Free Banking Era: A Re-examination', *The Journal of Money, Credit, and Banking*, 6 (May) pp. 141–67.

ROCKOFF, HUGH (1975) *The Free Banking Era: A Re-Examination* (New York: Arno Press).

ROCKOFF, HUGH (1975) 'Varieties of Banking and Regional Economic Development in the United States', *Journal of Economic History* (March), pp. 160–81.

ROCKOFF, HUGH (1986) 'Institutional Requirements for Stable Free Banking', *Cato Journal*, 6 (Fall), pp. 617–34.

ROLNICK, ARTHUR J. and WEBER, WARREN E. (1983) 'New Evidence on the Free Banking Era', *American Economic Review*, 73 (December) pp. 1080–91.

ROLNICK, ARTHUR J., and WEBER, WARREN E. (1984) 'The Causes of Free Bank Failures: A Detailed Examination of the Evidence', *Journal of Monetary Economics*, 14 (October), pp. 267–91.

ROLNICK, ARTHUR J., and WEBER, WARREN E. (1985) 'Banking Instability and Regulation in the U.S. Free Banking Era', *Federal Reserve Bank of Minneapolis, Quarterly Review*, 9 (Summer), pp. 2–9.

ROLNICK, ARTHUR J., and WEBER, WARREN E. (1988) 'Explaining the Demand for Free Bank Notes', *Journal of Monetary Economics*, 21 (January), pp. 47–71.

SCHULTZ, WILLIAM J., and CRAINE, M. R. (1937) *Financial Development of the United States* (New York: Prentice-Hall).

SCHWERT, G. WILLIAM (1989) 'Indexes of United States Stock Prices from 1802 to 1987', Cambridge MA: National Bureau of Economic Research. Working Paper (July).

SELGIN, GEORGE A. (1988) *The Theory of Free Banking: Money Supply Under Competitive Note Issue* (Totowa, NJ: Rowman & Littlefield).

SMITH, WALTER BUCKINGHAM, and COLE, ARTHUR HARRISON (1935) *Fluctuations in American Business, 1790–1860* (Cambridge Mass.: Harvard University Press).

SYLLA, RICHARD (1985) 'Early American Banking: the Significance of the Corporate Form', *Business and Economic History*, 14 (March), pp. 105–23.

TEMIN, PETER (1969) *The Jacksonian Economy* (New York: W. W. Norton & Company, Inc).

WHITE, EUGENE (1984) 'A Reinterpretation of the Banking Crisis of 1930', *Journal of Economic History*, 44 (March), pp. 119–38.

WHITE, LAWRENCE (1984) *Free Banking in Britain: Theory, Experience, and Debate, 1800–1845* (Cambridge and New York: Cambridge University Press).

Comment on Chapter 3
James A. Dorn

Monetary stability is a prerequisite for a smoothly functioning market economy. Erratic money produces price-level instability, which distorts market prices and interferes with the efficient allocation of resources. Moreover, without price-level stability, the banking system will be exposed to greater risk and uncertainty. A sound monetary system, providing for normal growth in the monetary base as real economic growth occurs, helps safeguard the banking system from monetary disturbances that can have systemwide effects. For these and other reasons, it is important to consider the operating characteristics of alternative monetary regimes, especially as they meet the test of price-level stability.

The US experiment with free banking (1837–63) offers a rich variety of lessons about the operation of a relatively unregulated banking system set within the framework of a commodity-based standard for the provision of outside money. These lessons and their implications for reforming the current discretionary fiat money regime are the focus of Hugh Rockoff's insightful chapter. In particular, his paper re-examines the following fundamental issues in the theory of money and banking:

1   Is a commodity-based monetary system preferable to a government fiat money régime in terms of achieving price-level stability?
2   Is a central bank necessary as a lender of last resort (LLR) or can a decentralized market mechanism protect against systemwide bank runs?
3   Should private bank notes be allowed to circulate freely as competing currencies?
4   Should free entry into banking be allowed?

In his analysis of these four issues, Rockoff is careful to note the data problems that confront anyone seriously interested in evaluating the nineteenth century US free-banking experiment.[1] He is also careful to point out that the US free-banking system differs significantly from F. A. Hayek's scheme for competitive private currencies (Hayek (1976, 1978)). However, by taking a comparative institutions approach – contrasting the monetary institutions that existed in antebellum America for the provision of outside and inside money with those that exist today – Rockoff is able to shed new light on the question of whether unregulated money and banking lead to chaos or order.

PRICE STABILITY UNDER ALTERNATIVE MONETARY RÉGIMES

Under a fiat money régime, in which there is no effective monetary rule to limit the growth of high-powered money, there is little reason to expect long-run price stability. Experience confirms this expectation. According to Peter Bernholz (1988, p. 11), 'a study of about 30 currencies shows that there has not been a single case of a currency freely manipulated by its government or central bank since 1700 which enjoyed price stability for at least 30 years running'.[2] This failure contrasts sharply with the success of countries that adhered to the rules of commodity-based standards and were able to maintain the long-run value of their national monetary units (see Bernholz (1988), p. 12; Gallarotti (1989)).

Under US free banking, the supply of base money was regulated by the operation of the semi-automatic gold standard mechanism. Although the United States was legally on a bimetallic standard, the passage of the Coinage Act of 1834 converted the United States to a *de facto* gold standard.[3] Unlike the performance of the Federal Reserve system, the gold standard operated to protect the long-run value of the dollar.[4] Even though the gold standard era was characterized by bouts of inflation and deflation, these price movements tended to be relatively mild and to offset each other over time (Bordo (1981). It is for these reasons that Rockoff favours a commodity-based standard over a discretionary fiat money standard.

Although the gold standard provided protection against persistent inflation, the US free-banking system was rocked by a major monetary shock in 1848, when gold was discovered in California, and experienced a significant banking panic in 1857. What interests Rockoff is the California gold discovery and the ensuing increase in the money supply – an increase of nearly 10 per cent per year over the 1848–56 period. Indeed, if the figures can be relied upon, the GNP deflator rose by only 2.82 per cent per year over this period while the index of consumer prices rose by a mere 0.89 per cent per year.

Accordingly, Rockoff estimates that velocity fell by 2.79 per cent per year between 1848 and 1857.

Rockoff first tries to explain the sharp decline in velocity by turning to the traditional determinants of the demand for money. But he finds that increasing real income per capita and declining nominal interest rates do not fully explain the acceleration of the decline in velocity that occurred over the 1848–56 period. To explain the 'residual', Rockoff turns to three additional factors: free banking, rising asset prices, and increased monetization of economic activity.

If free banking increased competition as the number of banks increased, and if banking services increased as a result, then it may be that free banking helped increase the demand for money and can help account for the larger than normal drop in velocity over the 1848–56 period. This is the hypothesis Rockoff proposes, but he is unable to find any convincing evidence to support it. Thus, he regards the fact that free banking co-existed with the mild inflation following the 1848 monetary shock as largely 'fortuitous'.

Having failed to show that free banking improved price stability by rendering better services and increasing the demand for money, Rockoff attempts to offer another explanation for the overly large decline in velocity and the mild inflation – one based on the increase in asset prices that occurred during the 1848–56 period. His argument is that the increase in asset prices increased the demand for money by increasing wealth and by raising the volume of financial transactions. This explanation is plausible, but it is also true that rising asset prices increase the opportunity cost of holding money. Individuals, therefore, have an incentive to shift out of money to alternatives, and velocity will rise, not decline. The net effect of rising asset prices on velocity, therefore, depends on the relative strength of the wealth effect and the substitution effect.

As a final attempt to explain the unusually large increase in the demand for money, Rockoff turns to the monetization hypothesis. He argues that there may have been an increase in the monetization of economic life during the 1848–56 period that accelerated the decline in velocity, and he offers some evidence to support this hypothesis. It seems unlikely, however, that the proportion of economic activity being conducted through monetary exchange increased to such an extent that increased monetization could account for the abnormally large drop in velocity. Also, it is not entirely clear why 'monetization' of economic activity should decrease velocity rather than increase it.

In trying to ascertain the stability of money and prices during the free-banking era, Rockoff faces the problem that the data may not accurately reflect the true behaviour of money and prices. The actual behaviour of money and prices over the 1848–56 period may have differed on the upside from that reported in Rockoff's Tables 3.1 and 3.4.[5] Moreover, Rockoff's analysis of the data does not distinguish between the free-banking system and other systems that co-existed with free banking during the 1848–56 period. In particular, the Suffolk banking system had a major influence on the money-supply process in New England and was closer to a laissez-faire banking system than the so-called free-banking system that operated in New York and other states.[6] It may be that a study of the operating characteristics of the Suffolk system could help explain the lower than expected inflation following the 1848 California gold discovery. If so, a stronger case could be made for the stability properties of a genuinely free banking system. However, Michael Bordo and Anna Schwartz (1989, p. 8) report that 'the Suffolk system was no bulwark against instability in the monetary system'. They agree that the Suffolk Bank 'provided a check on overissue by an individual bank', but they observe that the Bank's 'annual redemptions from 1834 to 1857 contradicts the theory of "self-correcting in-concert expansions"'. According to the authors, 'not only is there a clear upward trend in the figures, rising from $76 million in 1834 to $376 million in 1857, in line with a growing banking industry, but in addition every cyclical downturn in the period is registered in the time series'.[7]

The impact of monetary disturbances on velocity is important. Rockoff, however, chooses to focus on the secular trend of velocity and foregoes the opportunity to investigate the cyclical behaviour of velocity and its relation to the initial monetary shock in 1848. Reporting that velocity declined by 2.79 per cent *per year* from 1848 through 1856 disguises the fact that monetary velocity did not change by a uniform amount, as can be seen from Table 3.5.

In fact, velocity behaved in accordance with the pre-Keynesian theory of monetary disequilibrium, at first declining in response to the monetary shock and then increasing as inflationary expectations decreased the demand for money.[8] By omitting 1857 in discussing the price-level effects of the 1848 gold discovery, Rockoff omits a year in which velocity returned to its 1847 level, increasing from 6.61 in 1856 to 8.68 in 1857.

In sum, although the US apparently experienced a mild inflation

Table 3.5 Monetary velocity in the US free-banking era, 1847–59

Year	Monetary velocity[a]	Year	Monetary velocity[a]
1847	8.69	1854	6.57
1848	8.26	1855	6.83
1849	7.16	1856	6.61
1850	7.10	1857	8.68
1851	6.33	1858	6.74
1852	6.00	1859	6.99
1853	6.04		

[a] Calculated from Rockoff's Table 3.1, using columns 1, 5, 6.

following the California gold discovery in 1848, free banking cannot account for this 'fortuitous' result. Moreover, monetary disturbances were accentuated by changes in the velocity of money, though with a considerable lag following the 1848 gold discovery, but with virtually no lag following the specie drain and banking panic of 1857. Finally, it was the operation of the gold standard and not the principal characteristics of free-banking – free entry, the bond collateral requirement, and mostly voluntary reserve requirements – that limited the quantity of base money and kept price-level movements within tolerable bounds. On this basis, one can agree with Rockoff that a commodity standard is more likely to promote long-run price stability than a managed fiat money standard.

MONEY AND BANKING WITHOUT A LENDER OF LAST RESORT

The free banking era was characterized by the lack of an official central bank, the absence of government paper currency, no clearly defined lender of last resort (LLR), and variability in free-banking laws across states. A study of US free banking, therefore, can help answer the question of whether it is necessary to have an official central bank act as LLR to avert banking panics or whether a private, voluntary system can perform the LLR function more efficiently. An examination of the free-banking era also throws light on the question of what type of banking system is most apt to overcome a banking panic without a LLR.

In addressing these issues, Rockoff finds that most banks failed to redeem their notes in specie during the panic of 1857, including those in the free-banking system in New York and in the Suffolk system in New England. On this basis, he concludes that to minimize the risk of banking panics under a fractional reserve system, 'a central bank acting as a lender of last resort may be the only politically feasible institutional arrangement'. However, he also notes that a few branch-like systems (in Indiana, Ohio, and Kentucky) did not suspend specie payment during the panic. On this basis, he argues that branching and other voluntary arrangements should be encouraged to further reduce the risk of a banking panic and to minimize damages.

It is generally agreed that a fractional reserve banking system requires some mechanism to inject high-powred (outside) money into the banking system in the event of a liquidity crisis.[9] But the issue of whether this mechanism should be a central bank or a private market alternative is still unresolved. Rockoff could have shed further light on this issue by looking more deeply into the free-banking system's failure to maintain convertibility in 1857, and by examining the role of the Independent Treasury, the New York Safety Fund system, and the New England Suffolk system – all of which also failed to provide convertibility during the 1857 panic.

Under free banking, the bond collateral requirement was a poor substitute for a credible pledge to redeem private bank notes in specie. In the event of a specie drain, noteholders would have little confidence that their notes would actually be redeemed. With security prices falling and a deficiency of cash, free banks would be forced to suspend note redemption, as in 1857. The problem of averting a liquidity crisis was further evidenced by the fact that the bank reserves were concentrated in New York City, but no effective formal arrangement for supplying cash to city banks during a crisis existed in 1857.[10] Combined with the lack of any required reserve ratio for New York's free banks, each bank tended to over-extend its credit such that systemwide reserves were considered insufficient to stem a general run on banks (see Hedges (1938), pp. 131–2). Hence, the free-banking system, although reasonably efficient, was open to disturbances – both real and monetary – from outside the system. The bond collateral system, in particular, was not a self-correcting mechanism to assure that either over-expansion or monetary deficiency would be avoided.[11]

Although the free-banking system had no official LLR, mention should be made of the role of the Independent Treasury, which helped prevent the crisis of 1851, the stringency of 1853, and the crisis of 1854 from deteriorating into more serious banking panics, such as that of 1857. In each of these cases, the Independent Treasury acted like a central bank by engaging in open market purchases of government securities in the New York market.[12] By pumping new reserves into the banking system, the Treasury acted to counter the perverse elasticity of free bank notes under the bond security requirement. However, the Treasury's ability to do this was limited by its specie reserves. During the 1857 panic, for example, the Treasury failed to act as LLR for commercial banks.[13] Without a ready source of outside money (specie), either from the Treasury or from the New York Clearing House Association, city banks were unable to withstand the demand for specie occasioned by the failure of the Ohio Life and Trust Company, which kept sizeable reserves in its New York office (Hedges (1938), pp. 116–18). A general suspension followed.

To avoid banking panics, banks have to gain and maintain the public's confidence. Prior to the US free-banking system, New York State had instituted a Safety Fund (in 1829) to ensure that troubled banks would not cause a systemwide banking panic, in the event of a default on specie payment.[14] Under the Safety Fund system, each member bank had to pay a fixed percentage of its capital into an insurance fund, which was to cover both notes and deposits. By trying to insure both notes and deposits, the Fund over-extended itself, and the flat-rate premium created a moral hazard. Nevertheless, Hammond (1957, p. 562) believed that as a means for preventing bank panics the insurance principle underlying the Safety Fund system of banking was superior to the bond collateral principle of the free-banking system.

Another private alternative to free banking was the Suffolk banking system. This system was by far the freest and most efficient banking system in the United States during the free-banking era.[15] Its superiority rested on several factors: (1) its adherence to the convertibility principle; (2) its conservative and capable management; and (3) its self-regulatory structure, in which private self-interest could be harnessed for the benefit of the system as a whole as well as for noteholders. Unlike the free-banking system (with its bond collateral requirement) and the New York Safety Fund system (with its private insurance plan), the Suffolk system built confidence by establishing a reputation for actually redeeming all notes presented it. The Suffolk system was also self-regulating, and member banks, as well as the Suffolk Bank, had a stake in maintaining sufficient reserves to ensure redemption. Since country banks kept balances (redemption funds) in the Suffolk Bank and the Suffolk Bank was committed to redeem country bank notes, all parties had an incentive to comply with sound banking practices – and the clearing mechanism operated to provide New England with a relatively secure private currency system.[16]

Even so, a distinction must be made again between a single bank and the Suffolk system as a whole. The fact that adverse balances cause an individual bank to limit its credit and notes does not rule out over-expansion by the banking system as a whole, nor does it prevent a possible financial crisis and banking panic when credit and money later contract. And as we have already seen, the Suffolk system did not prevent monetary instability from affecting the behaviour of inside money.

In sum, none of the institutional devices operating in the nineteenth-century free banking era – the bond collateral requirement, the Safety Fund, the redemption guarantee and clearing mechanism of the Suffolk system, as well as the Independent Treasury – was able to prevent suspension during the panic of 1857. Rockoff's conclusion about the possible necessity of an official central bank as LLR in a fractional reserve banking system is therefore understandable. Yet, as he admits, the Federal Reserve also failed in its function as LLR during the 1930s, which was a far more severe business downturn than that experienced in 1857. The fact remains that the fundamental conditions for a stable banking system are a sound monetary system for the supply of outside money and a stable price level. As Bordo and Schwartz (1989), p. 32) emphasize, when price stability is absent, 'the performance and stability of banking systems under "self-regulation" will be in jeopardy' (see also Humphrey (1989)).

TOWARD A NEW MONETARY RÉGIME

The US free-banking experiment was a mixed bag, and it is not clear whether free banking promoted economic development or whether the country prospered in spite of it.[17] There was a major injection of high-powered money after the California gold discovery, a widespread banking panic, sporadic episodes of wildcat banking (more of a reputational effect than a major problem), perverse elasticity of the currency (owing to a defective bond collateral requirement), and increased transactions costs associated with the lack of a uniform currency with a stable value. Yet, for much of the free-banking era, the circulating media of those states with relatively sound free-banking laws performed satisfactorily (see Rockoff (1975)). New England's Suffolk system, which was closer to a laissez-faire system, performed even better than the so-called free banks – though it too was forced to suspend specie payment in 1857.

Any stability experienced in the banking system, however, rested largely on the performance of the gold standard, which determined the price level. Had free banking – that is, freedom to provide inside money subject to a bond security requirement – existed in a period with lower economic growth, a major monetary shock like the California gold discovery would have generated considerable inflation. That it did not do so in the US free-banking era was, as Rockoff put it, 'fortuitous'. The gold standard did produce reasonably stable prices over the long run but it was far from stable, as inflationary and deflationary episodes as well as financial crises attest. These and other problems indicate that the historical gold standard, as well as the free banking system it supported, can be improved upon.

Yet, the emergence of the Federal Reserve system in 1913–14 and its evolution into a pure fiat money régime without any anchor for the price level – or even any long-run commitment to achieve price-level stability as the *primary* objective of monetary policy – has itself led to a type of monetary chaos, since there is no effective monetary constitution (see Buchanan (1989); Dorn (1986)).

The question, then, is can we do better? If so, which way should we move? Towards more discretion in central bank policy or towards some type of monetary rule? Towards more regulation of banking or towards free entry? In Rockoff's mind the answers are clear: we can definitely do better in achieving price-level stability if we reform the present fiat money régime by introducing a monetary rule and we can improve banking by deregulation and branching. What we cannot do, argues Rockoff, is to go back to the free-banking era – 'even if we wanted to'. But we can use the lessons from that period to improve the current system. The key lesson, drawn from the operation of the gold standard, is that without a monetary rule of some sort there is no effective constraint on the inflationary impulses of modern democratic governments.

Although we cannot go back to the free-banking era, the failure of central banks operating under discretionary authority to achieve long-run price stability should make one hesitant to call for more rather than less government in the areas of money and banking. As

Richard Timberlake (1986, p. 638) observes: 'The history of monetary institutions reveals that every special intervention by government to regulate the monetary system – that is, to compromise market functions – has resulted in institutional changes that have both restricted freedom of enterprise in the production of money and reduced efficiency'. On this basis, Hayek (1976, p. 22) has concluded 'that the best the state can do with respect to money is to provide a framework of legal rules within which the people can develop the monetary institutions that best suit them'. And Friedman and Schwartz (1987, p. 311) have recently arrived at a similar conclusion, arguing 'that leaving monetary and banking arrangements to the market would have produced a more satisfactory outcome than was actually achieved through governmental involvement'.[18]

The failure of modern democratic governments to safeguard the long-run value of money by adopting a constitutionally based monetary rule has increased uncertainty in monetary affairs. By considering alternative monetary régimes that have existed, as well as those that might exist if the relevant theories could be put into practice, we can learn a great deal about the probable effects of alternative monetary institutions in achieving stable money and prices. In his analysis of the US free-banking era and its lessons for reforming the current fiat money regime, Rockoff has reinforced the point that monetary institutions matter. He has also reminded us that looking for real-world counterparts to our theoretical constructs is a risky business.

Notes

1. Bray Hammond (1957, p. 716) remarked: 'One must not expect too much of 19th century bank statistics'.
2. Bernholz is referring to the study by Parkin and Bade (1978).
3. Milton Friedman (1989, p. 5) notes, 'From 1834 on, gold coins circulated and gold was the effective standard'. See also Bordo (1981, p. 7, n. 30).
4. William Poole (1989, pp. 198–9) has argued that if long-run price stability is the relevant measure to test the performance of a monetary régime, then the classical gold standard must be ranked relatively higher than the government fiat money system as it has operatred under the Federal Reserve system.
5. Clark Warburton (1966, pp. 200–1) has noted that under-reporting of currency and deposits during the free-banking period biased estimates

of the money supply downward (see note f). The money supply figures given by Warburton for 1849 and 1859 are $316 million and $722 million, respectively. He believes both figures, especially the 1849 figure, are too low because of under-reporting by private banks. Rockoff's estimate of the money supply for 1859 is $565 million, a figure significanty below Warburton's, which is an underestimate as well.

6. In view of Hammond (1957, p. 556), 'The operations of the Suffolk Bank showed *laisser faire* at its best. With no privileges or sanctions whatever from the government, private enterprise developed in the Suffolk an efficient regulation of bank credit that was quite as much in the public interest as government regulation could be'. See also the interesting study by Karen Palasek (1988), who argues that the Suffolk system was much closer to unregulated banking than the so-called free-banking system.

7. In evaluating the Suffolk system, Bordo and Schwartz draw on the study by Dewey (1910, p. 89).

8. The pre-Keynesian theory of monetary disequilibrium held 'that except for secular trends changes in circuit velocity generally move, with a short time lag, in the same direction as changes in the quantity of money' (Warburton 1966, p. 268). For a general discussion of the theory of monetary disequilibrium, see Warburton, ch. 1.

9. See, for example, Timberlake (1965, pp. 158–9): 'Ordinary competitive processes in banking cannot protect society from bank credit fluctuations, because a fractional reserve banking system can create variable amounts of deposits against a given amount of reserves. Only when some disinterested controlling agency is formed to check the banking system's discretion can large variations in the money supply be tempered and unforeseeable changes in the demand for money be counteracted'.

10. The New York Clearing House Association, established in 1853, was still unsure of its powers and responsibilities in 1857, and so acted hesitantly and without enough force to stem the banking panic. The situation changed in 1860, when the New York Clearing House banks agreed to follow a policy of loan expansion based on Bank of England policy and to use Clearing House certificates to conserve on specie. These practices were very effective and helped prevent a crisis in 1860. Reserve requirements for New York Clearing House banks were also imposed in 1860, to equal 25 per cent of total liabilities. For a discussion of these factors, see Hedges (1938, pp. 132, 136–7).

11. On the weakness of the bond collateral requirement as a stabilizing force in the creation of inside money, see Hammond (1957, pp. 595–6), Hedges (1938, p. 25), McCulloch (1889, p. 125), and Selgin (1988, pp. 13–14). Rockoff (1986) also discusses some of the shortcomings of the bond security system, arguing that even though 'much sound banking was conducted under the bond security system in such states as New York and Ohio . . . the difficulties that beset it suggest that it is not the key to successful free banking' (p. 626).

12. See Hedges (1938, pp. 109–16) and Timberlake (1965, pp. 170–1).

13. The Treasury did issue notes, but without specie 'it lost much of its leverage for carrying out policy' (Timberlake (1965), p. 171). Although some economists would limit the LLR function to acting through the discount window to provide liquidity to prevent a banking crisis from turning into a monetary crisis, a case can be made that any measure to prevent systemwide bank runs comes under the LLR function, including open market operations (see Humphrey and Keleher 1984, pp. 277, 281).

14. The following discussion of the New York Safety Fund System is based largely on Hammond (1957, pp. 556–63).

15. For a discussion of the general characteristics of the Suffolk system, see Hammond (1957, pp. 549–56, 562–3). The follolwing analysis rests largely on his work.

16. Hammond (1957, p. 556) cites a New Yorker who in 1858 wrote that 'even with the aid of statutes and "revised statutes"', the banking system in New York was 'far inferior to that created by the voluntary Suffolk Bank system'. See also Haines (1966, p. 126).

17. Haines (1966, p. 128) describes the antebellum banking era as 'an era of monetary chaos', and states: 'The emphasis was on quantity of money rather than quality . . . [T]he tendency in many areas was to feel that if a little money was good, more must necessarily be better. The inevitable result was deterioration of the monetary system. General suspension of specie payments occurred in 1814, 1818, 1837, 1841, and 1857, and local difficulties were even more frequent. It was a period of irresponsibility, bank failures, monetary fraud, speculation, and confusion. The country grew, economically as well as geographically, but it was in spite of the monetary system, not primarily because of it'.

18. Friedman and Schwartz (1987, p. 311), however, 'continue to believe that the possibility that private issuers can . . . provide competing, efficient and safe fiduciary currencies with no role for governmental monetary authorities remains to be demonstrated. As a result we believe that this is the most important challenge posed by the elimination of a commodity-based outside money'. For a useful discussion of the case for competitive money and ways to implement it, see White (1983, especially pp. 297–9).

References

BERNHOLZ, PETER (1988) 'The Importance of Reorganizing Money, Credit and Banking When Decentralizing Economic Decision-Making.' Paper presented at the Cato Institute/Fudan University conference on Economic Reform in China: Problems and Prospects, Shanghai (September).

BORDO, MICHAEL D. (1981) 'The Classical Gold Standard: Some Lessons for Today'. *Federal Reserve Bank of St. Louis Review*, 63 (May), pp. 2–17.

BORDO, MICHAEL D., and SCHWARTZ, ANNA J. (1989) 'The Performance and Stability of Banking Systems Under "Self-Regulation": Theory and Evidence.' Paper presented at the Joint Universities conference on Regulating Commercial Banks: Australian Experiences in Perspective, Canberra, Australia (August 1–2).

BUCHANAN, JAMES M. (1989) 'Reductionist Reflections on the Monetary Constitution', *Cato Journal*, 9 (Fall), pp. 295–9.

DEWEY, DAVIS R. (1910) *State Banking Before the Civil War*, National Monetary Commission, 61st Cong., 2nd Sess., Senate Doc. No. 581 (Washington, DC: Government Printing Office).

DORN, JAMES A. (1986) 'Reforming the Monetary Regime', Introduction, *Cato Journal*, 5 (Winter), pp. 675–8.

FRIEDMAN, MILTON (1989) 'The Crime of 1873.' Working Paper No. E–89–12 (Stanford, Calif.: Hoover Institution, April).

FRIEDMAN, MILTON, and SCHWARTZ, ANNA J. (1987) 'Has Government Any Role in Money?', in A. J. Schwartz, *Money in Historical Perspective* (Chicago: University of Chicago Press) pp. 289–314.

GALLAROTTI, GUILIO M. (1989) 'Centralised versus Decentralized International Monetary Systems: The Lessons of the Classical Gold Standard.' Paper presented at the Cato Institute's Seventh Annual Monetary Conference, Alternatives to Government Fiat Money, Washington, DC (February 23–4).

HAINES, WALTER W. (1966) *Money, Prices, and Policy*, 2nd ed. (New York: McGraw-Hill).

HAMMOND, BRAY (1957) *Banks and Politics in America: From the Revolution to the Civil War* (Princeton NJ: Princeton University Press).

HAYEK, F. A. (1976) *Choice in Currency*. Occasional Paper 48 (London: Institute of Economic Affairs).

HAYEK, F. A. (1978) *Denationalisation of Money*, 2nd ed. Hobart Paper 70 (London: Institute of Economic Affairs).

HEDGES, JOSEPH E. (1938) *Commercial Banking and the Stock Market Before 1863*. The Johns Hopkins University Studies in Historical and Political Science, Series LVI, No. 1 (Baltimore, Md: The Johns Hopkins Press).

HUMPHREY, THOMAS M. (1989) 'Unsettled Issues in the Case for Free Banking', *Cato Journal*, 9 (Fall), pp. 461–5.

HUMPHREY, THOMAS M., and KELEHER, ROBERT E. (1984) 'The Lender of Last Resort: A Historical Perspective', *Cato Journal*, 4 (Spring/Summer), pp. 275–318.

McCULLOCH, HUGH (1889) *Men and Measures of Half a Century* (London).

PALASEK, KAREN Y. (1988) 'Institutional Constraints and Instability in New York and New England: Free Banking and Monetary Crises 1811–1863.' PhD dissertation, George Mason University.

PARKIN, MICHAEL, and BADE, ROBIN (1978) 'Central Bank Laws and Monetary Policy: A Preliminary Investigation', in *The Australian Monetary System in the 1970s*, pp. 24–39, edited by M. A. Porter (Melbourne: Monash University).

POOLE, WILLIAM (1989) 'Comment' [on 'Stability Under the Gold

Standard in Practice'], in *Money, History, and International Finance: Essays in Honor of Anna J. Schwartz* (Chicago: University of Chicago Press), pp. 195–200.

ROCKOFF, HUGH (1975) *The Free Banking Era: A Re-Examination* (New York: Arno Press).

ROCKOFF, HUGH (1986) 'Institutional Requirements for Stable Free Banking', *Cato Journal*, 6 (Fall), pp. 617–34.

SELGIN, GEORGE (1988) *The Theory of Free Banking: Money Supply Under Competitive Note Issue* (Totowa, NJ: Rowman & Littlefield).

TIMBERLAKE, RICHARD H., JR (1965) *Money, Banking, and Central Banking* (New York: Harper & Row).

TIMBERLAKE, RICHARD H., JR (1986) 'The Feasibility of Free Banking Institutions', *Cato Journal*, 6 (Fall), pp. 635–9.

WARBURTON, CLARK (1966) *Depression, Inflation, and Monetary Policy: Selected Papers, 1945–1953* (Baltimore, Md: The Johns Hopkins University Press).

WHITE, LAWRENCE H. (1983) 'Competitive Money, Inside and Out', *Cato Journal*, 3 (Spring), pp. 281–99.

Comment on Chapter 3

Anna J. Schwartz

Hugh has written a thoughtful account in which he looks back at banking and monetary developments in the United States in the 25 years before the American Civil War, when the federal government exercised no significant regulatory powers over banks. He inquires whether the relatively less or, more accurately, differently regulated banking system of that period is relevant to current interest in four proposals for reform of different aspects of existing monetary arrangements: (1) a return to a gold standard or some other commodity-based standard; (2) assigning the lender of last resort to a decentralized market mechanism; (3) authorizing private sector banks to issue currency; (4) opening up banking to free entry. His approach enables him to combine historical information with forward-looking analysis.

Hugh begins by summarizing the essence of the pre-Civil War free banking system that was adopted by nineteen states, twelve in the period 1848 to 1856: entry into banking was open to all, once minimum capital requirements were met, and bonds, usually issued by the state where the bank was located, had been bought and deposited with a state authority as backing for note issues. Individually chartered banks continued to operate in some states where they had begun operations before the enactment of the free-banking law, and in others with no free-banking law. Unit banking was the rule, with the exception of a few states that authorized branch banking. State usury laws were common. The monetary standard was bimetallic.

With this background, Hugh offers two preliminary observations. First, the free banking experience did not provide a test of Hayek's suggestion that, were government excluded from provision of money, private issuers would compete in providing not only the medium of exchange but also competitive forms of monetary base into which their issues would be convertible. Under free banking the monetary base was specie, uniform for all bank note issues. His second preliminary observation is that a commodity-based monetary system is not immune to disturbances. The disturbance during the free banking era was the discovery of gold in California and Australia.

125

Both observations, I believe, are valid. He then proceeds to analyse the impact of the gold discoveries.

VELOCITY THEN AND NOW

A table covering the period 1847–59, showing measures of wholesale and consumer prices and the GNP deflator, suggests that the new gold had a substantial impact on money and the base but only a mild impact on prices. The figures imply a sharp increase in real money balances, and a decline in velocity from 1848 to 1856 at the rate of 2.79 per cent per year.

Hugh tries to account for the behaviour of prices by the possible dispersion of the new gold through US balance of payments deficits and rejects the explanation. He tries to account for the behaviour of velocity by proposing determinants in addition to the usual real income and interest rate variables. Among other possible determinants, he considers improved banking services in the free-banking era, a boom in asset prices, the spread of the money economy, and the gold rush itself. In a money demand function for two periods (1821–58 and 1834–58), most of the variables are statistically significant, although their explanatory power is somewhat stronger for the longer period.

Hugh's conclusion is that the introduction of free banking contributed little to the rise in real balances in the gold rush expansion. He proposes the reverse linkage: rising demand for real cash balances prompted legislatures either to pass free-banking laws or to charter new banks more rapidly. That solution, of course, leaves unexplained the initial puzzle of sharp increase in real money balances.

I endorse his call for further research. Nevertheless, Hugh's comparison of 1848–56 with 1981–8, showing similarity in annual rates of growth of money, the GNP deflator, and real income, but the faster decline in velocity in the earlier period, is a *tour de force*. Whether banking deregulation, disinflation, greater interest elasticity, or still other unidentified forces led to recent increases in money demand, one of the uses of the past is surely that it shows nothing is new under the sun.

MONOMETALLISM V BIMETALLISM

In a following section, Hugh treats a counterfactual. Suppose there had been no gold discoveries and the US had been on a monometallic gold standard. Assuming that real income had risen and velocity fallen as they did, according to his figures a fall in prices would have ensued. A bimetallic standard would have been preferable in facilitating an increase in base money, and mitigating deflationary pressures. If a commodity standard is to be adopted, bimetallism wins in a contest with the gold standard. Looking back at the free-banking period, Hugh finds that the bimetallic standard set an upper limit to the monetary base that the existing fiat money system does not. That is an additional reason for choosing that standard. I agree completely.

CAN DIVERSIFIED PORTFOLIOS OBVIATE A BANKING PANIC?

Hugh centres his discussion of the role of a lender of last resort on the panic and suspension of specie payments in 1857. Although banks in states that permitted branching maintained convertibility during the panic, he does not accept the proposition that widespread branching would reduce the probability of panic to zero, and therefore concludes that a central bank as lender of last resort is probably required. All the same, he sees reason to encourage branch banking for the gains to safety that it provides. Again, I agree completely.

WHY AUTHORIZE PRIVATE SECTOR CURRENCY ISSUES?

Free banks were authorized to issue notes. Hugh asks, if that privilege was desirable in the past, does it merit support nowadays? He argues that one advantage of private sector currency issues is that seignorage accrues to private bankers, who may spend it more judiciously than government does. Under the free-banking system, however, the banks shared seigniorage with government in the form of higher bond prices. A second advantage of bank-issued currency, according to Hugh, is that changes in the public's desired proportion of notes to total money balances will have no effect on the money stock, provided the reserve ratios against notes and deposits are equal. Nevertheless, under those conditions runs on banks are still possible, should the public choose to hold specie rather than bank notes. In the existing monetary system, a shift by the public to currency, unless offset, depresses the sum of currency and deposits.

Eliminating this effect by authorizing private sector currency issues would yield little gain, Hugh indicates, because the proportion of notes to the money stock is now so small – under 7 per cent. He concludes that the main reason to support bank-issued currency is that banks are likely to be innovative issuers. I concur.

One other feature of the free-banking currency system, Hugh emphasizes, is that the bond security for note issues protected unsophisticated holders of the notes. That feature under current conditions, Hugh suggests, would provide protection to small depositors but not to others, for whom deposits would be unregulated. Since sophisticated depositors would bear risk and earn the returns on their funds, they would have an incentive to monitor the institutions they banked with.

THE EXTENT OF WILDCAT BANKING

In discussing note issue by wildcat banks, a frontier phenomenon that he regards as rare, Hugh compares two cases: (1) the nominal value of notes that could be issued exceeds the value of the bonds deposited, or (2) the value of the bonds deposited exceeds the value of the notes issued by a small margin. Although not stated explicitly, the point of the discussion appears to be the conditions under which wildcat note issues were profitable. Hugh describes the first case as unusual, in that banking regulations normally required the value of bonds to be deposited to exceed the value of notes issued and, in the unusual case, unfamiliar private notes could be circulated only at substantial discounts. This case was not therefore a road to riches for wildcatters. The second case could be profitable, according to Hugh, only if the notes could be used 'to leverage the purchase of a large mass of bonds, and to profit from the interest'. By this statement, I think he means, in line with Phillip Cagan's discussion of the profitability of national bank note issues, that the capital tied up in acquiring the bonds was the difference between the market price of the bonds and the amount of notes issued on that basis. The implication is that, in the absence of leverage, note issue was not necessarily profitable. Since the publication of Cagan's monograph, considerable controversy has developed concerning his leverage proposition.

It is not clear why Hugh refers only to two cases. Do they encompass the range of conditions of bond-secured circulation in all states? Until 1900, the condition of issue of national bank notes exemplified case (2). Thereafter, national banks received notes equal in amount to the par value of bonds deposited. The crucial variable affecting profitability was the difference between par and market value.

Hugh takes issue with recent studies emanating from the Minneapolis Fed absolving wildcat free banks of responsibility for bank failures on the ground that falling asset prices, independent of the banks' own behaviour, accounted for the failures. The Minneapolis writers fail to demonstrate that falling asset prices were an *ex ante* phenomenon, not *ex post* the occurrence of bank failures. Hugh also exposes the sleight of hand in the studies that rename wildcat banks mutual funds issuing small denomination securities, although the notes they issued contained no such descriptive phrase.

IN CONCLUSION

This chapter is rich in ideas about the past and the present. It provides valuable insights into the free-banking system. In Hugh's words, it was a 'system designed to minimize the role of government, maximize equality of economic opportunity, and protect the legitimate interests of unsophisticated users of the banking system'. He has extracted lessons from that system that teach the reader ways in which existing arrangements might be improved. In addition, the chapter offers suggestions for the future path of the monetary system. I found it well worth reading.

4 Experiments with Free Banking during the French Revolution

Eugene N. White

The French Revolution began a period of radical political, social and economic experimentation. Twice during the Revolution, when advocates of laissez-faire economic policies were in power, free banking flourished. While free banking in Scotland and the United States has been intensively studied, these experiements are not ideal for judging its merits. The French experience thus provides additional useful evidence on the viability of banking where there is free entry and the issuance of liabilities is unregulated.

The revolutionaries relinquished control of banking during two brief periods, 1790–2 and 1797–1803. In the first episode, notes were redeemable into government-supplied fiat money, while in the second, coin was exchanged for bank-notes upon demand. These experiments with free banking have been, for the most part, ignored or quickly dismissed by historians; however, these systems functioned reasonably well during their short existence. In spite of its apparent success, free banking did not survive long in France. The experiments were terminated because of the government's need to use paper money or a central bank to generate revenue in times of war.

This paper examines the unfamiliar history of French banking from the end of the *ancien régime* to the establishment of the Bank of France. This places the two free-banking episodes in their proper historical context, revealing the forces behind their inceptions and their demise. Following this exposition, France's experience is compared to the Scottish and American cases. This three-way comparison suggests that free banking did not completely escape from the problems surrounding deposit insurance today. In spite of its relatively unfettered character, banking was eventually limited in all countries either by prohibiting the issue of low denomination notes or by an insurance system for bank notes.

131

BANKING IN MID-EIGHTEENTH-CENTURY FRANCE

In mid-eighteenth-century France, there were no banks of issue. The public's memory of John Law and the Mississippi Bubble precluded the chartering of any institution with the tainted name of a bank. Banking thus meant private banking, which was divorced from government finance. This separation was primarily achieved by the division of the financial community into two distinct groups – the financiers, who were Catholic Frenchmen, and the bankers, who were pre-eminently Swiss Protestants.[1]

The financiers managed short-term government finance from the many venal offices of treasurer, accountant, and tax farmer they had purchased. Employing a variety of financial instruments secured by anticipated tax receipts, the financiers met the Crown's short-term borrowing needs. Excluded by their communion from government office, the bankers originally served as the intermediaries of the payments system. They transferred funds across regions, between currencies, and over time by means of bills of exchange. They were also active in foreign trade, speculation in precious metals, and insurance. However, this division of labour could not endure. The Crown's continual financial difficulties produced a growing volume and variety of securities that the bankers began to buy and trade. Eventually the monarchy was forced to acknowledge the bankers as legitimate creditors and permit them a role in the management of government finance.[2]

Government and private borrowing left France awash with all manner of financial instruments but no bank notes. The privilege of note issue could only be granted by the Crown, and it was not until 1776 that the monarchy was persuaded to give a charter to a bank of discount and issue. However, the legacy of John Law's debacle required that the name *banque* not be used and the new institution was called the Caisse d'Escompte.[3]

THE EARLY YEARS OF THE CAISSE D'ESCOMPTE

The Caisse d'Escompte was founded at a time of major fiscal reform for the French monarchy. After the Crown was forced into a partial bankruptcy in 1770, a wholesale reorganization of royal finances was begun. The controller-general and physiocrat Anne-Robert-Jacques Turgot produced a general plan to reorganize the tax system and deregulate trade. While this initiative failed, he agreed to charter the Caisse d'Escompte. Banking was not high on the physiocrats' agenda, but Turgot appears to have been persuaded to support the creation of the Caisse d'Escompte by Issac Panchaud, an influential banker. Like other anglophiles, Panchaud argued that England's economic prowess was derived from its superior institutions, including the Bank of England. Panchaud attributed the low rate of interest that prevailed in England and the Netherlands to their discount banks.[4] Borrowing at high interest rates, the Crown was particularly attracted by the idea of establishing an institution to lower them.

The decree authorizing the establishment of the Caisse d'Escompte was signed on 24 March 1776. The Caisse was organized as a limited liability public company with the right to discount bills of exchange and other commercial paper at a maximum annual interest rate of 4 per cent.[5] The bank could also trade in gold and silver, but it was excluded from all commerce in goods, foreign trade, and insurance. The Caisse accepted deposits and, more importantly, it gained the privilege of note issue. In accordance with Turgot's free-trade principles, it was not given a monopoly; but, in the absence of any other chartered banks, it gained a *de facto* monopoly. The bank was managed by seven administrators elected by the general assembly of stockholders, who met twice a year to examine the accounts and declare the dividend. The capital of the bank was set at 12 million livres.

The creation of the Caisse d'Escompte was a coup for the Swiss bankers, who bought most of the stock. Of the first seven administrators elected, five were Swiss bankers (including Panchaud) and only two were French Catholic financiers. The Caisse discounted bills of exchange and issued notes in denominations of 200, 300, 600 and 1000 livres, redeemable upon demand in coin.[6] These were very large denominations and were thus intended only for business transactions. While Panchaud had hoped for economy-wide benefits from easier credit supplied by this fractional reserve bank, it remained first and foremost a servant of the bankers. As shareholders, they received preferential access to discounts, giving their bills of exchange increased liquidity. Unlike other early central banks, the Caisse d'Escompte provided assistance to bankers, not credit for the state.[7]

At the same time as the Caisse d'Escompte was set up, the government's precarious financial position was threatened anew by France's participation in the American War for Independence. To tackle the difficult task of wartime finance, the king took the radical step of appointing as finance minister Jacques Necker, a leading Protestant banker. Necker did not need to use the Caisse d'Escompte's bank notes to finance the war because he was able to fund it almost entirely by borrowing.[8] Nevertheless, Necker did find the bank useful because it provided credit to the bankers who handled the distribution of new government securities.

To enable the Caisse to expand its operations successfully, Necker restructured the bank in 1779. The types of financial instrument the bank was permitted to discount were expanded to include fixed term loans, public securities, equities, and lottery notes. The discount rate ceiling was raised to 4½ per cent in wartime.[9] Most importantly, Necker was concerned that the Caisse's ability to increase its discounts would be limited by its ability to keep its bank notes in circulation. To expand their use and slow their return to the bank, Necker ordered the treasury and the tax farms to accept payments made in bank notes.[10]

The sale of government debt during the American war was enormously successful, and the Caisse d'Escompte profited by providing short-term credits to the bankers. The bank's dividend rose from under 3 per cent in 1777 to 8 per cent in 1782.[11] Bank note issue increased, but the Caisse continued to redeem its notes in coin. There was no impetus for inflation from money creation, and prices remained relatively stable.[12]

These developments did not, however, please everyone. Panchaud felt that the bank had strayed from its original purpose and complained that the Caisse no longer discounted commercial bills of exchange but only bankers' paper. It had become in his words, a 'banque des banquiers'.[13] Panchaud wanted the bank to act like a commercial bank that would provide credit to merchants not just bankers. He asserted that by accepting commercial paper, the Caisse could lower transactions costs and reduce interest rates.[14] Although his adversary, Necker, was forced to resign in 1781, Panchaud was unable to persuade the new minister to reorganize the bank. The nation was still at war and Necker's system of finance was too useful to be undone.

FROM BANKERS' BANK TO STATE BANK

The Caisse d'Escompte remained a bankers' bank, favoured by the state. Its continued independence was, however, threatened by the government's growing post-war deficits. In August 1783, the Minister of Finance found it increasingly difficult to borrow. Secretly, he approached the Caisse d'Escompte for a loan of 24 million livres. This temporary loan might have gone unnoticed had the bank not been speculating in silver. The rapidly expanded note issue, created by the loan and the speculation, quickly returned to the bank. Endeavouring to slow the redemption of bank notes, the bank slowed payment in coin and quietly obtained a decree from the Crown that would allow it to cease payments. [15]

Fearful of a full-scale run, the administrators ordered their accounts verified and made public. The independent report revealed not only the secret loan but also that credits to the government exceeded the bank's capital and that reserves were less than 10 per cent. The public now saw that the bank's solvency was linked to that of the state. [16] If the Crown had defaulted, as it had in 1770, the bank would have failed. Embarrassed by this disclosure, the government repaid the bank.

Although there were problems with the existing bimetallic standard, it effectively prevented the government from using the bank as a significant source of credit. The Caisse d'Escompte might be a closely held bankers' bank with a monopoly of note issue, but its need to redeem its bank notes on demand for coin disciplined the bank from over-issuing notes. The distrustful Parisian public needed only to hear a rumour that the Crown was trying to quickly borrow from the bank and a run would halt the loan. Unlike the British government, the French Crown could not borrow from its bankers' bank. Out of power, Necker warned against trying to make the Caisse into a Bank of France that could lend short-term to the government. [17] The Bank of England could only do this because of the public's high degree of confidence in government securities, a confidence which was lacking in France.

The Caisse d'Escompte soon recovered from this affair, but the monarchy's financial position continued to deteriorate. A crisis erupted in August 1788, when the Crown was unable to meet obligations that were due. Loménie de Brienne, the succeeding finance minister, responded by suspending some payments and ordering others to be made in a mixture of coin and interest-bearing promissory notes. Having discounted government tax anticipations, the Caisse was perceived to be in a precarious position, even though the government promised to repay the bank in coin. [18]

This crisis returned Necker to power, but he was unable to solve the Crown's financial dilemma. Even though he had condemned it, Necker sought assistance from the Caisse d'Escompte in September 1788. Necker returned again and again for loans, giving the bank the authority to suspend payments. By the end of 1789 the Caisse's note issue had reached 129 million livres. Although it was required by statute to hold 25 per cent of its issue in reserves, it had only 5 million livres left.[19] The Caisse's bank notes had become fiat money.

THE REVOLUTION, PAPER MONEY AND THE FIRST EXPERIMENT WITH FREE BANKING

While ruinous to the Caisse d'Escompte, the credit supplied to the Crown was insufficient to cover the deficit. Once the National Assembly had seized control of the nation's finances, it was faced with finding a solution. Seeking alternative sources of revenue, the Assembly decided in early November 1789 to expropriate the enormous properties of the Church.[20] Necker attempted to take the initiative back from the National Assembly and proposed the conversion of the Caisse d'Escompte into a Banque Nationale. This new institution would make advances at 3 per cent to the government. The state would then repay the bank with funds from the sales of the nationalized lands.[21]

The idea of establishing a national bank was derisively greeted as an attempt to re-establish John Law's bank. However, the assignats that the National Assembly decreed bear a strong resemblance to the notes that Necker's Banque Nationale would have created. These notes came in denominations of 200, 400, and 1000 livres, bore 3 per cent interest, and were legal tender. They were intended only as a temporary issue to be retired by the sales of nationalized lands and receipts of extraordinary taxes. This would have been a sound scheme if the Assembly had found some way to eliminate the deficit. Instead the quantity of assignats grew with the deficit and eventually exceeded the value of the land available for redemption.

The difficulty of eliminating the deficit was not apparent to all, and the government sincerely hoped to retire the notes of the Caisse d'Escompte. Yet, the precipitous drop in tax receipts and the delay in the printing of the assignats forced the government to continue borrowing from the Caisse d'Escompte. By 31 December 1790, loans from the bank had reached 400 million livres.[22] Once the printing presses of the revolution were set in motion, these notes began to be replaced by assignats.

While the revolutionaries co-opted the Caisse d'Escompte and transformed its note issue into the legal-tender assignats, they unwittingly permitted the emergence of a system of banking with free note issue. The uncertainties of the Revolution and the inflation began by the assignats caused a gradual disappearance of coin and pushed France off its bimetallic standard. As the assignats were printed only in lage denominations, a shortage of small denomination media of exchange appeared. While the central government was preoccupied with other matters, several towns organized *caisses patriotiques* or patriotic banks, where assignats could be exchanged for smaller denomination notes, known as *billets de confiance* or bills of confidence.

The number of *caisses patriotiques* grew very rapidly. There was relatively little government interference because the Revolution had embraced laissez-faire and eliminated the old régime's business regulations. In 1790 and 1791 the National Assembly reaffirmed its laissez-faire principles and refused to interfere in banking. It decreed that there was no government guarantee for the solvency of the *caisses* and that the *billets* were not legal tender.[23] The number of *caisses* grew very rapidly, exceeding 1600 by the end of 1792, as entrepreneurs, in addition to local authorities, began to open them.[24]

The first *caisses* were 100 per cent reserve banks, charging a small transactions fee. Private entrepreneurs, however, soon recognized the profitable opportunities available in operating fractional reserve banks. By 1792 all the leading *caisses* in the large cities were fractional reserve banks. Although towns, merchants, manufacturers, and even theatres, grocers and printers established their own *caisses*, some larger banks were organized by the private bankers. The two largest *caisses patriotiques* in France were the Caisse Patriotique de Paris and the Maison de Secours, both located in Paris. The Caisse Patriotique de Paris was founded by Etienne Delessert, a leading banker and administrator of the Caisse d'Escompte, and several Genevans.[25] On the other hand, the Maison de Secours was organized by Parisian lawyers and officials.[26]

The fractional reserve banks operated freely, and some even minted their own non-full-bodied coin. Throughout 1791, the *caisses patriotiques* were considered quite successful. While the *billets de confiance* were not legal tender, they were widely accepted, often beyond the towns and *départements* of origin. If the government had solved its deficit problem, it would have been able to limit the emission of assignats, thus giving the *caisses* a controlled backing for their notes. A stable régime might have emerged, with the government supplying the outside money and the free banks the inside money.[27] This did not happen, and although the *caisses* had solved the shortage of low denomination media of exchange and gained the public's confidence, they came under attack in 1792.

There were complaints in the popular press about the counterfeiting, fraud and inflation caused by the *caisses patriotiques*. Although it is impossible to measure the extent of counterfeiting, the problem was apparently more severe for the *caisses patriotiques* than it had been for the Caisse d'Escompte. The notes issued by the Caisse and even the first years' issue of assignats were in very large denominations. All these notes were used primarily for government, mercantile and financial transactions. In contrast, the *billets de confiance* were in very small denominations and were employed by the general public in their daily purchases. The critics of the *caisses* charged that printing low denomination bank notes allowed counterfeiting and excessive note issue because the largely illiterate public did not act as discriminating noteholders.

The *caisses patriotiques* were also accused of speculating and hoarding commodities by an excessive note issue that drove up prices. Yet, there is no evidence to suggest that the leading *caisses* were engaged in any other business than discounting commercial bills. At their peak, the *caisses* probably issued no more than 140 million livres of bank notes, only a fraction of the 1,369 million livres of assignats in circulation at the end of 1791. The *caisses* acted as fractional reserve banks that retained steady reserve ratios, and it was the growing quantity of assignats that increased the *billets de confiance* and inflation.[28]

While the problems of counterfeiting and over-issue of the *billets de confiance* received considerable attention, they do not appear to have been widespread enough to have threatened the banks. Futhermore, some *caisses patriotiques* campaigned to inform the public about how to identify counterfeits and published their balance sheets to demonstrate their solvency. The general soundness of the *caisses patriotiques* is revealed by the fact that when they were closed, very few needed government assistance to reimburse their noteholders. However, the brevity of the experiment in free banking makes it difficult to judge whether the *caisses* would have encountered graver problems. The answer depends on the vigilance of the public and whether banks were eager to protect their reputation.[29] If the public holding *billets* reacted as promptly as the noteholders of the Caisse d'Escompte, one of the requirements for ensuring the continuous redemption of bank notes would have been fulfilled. If on the other hand, the public failed to monitor their bank notes adequately and quickly return them for redemption, counterfeiting, fraud and inflation might ensue.

Public confidence in the *caisses patriotiques* was not destroyed by any actions of the banks but by increasingly erratic government policy. Runs on the *caisses* were precipitated by the refusal of some tax collectors to accept *billets de confiance* and a proposal in the Assembly to require bank reserves be deposited with local authorities. As attacks in the press stepped up and noteholders lost confidence, the National Assembly voted on 8 November 1792 to liquidate the *caisses* by the end of the year. The closure of all banks of issue had two benefits for the revolutionaries. First, blaming them for inflation deflected the public's attention from the primary cause of inflation, the rise in the quantity of assignats in circulation. Secondly, by forcing the prompt retirement of the *billets de confiance*, the revolutionaries increased demand for assignats, thereby raising the potential seigniorage from their issue.

The assignat-generated inflation led to hoarding and capital flight. The government responded with price controls, rationing, and an assault on all forms of private finance. By mid-1793, all stock associations were dissolved, trade in specie was prohibited, and the banks and the bourse were closed.

THE SECOND EXPERIMENT WITH FREE BANKING

After the Terror, the Directory began to move back to the original free enterprise tenets of the Revolution. Included in the Directory's reforms was a repeal of the anti-banking laws in 1796. The disastrous co-option of the Caisse d'Escompte, leading to the assignat inflation, favoured the re-establishment of independent banks of issue. Numerous pamphlets supported this position. Saint-Aubin, for example, argued that recent history had shown that it was impossible for there to be any connection between the government and the banks. The government would always be tempted to obtain loans that would force more notes than could be sustained into circulation. Banks must thus be completely independent of the government.[30]

The first of the new banks of issue was the Caisse de Comptes Courants, established in Paris on 26 June 1796. This was in essence a revived Caisse d'Escompte, organized by bankers, some of whom had been administrators in the Caisse. With a capital of 5 million francs, it received the deposits of private bankers, discounted commercial paper up to 90 days, and issued 500 and 1000 franc notes redeemable in coin.[31] A competitor, the Caisse d'Escompte du Commerce, opened in 1797 with a capital of 6 million francs.[32] The following year another large bank, the Comptoir Commercial, was opened in Paris. This discounted commercial paper and issued bank notes in denominations of 250, 500, and 1000 francs.

These new banks served, first, the private bankers and, secondly, the commercial community but not the general public. Like the Caisse d'Escompte, these banks were established by bankers who faced substantial risks dealing in bills of exchange. By subscribing to the shares of a bank, a private banker obtained access to a rediscount agency. The notes received from a bank were widely accepted because of the short duration and generally high quality of the assets. The central importance of mutual assistance is evident in the banks' discount policies, which rationed credit according to the number of shares held.[33]

Ouside Paris, one bankers' bank was established in Rouen, the Société Générale du Commerce. This institution discounted bills of up to 25 days and issued notes of 100, 250, 500, and 1000 francs. Compared to the Paris banks, it was relatively small, with a circulation that never exceeded 200,000 livres. By contrast, the Caisse de Comptes Courants and the Caisse d'Escompte du Commerce each reached a circulation of 20 million francs.[34]

The structure of this second free-banking system was very similar to that of the *caisses patriotiques*. In both there were two or three dominant banks in Paris whose bank notes accounted for a substantial percentage of all notes issued. The remaining banks, both in Paris and in the provinces, were relatively small. These minor banks may have been numerous, although their number has yet to be determined. Many of them issued small denomination notes redeemable in copper coin, in contrast to large banks, whose high denomination notes were redeemed in silver or gold coin. In Paris, the Factorie du Commerce issued notes of 10, 15 and 20 francs.[35] One bank in Tours issued notes ranging from 10 to 100 francs and established offices in five nearby towns for redemption.[36] Other towns with small banks included Rouen, with three, and Saint Quentin, Troyes, and Nantes, with one each. These were not bankers' banks and they gave credit to merchants. Their notes were used by the general population for daily transactions and were even accepted by government tax collectors. In the absence of these intermediaries, the failure of the large banks to issue small denomination notes would have imposed a high resource cost on the general public by forcing it to rely exclusively on the use of coin.

There was intense competition among all banks. In Rouen, each of the three small banks attempted unsuccessfully to obtain exclusive privileges from the local government, while the Société Générale endeavoured to have them all suppressed.[37] The large banks found the government sympathetic to their interests. The Minister of the Treasury, Barbé-Marbois, viewed the small banks as a plague, and his successor, Mollien, was appalled that many low denomination bank notes circulated at small discounts.[38] Nevertheless, these small banks managed to survive because the government feared offending those who used their notes – the merchants and the workers.

This intense criticism of the smaller banks does not, however, appear to have been justified. There were apparently no widespread failures or extensive counterfeiting.[39] Unfortunately, as in the case of the *caisses patriotiques*, the brevity of the experiment does not permit any final judgement on the importance of these problems. Among the large banks, the strong mutual interests of bankers seem to have ensured noteholders of a high degree of safety. The most serious threat to any bank occurred in October 1798, when the director-general of the Caisse de Comptes Courants issued 2½ million francs for his own use and then fled. The evening this was discovered, the administrators of the Caisse asked the government for assistance. The Minister of Finance replied that, while the government was in no way responsible for the bank's dilemma, he would give a loan of 1.2 million francs because the Caisse provided an essential public service. At the same time, the shareholders declared that they would guarantee the bank's liabilities, and many deposited coin with the Caisse. This prevented a run on the bank and the excess banknotes were honoured and retired from circulation.[40]

THE BANQUE DE FRANCE AND THE ELIMINATION OF FREE BANKING

The coup d'etat of 18 Brumiare (10 November 1799) that made Napoleon the First Consul marked a renewed effort by the government to control the banking system. Napoleon apparently desired to have 'his own' bank, and approached the bankers Jean-Barthélemy Lecoulteux de Canteleu and Jean-Frédéric Perregaux about creating a new institution. These bankers, who were directors in the Caisse de Comptes Courants, drew up an ambitious plan to establish a bank of discount and issue with a capital of 30 million francs. To float this huge enterprise, the bankers convinced the stockholders of the Caisse des Comptes Courants to dissolve the bank on 18 January 1800 and buy shares in the new Banque de France.[41]

The new bank was to be administered by a council of fifteen regents, with its management entrusted to three regents and super-vision to three censors. Not surprisingly, the Banque de France was dominated by the bankers. Of the thirty-eight regents during the Consulate and Empire, twenty were bankers.[42] The general assembly of the 200 largest stockholders was to represent all shareholders, thus concentrating the power of the great bankers.[43]

There was no rush to invest in this new bank. By the end of 1800 only 7.6 million francs of its capital had been subscribed, and it was not until 1802 that all shares had been sold. With the recent memory of the Caisse d'Escompte and the assignats, the Banque de France's close and obvious links to the government inspired considerable hostility in the business community and the press.[44] The Banque de France did have certain advantages over its precursor. It was not subject to any fixed reserve requirements and it was free to vary its rate of discount. Furthermore, the bank enjoyed the favour of the new government. The Finance Minister deposited various funds with the bank and used the security deposits of tax collectors to buy stock, conferring on it considerable advantages over its Paris rivals.[45]

In spite of this obvious favouritism, Perregaux argued that the bank operated independently of the government and was not obliged to it. In 1803, the Banque de France even dared to refuse a 20 million franc loan to the government, and Perregaux declared that public confidence would be totally ruined if the loan were conceded.[46] To secure control of the Paris market, the bank attempted to destroy the competition. Twice the Banque de France collected several million francs of notes of the Caisse d'Escompte du Commerce for surprise presentation. When the Caisse resisted successfully by paying out coin for these notes, it was closed by armed force. The other large Paris banks were also coerced to dissolve and convert their shares into shares of the Banque de France, while the small banks were liquidated.[47]

In the process of eliminating these rival banks, the Banque de France was given in 1803 the exclusive privilege of issuing bank notes in Paris for 15 years. Its capital was raised to 45 million francs, and the lowest denomination note it could issue was set at 500 francs. Tight rules for paying dividends greater than 6 per cent were specified, imposing a limit on the shareholder's ability to benefit from the bank's monopoly note issue. Shareholders' were also denied any special rights to discount. Now any merchant, manufacturer or banker meeting the minimum requirements could discount his paper. In addition, seven of the bank's fifteen regents and the three censors were to be chosen from shareholding merchants or manufacturers. This change reflects the increased influence among Napoleon's advisors of Crétet, who wanted merchants to have equal access to credit.[48] At the same time as these changes occurred, the departmental banks came under government control, and they were prohibited from issuing any notes less than 250 francs.[49]

Although this legislation only gave the bank a monopoly of note issue in Paris, it became the pre-eminent bank of issue, the circulation of the remaining provincial banks being slight by comparison. The Banque de France also became the government's bank, rather than the bankers' bank. Advances to the Treasury rose from 22.6 million francs in 1800 to 274.3 million francs for 1804–5.[50] Even though the total commercial discounts rose from 111.8 to 630.9 million francs, perhaps 80 per cent of these were obligations of the tax farmers.[51] This growth reflected the government's increased wartime needs and the Treasury's difficulty in raising revenue.[52]

The Treasury's demands on the bank reduced its liquidity, and a run on the bank began in late September 1805. It was slowed when the bank began a partial suspension of payments on 24 September and restricted daily redemption to one bank note. This resulted in the bank notes being traded at a 10 to 15 per cent discount.[53] The Banque de France survived the crisis, and the government recognized that adherence to the bimetallic standard, re-established in 1803, limited its ability to borrow from the bank.

After the crisis of 1806, Pierre Samuel du Pont de Nemours took the opportunity to publish a pamphlet extolling free banking.[54] Surveying previous panics, du Pont argued that if a bank prudently selected its portfolio, its notes would always be freely redeemable. The problem was simply that banks were very useful to governments, and granting loans to governments endangered banks. At best, banks could help the state market its loans. Du Pont concluded that banks could only be completely safe if they were wholly independent of the government.

Napoleon disdainfully rejected this advice and acted on his belief that the bankers had been principally responsible for the crisis. From now on the state would take a greater role. In Napoleon's words, 'The bank does not solely belong to the stockholders, it also belongs to the state that gave it the privilege to print money'.[55] To reconstruct the Banque de France, Napoleon issued a decree on 22 April 1806 that placed at the head of the bank a governor and two deputies whom he nominated. For governor, he chose Crétet, who had spoken out against the dominance of the bankers. In addition the bank's capital was raised to 90 million francs and its privilege of note issue was extended to 25 years.[56]

Loans to the government once again drastically increased in the crisis years of 1812–14. In 1814, another panic broke out but was contained by a restriction of payments, while the bank was bolstered by a loan from private Paris bankers.[57] The Banque de France's position as the preponderant bank of issue was challenged after 1814 but never severely threatened. Under the Restoration, the bank gained a greater measure of independence but at the cost of additional competition. Three departmental banks were chartered in Rouen, Nantes and Bordeaux. Other banks were later established in Lyon, Marseille, La Havre, Lille, Toulouse and Orléans. Over time, their growth might have threatened the pre-eminence of the Banque de France, but, in 1848, the bank regained its monopoly position. Its competitors were forced to merge with the bank, which was given the exclusive privilege of note issue.[58]

LESSONS FROM FRENCH FREE BANKING

One notable feature of French free banking was the absence of any apparent interest in the insurance of bank notes or deposits. In this respect France seems to have been like Scotland. Given the enormous problems associated with bank liability insurance, this suggests that Scottish and French free banking may provide some guidance for redesigning current banking systems.

While these banking systems avoided insurance schemes, they were apparently not free of the problems that have led to the adoption of deposit insurance in the twentieth century. This has not been recognized because of one important eighteenth-century regulation that contravened the ideal of laissez-faire has been overlooked: the minimum legal denomination of note issue. The purpose of a legal minimum denomination was to exclude all but businessmen and the well-to-do from using bank notes.

In Scotland, the minimum denomination of notes was set at £1. This regulation was a consequence of the 'small note mania' of the early 1760s, when many little banks issued very low denomination notes.[59] These small intermediaries were attacked for their excessive and varied note issue. Included among the contemporary enemies of these banks was Adam Smith, who believed that bank notes should not be issued for less than £5. He wrote:

> Where the issue of banknotes for such small sums is allowed and commonly practised many mean people are both enabled and encouraged to become bankers. A person whose promissory note for five pounds or even for twenty shillings, would be rejected by every body will get it to be received without scruple when it is issued for so small a sum as a sixpence. But the frequent bank-ruptcies to which such beggarly bankers must be liable, may occasion a very considerable inconvenience and sometimes even a very great calamity to many poor people who had received their notes in payment.[60]

Smith's concern was that the common people would not monitor the bank notes they used. Small denomination bank notes would pass continuously from hand-to-hand and rarely be returned for redemption. This would allow unscrupulous bankers to expand their note issue without the discipline that the market imposed on banks that circulated only large denomination notes.

Smith's simple solution was to exclude the common people from banking services. In the more democratic nineteenth-century United States, the response was different. Banking statutes did not fix the minimum denomination, and any latent powers given to regulators were vague.[61] Bank notes were widely used in the United States, but the public feared the receipt of worthless paper. Before free banking was generally adopted, several states – New York, Vermont, Michigan, Ohio and Iowa – set up systems to insure bank notes and sometimes deposits.[62] These guarantee systems tended to suffer from the same problems as modern deposit insurance. Once a state enacted a free-banking statute, the insurance system was allowed to wither. Under free banking, however, bank notes could only be issued if a bank had purchased specific bonds and deposited them with the authorities so that, in the event of a failure, they could be sold and the noteholders reimbursed. This system of guarantee worked reasonably well, depending largely on whether the state carefully chose the bonds.[63] The bond-backed note issue of free banks was thus a substitute for the insured notes of the chartered banks. In the United States, where there was no effective limitation on the minimum denomination, some form of protection for the common man was a political necessity.

In France the minimum denomination of notes was an issue of continuing importance. The pre-Revolutionary Caisse d'Escompte issued only very large denomination notes, and initially the revolutionaries only created large denomination assignats. Even though the assignats were irredeemable fiat money, the revolutionaries were extremely concerned that the common people would not pay attention to the notes that they received, permitting counterfeiting. When the *caisses patriotiques* began issuing very low denomination *billets de confiance*, all the complaints about fraud and counterfeiting focused on the poor people's indifference about the notes they used. The demand for *billets de confiance* soon forced the government to issue its own low denomination assignats.

During the second experiment with free banking in France, the big banks, government officials and economists all feared the consequences of small banks issuing low denomination notes. The liberal economist Jean-Baptiste Say recognized the conflict with the laissez-faire ideal and wrote in defence of the suppression of these banks:

> Does the government have a right to forbid private firms from issuing small notes that the public is willing to receive? Should it violate the freedom of enterprise it has pledged to uphold? Without a doubt, it should because it is likewise authorized to condemn a private building that threatens the public's safety.[64]

This view helped to secure the Banque de France its monopoly and the few regional banks of their local monopolies with very high minimum denominations for their notes. Free banking with no denominational controls did not endure long enough during either experiment to see if a demand for bank note insurance would have developed.

Free banking with minimum denominations may thus not be truly free banking in the sense that the term is generally accepted among economists today. Regulation of this sort may be simply eliminating a large portion of the population from using the banking system in order to avoid any potential problems created by an inadequate monitoring of banks.

Although these concerns were present, the brief French experiments with free banking were not abandoned because of any systemic defects. Laissez-faire banking came to an end because the government needed to fund its deficits. The *caisses patriotiques* were blamed by the government for causing inflation, all the while it was increasing the supply of outside money. Napoleon ended the second period of free banking, granting the Banque de France special privileges and eliminating its rivals, thereby increasing its power to lend to the government. Free banking was simply not sustainable in the turbulent years of the Revolution and Empire, when governments needed to mobilize all sources of revenue.

Notes

1. See Herbert Lüthy (1961) *La Banque Protestante en France de la Révocation de l'Edit de Nantes à la Révolution* (Paris: SEVPEN).
2. Jean Bouvier (1970) 'Vers le Capitalisme Bancaire: Expansion du Crédit après Law', in Ernest Labrousse, *et al*, (eds) *Histoire économique et social de la France* (Paris: Presses Universitaires de France), Vol. II, pp. 267–321.
3. The Caisse d'Escompte is usually translated as the Discount Bank.
4. Robert Bigo (1927) *La Caisse d'Escompte (1776–1793) et les Origines de la Banque de France* (Paris: Presses Universitaires de France), pp. 40–3.
5. The *Arrêt du Conseil* can be found in Gustave Schelle (1923) *Ouevres de Turgot* (Paris: Librairie Félix Alcan), Vol. V, pp. 354–7.
6. Jean Lafaurie (1981) *Les Assignats* (Paris: Le Leopard d'Or), p. 79.
7. Charles Goodhart (1988) *The Evolution of Central Banking* (Cambridge, Mass.: MIT Press), p. 4.
8. See Eugene N. White (1989) 'Was There a Solution to the Financial Dilemma of the Ancien Régime?', *Journal of Economic History*, Vol. 49, No. 3 (September).
9. Jacques Necker (1820) *Ouevres complètes* (Paris), Vol. 3, pp. 49–51.
10. Bigo, *op. cit.*, p. 57.
11. Laffon de Ladebat (1793) *Compte Rendu des Opérations de la Caisse d'Escompte* (Paris), Table VII.
12. Ernest Labrousse (1976) 'Les "bons prix" agricoles du XVIIe siècle', in Ernest Labrousse, *Histoire Economique et Social de la France* (Paris: Presses Universitaires de France, Vol. II, pp. 386–7.

13.   Lüthy, *op. cit.*, pp. 461–2.
14.   Robert D. Harris (1979) *Necker, Reform Statesman of the Ancien Régime* (Berkeley: University of California), p. 203; and Bigo, *op. cit.*, pp. 66–7.
15.   Bigo, *op. cit.*, pp. 75–83.
16.   Bigo, *op. cit.*, pp. 81–3.
17.   Jacques Necker (1820) 'De l'Administration des Finances', *Ouevres Complètes*, Vol. 5, pp. 525–30.
18.   Bigo, *op. cit.*, pp. 113–34 and Laffon de Ladebat, *op. cit.*, pp. 24–6.
19.   Laffon de Ladebat, *op. cit.*, pp. 33–4 and Table 7.
20.   Jacques Godechot (1968) *Les Institutions de la France sous la Révolution et l'Empire* Paris: Presses Universitaires de France), pp. 175–8.
21.   Jacques Necker (1820) 'Projet d'une Banque Nationale', *Oeuvres Complètes* (Paris), Vol. 7, pp. 149–97.
22.   Lafaurie, *op. cit.*, pp. 83–4.
23.   Jean Bouchary (1941) *Les compagnies financières à Paris du XVIIIe siècle* (Paris), Vol. 2, pp. 11–14.
24.   Eugene N. White, 'Free Banking During the French Revolution', *Explorations in Economic History* (1990), Table 1.
25.   Bouchary, *op. cit.*, pp. 53 and 59; and Lüthy, *op. cit.*, p. 449.
26.   Bouchary, *op. cit.*, p. 73.
27.   It has been argued that currency backed by tax receipts or land sales will produce a régime of price stability. See, Bruce Smith (1985) 'Some Colonial Evidence on Two Theories of Money: Maryland and the Carolinas', *Journal of Political Economy*, XCIII; and Eugene N. White (1987) 'Fueron Inflacionarias Las Finanzas Estatales en el Siglo XVIII? Una Nueva Interpretacion de los Vales Reales', *Revista de Historia Economica*, Vol. 3, No. 3.
28.   It is impossible econometrically to detect an inflationary impulse from the *billets de confiance* in time series analysis or in a cross-section across *départements*. For a more complete analysis, see White, 'Free Banking'.
29.   This may also be stated as the banks having a low rate of time preference. Goodhart, *op. cit.*, pp. 57–60.
30.   Saint-Aubin (1795) *Des banques particulières* (Paris).
31.   Alphonse Charles Courtois fils (1881) *Histoire des Banques en France* (Paris: Librairie Guillaumin), pp. 109; and André Liesse (1909) *Evolution of Credit and Banks in France* (Washington DC: Government Printing Office), pp. 11–12. After the hyperinflation, the unit of account changed from livres to francs.
32.   Courtois, *op. cit.*, pp. 109–10 and Liesse, *op. cit.*, pp. 13–14.
33.   In its first incarnation, the Banque due France was much like its rivals. Discounts were limited to 90-day three-signature paper, with 5000 francs of credit available per share and a maximum of 15,000 francs for non-shareholders. Maurice Lévy-Leboyer (1976) 'Le crédit et la monnaie: l'évolution institutionelle', in Ernest Labrousse, *Histoire Economique et Sociale de la France* (Paris: Presses Universitaires de France), Vol. 3, pp. 352–3.
34.   Courtois, *op. cit.*, pp. 110–11 and Liesse, *op. cit.*, pp. 12–14.

35. Guy Thuillier (1983) *La monnaie en France au début du XIXe siècle* (Geneva: Librarie Droz), p. 214.
36. *Ibid.*, pp. 388–90.
37. *Ibid.*, pp. 392–4.
38. *Ibid.*, pp. 216–17. This is, of course, exactly how bank notes circulated in the American free-banking era. See, Hugh Rockoff (1974) 'The Free Banking Era: A Re-Examination', *Journal of Money Credit and Banking*, 6.
39. Thuillier, *op. cit.*, p. 218, footnote 20.
40. Jean Bouchary (1943) *Les Manieurs d'Argent à Paris à la fin du XVIIIe siècle* (Paris: Marcel Rivière), Vol. III, pp. 233–8.
41. Liesse, *op. cit.*, pp. 17–19, Courtois, *op. cit.*, p. 111.
42. In spite of the Revolution, the Protestant bankers still played a prominent role, and five of the bankers were Swiss-born. Romuald Szramkiewicz (1974) *Les Régents et Censeurs de la Banque de France nommés sous le Consulate et l'Empire* (Genève: Librairie Droz), pp. XLIII–XLVII.
43. Courtois, *op. cit.*, pp. 111–12 and Liesse, *op. cit.*, pp. 19–20.
44. Bigo, *op. cit.*, p. 234.
45. Napoleon and his circle bought sixty-seven of the original 1000 shares. Bouchary, *Les Manieurs*, *op. cit.*, III, p. 52.
46. *Ibid*, III, p. 52–54. However, Perregaux seems to have played an ambiguous role, as he sent regular secret reports to Napoleon.
47. Liesse, *op. cit.*, pp. 24–5.
48. Bigo, *op. cit.*, p. 245.
49. Courtois, *op. cit.*, pp. 115. The small banks were unwilling to be put out of business. In 1805, the Minister of the Treasury had to issue a special decree to enforce the closure of the small banks in Rouen. Thuillier, *op. cit.*, p. 219.
50. Courtois, *op. cit.*, pp. 342–3. These figures represented the value of all loans or discounts given, and are not the stock at one point in time.
51. Liesse, *op. cit.*, pp. 28–9.
52. The bank's problems also increased because of credits given to the government's leading contractor, Gabriel-Julien Ouvrard, for speculation in specie.
53. Bigo, *op. cit.*, pp. 266–70, Courtois, *op. cit.*, pp. 118–19 and Liesse, *op. cit.*, pp. 29–30.
54. Pierre Samuel du Pont de Nemours (1806) *Sur la Banque de France* (Paris).
55. Bigo, *op. cit.*, p. 276.
56. The bank was also given the power to organize branches. It established offices in Lyons, Rouen and Lille, but they remained small operations, and the first two were closed in 1817 and the last in 1813. Liesse, *op. cit.*, pp. 33–4.
57. Courtois, *op. cit.*, pp. 124–30 and Liesse, *op. cit.*, pp. 41–2.
58. The combined note issue of these banks rose from 33 to 90 million francs between 1837 and 1847, while the Banque de France's maximum note issue only grew from 217 to 288 million francs. Courtois, *op. cit.*, pp. 341–3.

59.   Sidney G. Checkland (1975) *Scottish Banking. A History 1695–1973* (Glasgow: Collins), pp. 104–6, 118–21.
60.   Adam Smith (1937 [1776]) *The Wealth of Nations* (New York: Modern Library), p. 307.
61.   See the New York model statute in Hugh Rockoff (1975) *The Free Banking Era: A Re-Examination* (New York: Arno Press), pp. 70–9.
62.   Charles W. Calomiris (1989) 'Deposit Insurance: Lessons from the Record', *Federal Reserve Bank of Chicago: Economic Perspectives* (May/June), pp. 10–19.
63.   Arthur J. Rolnick and Warren E. Weber (1984) 'The Causes of Free Bank Failures: A Detailed Examination', *Journal of Monetary Economics*, 14, pp. 267–91.
64.   Jean-Baptiste Say (1803) *Traité d'économie politique* (Paris), Vol. II, pp. 40–1.

Comment on Chapter 4

Forrest Capie

Eugene White makes the task of the discussant difficult. He writes clear, well-argued and supported accounts that leave little to be cleared up and with which I find it difficult to disagree. This chapter is no exception in its neat blend of unobtrusive analysis and careful history.

Eugene White has provided us with a fascinating account of the emergence and development of banking in France before and during the Revolution, and somewhat beyond. There are two periods in which free banking developed. These appeared to work quite well, contrary to the prevailing historical orthodoxy, with only limited fraud and counterfeiting – certainly nothing on a scale to threaten the system. Free banking did not fail in either of these episodes, but rather it was brought to an end by the overriding needs of the State. History has not been kind to the private banks in the Revolution and Empire periods, and White provides a revision to some of these views.

I do have some questions and suggestions for elucidation. They can perhaps be best arranged chronologically, relating first to the years before the Revolution, then to the period that is the central focus of the paper, and lastly to the period beyond 1806.

The first question concerns the nature of the French monetary and banking system and its relation to the economy in the eighteenth century. It is clear that John Law's escapades had soured the French to banking. But the French economy performed moderately well in the eighteenth century – economic historians warn us against drawing too great a distinction between French and English output growth. The vast literature on the Industrial Revolution in England, and the emphasis given to the fact that this experience was the first of its kind, have obscured the nature of economic development in both countries. This turns out to have more similarities than differences, with both countries making steady progress in the course of the eighteenth century. The data show that prices were rising on a gently upward trend from the 1730s to the 1780s. So reasonable output growth and slight excess money per unit of output is implied. The question is, then, were there firms performing the functions of banks even if they were not called banks, and if not, did it matter? The reason the question seems important is that the answer might help us place the free-banking episode in clearer perspective. This is so, since we would have a clearer understanding of what preceded it, and discover more about firms performing banking functions but not called banks.

In the core of the paper there seem to be two main issues worth exploring. The first of these concerns the degree of success that attaches to the free-banking experience. Larry White set out some criteria against which a free-banking experience could be assessed. He listed four areas: note over-issue, convertibility, provision of the unit of account, and stability. While much of Eugene White's paper is not explicitly an examination of the hypotheses on these issues, and some of his remarks are based on other work he has done, it may be worth setting the French experience against these tests. Firstly, it seems that French banks did not over-issue, and that competition among the banks of issue did not produce inflation. The related question on whether or not there are economies of scale in note circulation and on note issue being a 'natural monopoly' is not touched on, perhaps because that would take longer to develop. Secondly, French banks did issue convertible notes – convertible into assignats, and it seems, convertible on demand. Thirdly, the occasion for them to be concerned with the provision of the unit of account did not arise; and in any case this is something that would take time to evolve. On the question of banking stability there seem to be no grounds for complaint.

What I thought was striking was that both free-banking episodes took place largely in a period of inconvertibility, though we need some clarification on this, since exactly what the nature of convertibility was in these years is not clear. It seems that when Necker was making demands for funds from the Caisse d'Escompte in 1788, that this must have resulted in a *de facto* suspension of the metallic standard. However, my reading of the paper seems to suggest that it was the issue of assignats in the early 1790s that pushed France off the metallic standard. If it were the case that free banking in 1790–2 operated in a period of inconvertibility, this would surely strengthen the case for claiming it a success; for, as White argues, if only the state had been able to control its issue of assignats, there could have been an example of a stable and generally successful experience in spite of inconvertible paper money.

The second episode of free banking stretched from 1796 to 1806, and most of this period appears to have been one of inconvertible currency. So the experiment is surely being judged in the most severe conditions. Some free-banking episodes (such as in Scotland and North America) took place when a metallic standard was in place and the banks there clearly operated under that discipline. So the questions here are, is this French experience in fact a tougher test of free banking, and was the test successfully passed?

Another question that I would like to raise relates to the emergence of the central bank. Is it really the case, as the evidence presented here suggests, that a central bank was on the point of emerging, as a result of evolution, in Paris at this time? The French had had some nasty experiences with the state and finance in the eighteenth century, and while the Revolution was seen as a new age when old attitudes were being swept away, making way for enlightened and rational behaviour, the deep suspicion of the State still lingered. (On second thoughts perhaps that is the enlightened and rational stance.) The evidence that seems to come through strongly is that in spite of promises by the Crown, and in spite of constructed safeguards to prevent the state behaving improperly, the State persisted in trying to secure loans and ultimately demanded funds. In 1776 the Crown extracted a loan; in 1783 a secret loan was obtained; and in 1788 Necker obtained further funds to such an extent that it appears to have pushed the country off the metallic standard. In other words, is this experience not an example of the State insisting on a bank that it could be sure of raising funds from, rather than an evolution? In support of this point could it not be argued that the French, given their particular history in the eighteenth century, would never voluntarily have accepted a bank proposed by the State essentially for the State's purposes.

The question on the period beyond that covered in the paper is the following. The French had for long been suspicious of the State and its interference in finance; and, as White argues, it was only in time of war that the State found that free banking represented an intolerable constraint on its fund raising. Given too that free banking appears to have been a comparative success and was probably judged so by the public at the time, and Napoleon was keen on free markets and sound money, why then is it that it did not re-emerge in the nineteenth century?

Comment on Chapter 4
Didier Bruneel

As you can imagine, the very idea of free banking is a nightmare for a central banker, and here I am with a very challenging paper telling me, I quote, that 'the French experience provides useful additional evidence on the feasibility of a free-banking regime'. When I received this paper my first reaction was to search for historical errors or mistakes made by Professor White. But after a short while I realized that he knows this period of French history a lot better than I do. So I won't try to argue about the facts themselves but only about Mr White's interpretation of them.

I will go back to the two French experiences that he has described and I will try to show you two points:

1 That these experiences are not good examples of free banking.
2 That even if we accept them as free banking, they were not successful, not only because they took place in the turbulent years of the Revolution and Empire, when government needed to mobilize all sources of revenue, but also for the traditional reasons that free banking was not successful in other countries – bank failures, lack of confidence, counterfeited notes and so on.

According to Mr White himself, free banking is characterized by two elements: (1) free entry, and (2) unregulated issue of liabilities in the absence of a central bank. With regard to the first element, and the bills of confidence of 1790 to 1792, it is true that free entry was granted, mainly for philosophical reasons. Cambon, for example, asserted that: 'Any individual is entitled to enjoy freely the confidence of his fellow citizens; this confidence is his property: it is therefore impossible to ban the issue of bills of confidence'.

As a matter of fact, issuers could just as well be public authorities (departments, districts, local funds) as private entities (patriotic funds, *caisses de bonne foi*, funds based on confidence) private individuals (manufacturers, merchants, bankers, shopkeepers, café-owners); and 5,800 types of bills or notes of all forms and all colours were issued. Private issues had to be covered by metal or by assignats

155

(the legal tender note issued by the government) and the bills of confidence were not legal tender.

Two reasons explained their success at the beginning:

1 There were no coins, no gold, no silver any more at this time, and the assignats had only high denominations (50 to 2000 livres). So there was a need for something with a small denomination. The bills of confidence had such a small denomination (between 6 deniers and 25 livres for most of them), and they just played the role of the missing coins.
2 Since bills of confidence were not legal tender, one could refuse to receive them in payment. But those who dared refuse them swiftly became 'suspect' and during the Revolution becoming a suspect was a good way to lose one's head.

The failure of the system was caused by the misuses that were committed: for example, notes were issued uncovered, and notes stamped 25 livres were sold for 4 livres (at issue). In addition, there were many failures and scandals. One of the most famous was the failure of the 'Maison de Secours', which Mr White held up as an example in his paper. The panic was such that the *billets de confiance* (bills of confidence) were called *billets de défiance* (distrust bills).

Counterfeiting was surely a big problem. We do not have specific statistics about counterfeited bills of confidence but during this period counterfeited notes were made almost everywhere, and in Paris 160 counterfeiters of assignats were sentenced to death in 1792. To quote an official, the only protection against counterfeiters was the dislike of the citizens for the paper, either good or false.

With regard to the second experience beginning in 1796 everything was different. Free entry did exist but the number of banks was very small. The notes in circulation amounted only to 70 million in 1802. At that time, the money supply (in gold or silver) was about 2 to 3 billion. These notes were usually of high denominations (essentially 500 to 1000 F) and therefore were not spread among the general public. They were not legal tender but could be exchanged for gold on demand.

These elements are in accordance with the theory of free banking, but I want to stress two points:

1 In 1798 the Caisse des Comptes Courants, one out of the two biggest banks, had to ask for the help of the Treasury when the

general director fled after having issued notes for his own use for an amount of more than 2 million.

2 The role played by the Banque de France immediately after its creation in 1800 makes it impossible to draw any conclusion in favour of free banking.

It is obvious that in the mind of Napoleon the issue of paper should be realized by a bank having a monopoly and close links with the Treasury. A few months after its creation the Banque de France was issuing 60 per cent of the paper in circulation having *de facto* a kind of monopoly.

From the outset the Bank of France has had close links with the Treasury, which subscribed for 5,000 shares out of a capital of 30,000. As early as 1800, the Bank had serviced the lottery, government securities and pensions. In exchange the Treasury soon asked for temporary advances. And as early as 1803, the Banque de France had been entrusted with the issue privilege for Paris.

Let us summarize. Free entry was really accepted during the first experience but only for issuing notes with a small denomination. The experience ended up with failures of issuers, lack of confidence and counterfeiting. Free entry was not really accepted during the second experience. The amount of notes issued was very small and it is difficult to say that free banking played a role during such a short period.

To conclude, I would remind you that for a long time there has been a tendency in France to centralize and control everything. As an example of this tendency, a plan for a 'Banque Générale du Royaume de France' under the name of Banque de France was presented to Henri IV in 1608. Had this plan succeeded, the Banque de France would have been established one year before the Bank of Amsterdam and 86 years before the Bank of England.

5 The Evolution of Central Banking in England, 1821–90

Kevin Dowd

INTRODUCTION

The revival of interest in free banking has made clear how important it is to re-evaluate our monetary history. One of the reasons why so many economists support state intervention in the monetary system is that they believe that history shows that monetary laissez-faire is inherently unstable, and that central banking evolved to counter that instability.[1] It is now becoming increasingly apparent that the first view is unsupportable, and that the relatively unregulated banking systems of the past have a good record of stability.[2] The evidence suggests, in fact, that they have a superior record to contemporary or later banking systems which were more heavily regulated. A question then arises: if monetary laissez-faire is not inherently unstable, it must follow that central banking could not have evolved to counter the market's inherent instability, and we are left wondering why central banking *did* evolve.

This paper tries to shed some light on this question by examining the growth of central banking in England between the resumption of specie payments by the Bank of England (1821) and the Baring crisis (1890). This period was chosen because – at the risk of a slight exaggeration – it marks the transition of the Bank from a 'merely' privileged institution to a recognizable central bank. It is true, of course, that in the quarter century before 1821, and perhaps even earlier,[3] the Bank had accumulated considerable experience of central banking,[4] and it was in this period also that the theory of central banking was first developed; but these factors appear to have had comparatively little direct influence on the subsequent development of English central banking. The resumption of specie payments was intended to restore the situation of 1793, and relatively little remained after that of the Bank's earlier central-banking role. At most, the Bank had some ill-defined public responsibility, and even

159

that was controversial. Most of the theory of central banking was subsequently forgotten and had to be rediscovered later. In short, the modern system of central banking in England to a large extent developed *after* 1821.

Its roots, however, go back to the Bank's privileges of the late seventeenth and eighteenth centuries. The Bank's privileges gave it a size and security which no other institution could match, and this size and security gave its notes a competitive advantage over the notes of other banks. The Bank also pursued a policy of using its market power to discourage rival issues, and by the end of the eighteenth century it had succeeded in eliminating other London note issues. These factors in turn encouraged the other banks to use Bank notes as reserves, and the Restriction completed the process by which Bank liabilities became the principal reserve medium of the English banking system. The fact that the other banks used Bank liabilities for their reserves meant that the Bank could control their total reserves, and this control is the key factor in the Bank's subsequent development. It made the other banks dependent on the Bank – because they might need more reserves from it – and their dependence forced them to defer to it and acknowledge its hegemony. A second consequence of this dependence was that it eventually forced the Bank to accept the role of lender of last resort for the banking system. Both the Bank's hegemony over the banking system and its lender of last resort function thus derived ultimately from the same source – the Bank's control over other banks' reserves – which in turn stemmed from the Bank's earlier privileges.

These developments took place in an environment of periodic crisis that was largely caused by legislative restrictions on banking. Two kinds of restriction particularly stand out. Until 1826 all English banks other than the Bank of England were restricted to partnerships of six or fewer people. In an industry characterized by extensive economies of scale, this meant that English banks were small and under-capitalized, and very vulnerable to failure. It was in these circumstances that the Bank of England established its hegemony in London. The restrictions on joint stock banking were relaxed in the early nineteenth century, but the banks also had to live with restrictions on the note issue, and these restrictions were tightened by the Bank Charter Act in 1844. The restrictions on the note issue made it difficult to satisfy changes in the public's demands for bank liabilities, and gave rise to the possibility of panics in which the public would clamour for more Bank notes than the Bank could provide. It is significant that in three of these crises – those of 1847, 1857, and 1866 – what caused the panic to abate was a government promise to remove the restriction and allow the Bank to issue the additional notes that the public wanted.

The early development of central banking in England is therefore easily summarized. Legislative restrictions enabled the Bank of England to establish a position of unique strength, an important feature of which was the other banks' dependence on reserves provided by the Bank. By weakening the other banks, legislative restrictions also made the banking system prone to crises, and reduced the banks' ability to handle them. When crises occurred, the banks therefore had little option but to turn for assistance to the Bank of England. The Bank at length accepted the principle that it should provide that assistance, but the price it exacted was the acknowledgement of its hegemony over the monetary system. The process was complete by the time the Baring crisis occurred, and there were no further developments in British central banking until August 1914.

THE EARLY HISTORY OF THE BANK

The Bank of England was initially established in 1694 to provide the government of William III with a loan to fight Louis XIV. The circumstances in which it was founded are most instructive: three decades earlier, Charles II had had to rely on loans from London bankers, and he ran up large debts which he could not repay. His default in 1672 then destroyed the government's credit for many years. As a consequence, William III in the 1690s found it extremely difficult to raise loans, so he fell in with a scheme suggested by a Scottish financier, William Paterson, to establish a bank – the Bank of England – to lend the government money in return for the grant of certain privileges. Over the following years, the Bank's charter and privileges were gradually extended in return for a series of loans to the government: 'The early history of the Bank was a series of exchanges of favours between a needy Government and an accommodating corporation' (Smith (1936), p. 9). Apart from periodic increases in the Bank's capital and authorized note issue, the most significant of these provisions were the monopoly of the possession of the government's balances (1697), the granting of limited liability to the shareholders (1697), the restriction of other banks in England and

Wales to partnerships of no more than six partners with unlimited liability (1708; reaffirmed and strengthened in 1742), and the management of the National Debt (1751) (Smith (1936) (pp. 9–10)). As one historian put it, 'It is . . . evident that throughout the 18th century and early years of the 19th the Bank of England's first interests were the guarding of its monopoly issuing of notes, and the strengthening of the bonds which united it to the state by taking every advantage of the financial weakness of the Treasury' (Richards (1929), p. 199).

The Bank made good use of its privileges to build up a large business and establish its own supremacy. 'Possessing so many advantages the Bank easily overshadowed its competitors, and, as Bagehot has stated, "it inevitably became *the* Bank in London . . ."' (Richards (1929), p. 200). It used its market power to induce the other London banks to abandon their note issues sometime after 1772, even though the issuing of notes was normally a lucrative business and the banks retained a legal right to issue notes until 1844 (Powell, (1915, p. 229, no. 2)).[5] The elimination of the rival note issues in London shows both the extent of the Bank's power over the London banks and its willingness to use that power to further its own private interests. Promoting its own issues against those of other banks seems to have been consistent Bank policy.[6]

At the same time as they abandoned their own issues, London banks turned to Bank of England notes to redeem their own liabilities. Part of the reason for this was that notes were less costly to store and move than gold. In addition, the public would have preferred notes to gold for the same reasons, and so a bank that offered to redeem its liabilities with gold instead of Bank notes would have put itself at a competitive disadvantage. So would a bank that offered as redemption media financial instruments issued by some institution other than the Bank – without the Bank's privileges, no other institution could offer instruments that would have been as secure in a crisis. The banks were therefore driven to use the liabilities of the Bank of England as their own reserve media. This development is highly significant because the Bank of England's control over the other banks' reserves was to provide the basis on which the lender of last function was to evolve. Indeed, one could go further and say that it was to provide the basis from which the monopoly of the note issue was to develop into a modern central bank.[7]

Then came the French revolutionary war[8] and the government's attempts to finance much of its expenditure by loans from the Bank. When it had been founded, the Bank had been forbidden to lend to the government without the express permission of Parliament,[9] but despite this injunction the Bank had been in the habit of making loans against Treasury bills made payable at the Bank. Perhaps because it anticipated further government demands for loans, the Bank in 1793 requested the government to pass an Act of Indemnity to protect it against liability for the loans it had made in the past, and for future loans up to a certain amount. The Prime Minister, Pitt, lost no time putting such a bill through Parliament, but he deliberately left out the clause limiting the loans the Bank could make without Parliamentary approval. Pitt

> was now armed with the unbounded power of drawing upon the Bank; with nothing to restrain him, unless the directors should take the audacious step of dishonoring his bills. The bank was henceforth almost at his mercy, and ... he plunged into that reckless career of scattering English gold ... across Europe (MacLeod (1896), p. 105).

The Bank directors repeatedly complained about Pitt's incessant demands for loans, but they dared not refuse him, even though the loans threatened to push the Bank itself into failure. At last, the landing of French troops in Wales in February 1797 provoked a run on gold that the Bank lacked the resources to withstand, and the Bank had no choice but to appeal to Pitt for assistance. The government responded with an Order in Council – afterwards ratified by Act of Parliament – ordering the Bank to suspend [specie] payments. In effect, the government had driven the Bank into failure and then legalized its bankruptcy to keep it in business.[10]

There followed the long period of the Restriction (1797–1821), in which the Bank operated an inconvertible currency. The combination of legal tender,[11] the issue of small notes by the Bank,[12] and, perhaps most significantly, the depreciation of the Bank's notes,[13] all helped to further the use of Bank notes (and deposits) as the principal – and only significant – reserve medium of the other banks. In effect, the Bank of England became the monopoly supplier of base money, and therefore had the power to manipulate the reserves of the banking system as it pleased. Since, furthermore, the Bank was no longer subject to any commitment to redeem its liabilities for gold, it also had ultimate control over prices. The Bank's directors generally understood that their policies could have considerable influence on financial conditions, but they had much less understanding of the extent of that influence or how it should be used, and many of them believed that the Bank could do nothing to disturb prices provided it restricted its discounts to self-liquidating bills – the 'real bills' fallacy.[14] Consequently, both the Bank's policies and the real bills doctrine came in for much criticism, and the controversy gave rise to some notable contributions to monetary theory. Two contributions stand out. In 1802, Henry Thornton's *Paper Credit* provided a blueprint for managing a central bank on an inconvertible standard. It also gave a detailed analysis of the lender of last resort function,[15] and a devastating attack on the real bills fallacy. Also notable was the Bullion Report (1810) which made clear the Bank's responsibility for the depreciation of its notes and provided a famous and influential critique of the real bills doctrine.

The end of the Restriction period was signalled by the Resumption Act of 1819, which stipulated that the Bank should restore convertibility by 1 May 1823. In the event, it actually resumed payments 2 years before then. An earlier Act of 1816 had specified that the issue of notes under £5 was to cease 2 years after the resumption of convertibility, but the Bank anticipated this deadline as well by ceasing to issue small notes on resumption (Clapham (1944), pp. 75–6). Another Act of 1819 tried to restore the Bank's earlier degree of independence by requiring that it obtain explicit Parliamentary approval before lending to the government (Andreades (1909), pp. 241–2), and Bank notes again ceased to be legal tender (Smith (1936), p. 13). The Bank's legal position was now similar to what it had been in 1793.

As in 1793, many people also regarded it as having some kind of special responsibility towards a monetary system based on the gold standard, and much of the monetary theory developed in the Restriction period slipped into oblivion.[16] The only real difference with 1793 was that banks and their customers were now more used to using Bank notes to redeem their liabilities,[17] and Bank notes remained very significant in banks' reserves, even though the ban on small notes forced them to accumulate coins to redeem deposits of less than £5. The greater use of Bank liabilities as reserves implied that the Bank had a more powerful 'lever' over the monetary system than it had before the French Wars.

THE DETERMINANTS OF BANK POLICY

Before proceeding much further it is perhaps useful to consider in more detail the objectives of Bank policy and what determined them. The Bank's policy was a response to two sorts of pressure. On the one hand, there was pressure from the shareholders for the Bank to maximize their profits, and while the directors could – and often did – withstand a certain amount of pressure from that direction,[18] they could not defy an organized majority which was set on a definite policy. On the other hand, the Bank had a close if informal relationship with the government, and it had to take government wishes very seriously. The government would make frequent requests of the Bank, and though it was often ready to modify its requests in the light of the opinions of the Bank management, it nonetheless expected its requests to be obeyed. The Bank understood this, and was reluctant to flout the government openly, even though the government had no formal authority over it, and I have already discussed how the Bank acceded to Pitt's requests in 1793–7, even though they threatened to drive the Bank into default, and indeed eventually did so.

There appear to be several reasons for this willingness to accommodate the government. One was the government's legislative power: it could always bring in legislation to get its way, if necessary, and it was more convenient for both sides if the Bank simply gave in. Moreover, the Bank could ill afford to antagonize the government because it was dependent on it to make sure that its charter and privileges were periodically renewed, and it would always want to retain the government's goodwill in case a crisis should occur and the Bank needed help. A second source of the government's influence over the Bank was its power of patronage (i.e. its power to offer jobs and honours). Patronage worked by 'buying off' key individuals, and governments of the period used it very effectively.[19]

Pressures from shareholders and government were not the only determinants of Bank policy. One must also consider the self-interest of the directors themselves. Most members of the court earned their living working in City firms, and their principal concern would have been the well-being of their own firms. As a result, they would have had some interest in ensuring that the Bank provide the market with any support it might need. Since controversy might lead to their replacement, they also had some incentive to avoid policies that would provoke adverse criticism. We shall have more to say on this below.

These conflicting interests and pressures produced a Bank policy that was a compromise between maximizing – or, more precisely, satisficing – profits to satisfy shareholders, keeping the government content, and occasionally supporting the market in a crisis. The relative importance of these objectives varied:

> Up to about 1825 the Bank definitely aimed at high profits for its Proprietors, and resented any imputation of public responsibility, except to keep itself in a sound position and to give a preference to the Government in making its advances ... At the same time, it must be admitted that the Directors were wise enough to withstand the desire, very pertinaciously expressed by some of the Proprietors, for maximum dividends and the distribution of all available profits (Dodwell (1934), p. 57).

Despite conflicts with other objectives, the Bank nonetheless had little difficulty in making a decent profit until well into the nineteenth century. The absence of real competition enabled it to make 'a comfortable income for its stockholders, without exerting itself a great deal' (Sayers (1958), p. 11), but this changed after rival joint stock banks were allowed. As Sayers (*loc. cit.*) put it,

> in the middle decades of the nineteenth century circumstances ceased to support its profits in quite the old easy way. Though London's business, with the country's, was undergoing spectacular expansion, the staid ways of the Old Lady of Threadneedle Street were uncompetitive, and new business went rather to the rising young men of the joint-stock banks. The decisions that followed the crash of 1857 accentuated the loss of discount business ... [and its dividends were] a doubtful satisfaction to stockholders who could see how well the shareholders in some of the new joint-stock banks were faring.

We now return to the 1820s.

THE 1825 PANIC AND THE ACTS OF 1826

In 1825 there was a major financial crisis – after a period of considerable expansion of their issues by the Bank of England and the private banks,[20] and, perhaps more significantly, after large amounts of speculative British investment in South America. The collapse of the investment boom in mid-1825 left many British financial firms in serious difficulties. The apprenhension mounted in the autumn, and there were large bank failures in November. On 5 December it then became known that one of the leading City finances houses – Poles & Co. – was in serious difficulties. The Bank arranged for assistance for Poles, and the firm struggled on for a while. In the meantime, the crisis gradually worsened. In London it reached its peak in the week from Monday the 12th to Saturday the 17th, when the storm 'raged with an intensity which it is impossible for me to describe' (Richards, the deputy governor; quoted in MacLeod (1896, p. 122)). On the Monday and Tuesday the demand for cash was so great that it was said to be impossible to convert even the best government securities into cash on any terms.[21] The public were clamouring for Bank notes and gold coins, and neither could be produced fast enough, though the printers were working overtime and the Mint was coining sovereigns furiously (Clapham (1944), p. 100).[22] That same week the government refused the Bank any form of assistance – the Bank would have to meet demands for redemption until it ran dry – and the Bank decided to reverse the contractionary policy it had followed since May. In the famous words of a Bank spokesman, Jeremiah Harman:

We lent by every possible means and in modes we had never adopted before. We took in stock as security; we purchased exchequer bills, and we made advances on exchequer bills; we not only discounted outright, but we made advances on deposits of bills of exchange to an immense amount; in short, by every possible means consistent with safety of the bank; and we were not on some occasions over-nice ... we rendered every assistance in our power (quoted in McLeod (1896, p. 123)).

The Bank's expansionary policy 'and the resultant issue of £5 million of notes, snatched the country from the brink of the cataclysm which it already overhung' (Powell (1915), p. 330). By the end of the Saturday, the Bank had apparently run out of notes,[23] but a new batch arrived from the printers on the Sunday, and a consignment of gold arrived from France on the Monday, 17th December. That day Poles failed, and with it some other London banks, and forty-four country banks for which Poles was the correspondent. Despite these events, the panic in London started to abate, and though the panic in the provinces at first got worse, the whole country had calmed down by the end of the week.

Bagehot was later to describe the panic as so tremendous that its consequences were well-remembered after nearly 50 years. The Bank had come within an ace of failure,[24] and in Lord Bentick's colourful phrase, the country had come 'within twenty-four hours of barter' (Powell (1915), p. 330). The 'wreckage was already frightful', and by the end of the year seventy-three leading English banks had suspended business, many of them never to resume, while the next year saw an extraordinarily high number of business bankruptcies (Clapham (1944), pp. 102, 109). The toll that it took on the participants can be gauged from another comment of Richards, the deputy governor, that after it was over 'those who had been busied in that terrible scene could recollect that they had families who had some claim upon their attention. It happened to me not to see my children for that week' (quoted in Powell (1915), pp. 330–1)).

The crisis gave rise to considerable controversy, and the government determined to legislate.[25] Two Acts resulted. The first, in March 1826, forbade banks to issue any new notes under £5, and to re-issue any such notes after 5 April 1829 (Clapham (1944), p. 106). The banning of small notes reflected a widespread opinion that their issue had been a major contributory factor to the commercial crisis (MacLeod (1896), p. 126). The second Act, in May 1826, authorized the formation of joint stock banks with the right to note issue, provided that they had no office within 65 miles of London (Clapham (1944), p. 107). The Court of the Bank disliked this measure, but could do nothing about it (Clapham (1944), p. 105). This Act also encouraged the Bank to set up branches in the country by giving it explicit authorization to do so.[26] The Bank then proceeded to set up branches in the provinces, but it is worth noting that it took government prompting and the threat of competition to make it do so.

1833 BANK CHARTER ACT

In 1832 a Parliamentary Committee of Inquiry was set up to examine the Bank's charter, which was due to expire the next year.[27] One of the key issues in the discussions was how far the Bank should pass up profit opportunities to promote the wider interest. There seemed to be a large body of opinion that the Bank's responsibilities were greater than those of an ordinary bank, but there was no agreement as to what they were. As Fetter (1965, p. 152) writes, the Bank was a monopoly, but it was not clear either to Government, the public or the management and the stockholders of the Bank whether the price that it paid for that monopoly was simply the direct services rendered to Government, or whether it had a larger responsibility to the banking community, and even to the whole economy. The answers to these questions, ever present though rarely stated directly, were made increasingly complex by the shift in public opinion, gathering strength in the 1820's and reaching high tide in the 1850's, that anything savouring of monopoly, of state direction, even of action that was not directed to the maximizing of profit, was undesirable. It is no wonder that in such a situation there was no clear and consistent opinion about the Bank's responsibilities...

The Parliamentary Inquiry led to the 1833 Bank Charter Act, the main features of which were as follows:

1   The Bank's charter was renewed until 1855, with the proviso that the government had the right to suspend it after 12 years.
2   Bank notes were to become legal tender, except at the Bank itself. This measure was intended to protect the Bank's gold reserves against internal drains by making it legally possible for other banks to satisfy demands for redemption without the need to draw gold from the Bank.
3   The Act affirmed the legality throughout England and Wales of joint stock banks that did not issue notes, i.e. the Bank's joint-stock monopoly was explicitly restricted to note-issuing banking. This measure thus eliminated the uncertainty that had surrounded the legality of non-note-issuing joint stock banks in London. The Chancellor, Lord Althorp, rejected the Bank's appeals to have its joint-stock monopoly extended to cover deposit banks (MacLeod (1896), p. 49).
4   At the Bank's request, bills of exchange and promissory notes with no more than 3 months to run were freed from the usury laws that restricted interest rates to a maximum of 5 per cent.[28] This was very significant because it gave the Bank free rein to use its discount rate to protect its reserve.
5   The Bank was to furnish the Exchequer with weekly returns regarding the amount of its bullion and its note circulation and deposits, and the monthly averages were to be published each quarter in the *London Gazette* (Andreades (1909), p. 262;

Dodwell (1934), p. 58). There was a gradual increase in the early nineteenth century in the amount of information the Bank was required to furnish,[29, 30] which appears to indicate a 'growing recognition of its special position and public responsibility' (Dodwell, (1934), p. 58).

THE PALMER RULE AND THE BANK CHARTER ACT OF 1844

The 1832 Inquiry witnessed the first public explanation of a rule of thumb that the Bank claimed to have been following since 1827 (Viner (1937), p. 224). This was the famous 'Palmer rule', according to which the Bank sought to maintain a gold reserve ratio of one-third against the sum of its note and deposit liabilities. The other two-thirds of the Bank's assets would be its holdings of securities, and the underlying idea was that outside of exceptional circumstances which might require the use of Bank 'discretion', the volume of securities would be held constant. A fall in reserves would then be self-correcting: the fall in reserves would lead to a reduced money supply, lower prices, a restoration of the exchanges, and an influx of gold.[31] The Bank's attempts to follow the rule were not particularly successful, however, and the rule was frequently breached in practice because the Bank was unable to 'fine-tune' its reserves or its liabilities to the degree that they seemed to require.[32]

    An interesting question is why the Bank's managers chose to submit themselves to the discipline of something like the Palmer rule. One explanation is that they genuinely believed that the Bank's 'optimal policy' was to follow the 'right' simple rule, and at the time believed that the Palmer rule was the right one.[33] Another explanation, not entirely inconsistent with the first, is that they believed that a rule would give them some protection against criticism of their policies. To the extent that they could persuade their shareholders that the rule was 'right', they had a defence against the criticism that they should be doing more to increase profits instead; to the extent that they could persuade Parliament and the public, they had a defence against the charges of monetary mismanagement which were often levied at the Bank, and which were dangerous to the Bank because of the possibility that they might lead to legislative intervention to curtail its power or privileges.[34]

    The monetary disturbances of 1836–9 and the continued controversy over the Bank's policies led to suggestions for a new rule that proponents claimed would eliminate the main source of monetary instability. This rule – the currency principle – was apparently first set out by Loyd (1837).[35] The idea was to give the Bank (or a government bank) a monopoly of the note issue, but with a 100 per cent reserve requirement, and leave the Bank in all other respects free. The currency principle was based on the notion that monetary disturbances were due to over-issues of notes, and could be eliminated if the currency issue was made to behave as if it were purely metallic. By this stage, the inadequacies of the Palmer rule were becoming obvious, and the Bank management was sensitive to the claim of the currency school that it was an inappropriate rule to follow. The management would also have been aware that the Palmer rule could provide it with little defence against criticism if it was unable to adhere to it in practice. Far from protecting it, the Palmer rule had left the Bank management open to the additional charge of incompetence in failing to meet its own stated objectives. The doctrines of the currency school seemed to offer the Bank a solution to these problems, and the Bank management soon embraced them.[36]

In January 1844 the Governor and Deputy Governor of the Bank submitted a memorandum to the Prime Minister, Peel, that contained what were to become the major provisions of the 1844 Bank Charter Act. Peel was a supporter of the currency school,[37] and, having realized that the ideas he was moving towards were already present in the minds of the Bank management, he seized on their suggestions and had little difficulty persuading the Cabinet to go along with him. The result was the Bank Charter Act passed later in the year. This Act separated the Bank into an Issue Department responsible for the note issue, and a Banking Department responsible for everything else. The Issue Department was obliged to observe a 100 per cent marginal reserve requirement, and the Banking Department was left free to do as it wished. In addition, the note issues of other banks were to be frozen, so that the Bank now had an effective monopoly of the English note issue.[38]

One of the most important consequences of the Act was that it encouraged the directors to believe that it freed them of any responsibility towards the rest of the banking system (Dodwell (1934), pp. 62–3). The Bank had surrendered its freedom over the note issue in return for what many of the directors would have seen as a confirmation of its freedom over the rest of its business.[39] As

Hawtrey (1938, p. 20) observed 'pushed to its logical conclusion', the Act

> meant that the Bank would no longer undertake to be the lender of last resort. It would be free, on the one hand, to refuse to discount bills beyond such limit as seemed convenient, and, on the other, to get its share of the discounting business of the market, and for that purpose to offer to discount bills at a competitive rate.

THE CRISES OF 1847, 1857 AND 1866

The critics of the currency school had always claimed that its recommendations would not prevent crises, and it was not long before they were proved right. The disastrous potato crops of 1845 and 1846 had given rise to large exports of gold to pay for imports of corn. The Bank's gold reserves fell, and a rise of discount rate to 3½ per cent in January did nothing to stop the outflow. Bank rate was raised to 5 per cent in April when the Banking Department's reserve had fallen to just over £2½ million. The market then panicked, the Bank rationed its discounts, and the market discount rate rose to 10 or 12 per cent. At this point gold started to come into the Bank's reserve again, and the market calmed down. Later in the year, however, a series of failures led to renewed apprehension and further falls in the Bank's reserve. In October the Bank raised its discount rate to 5½ per cent and again rationed its discounts. The market panicked again, and this time some of the banks began to fail.

The City clamoured for the suspension of the 1844 Act to enable the Bank to issue extra notes. Powell (1915, p. 363) reports the bankers' appeal to the Chancellor, Sir Charles Wood: 'Let us have notes. We don't mean, indeed, to take the notes, because we shall not want them; only tell us that we can get them, and this will at once restore confidence'. The government held out for a while, but at last gave in. On Saturday, 23 October, the government informed the Bank that a Bill of Indemnity would be presented to Parliament should the Bank issue notes in excess of those allowed under the 1844 Act. As a condition, the Bank was to raise the discount rate to 8 per cent. The publication of the government letter the next Monday instantly abated the panic.

The certainty that money could be got took away all desire to have it. The Bank prepared ... additional notes, but there was no need to use them. Notes which had been hoarded under the impression that the limit fixed by the Act of 1844 would shortly be reached and that the Bank would be unable to assist the commercial world, were brought out in a mass from their hiding places; the same thing happened with regard to gold (Andreades (1909), pp. 336–7).[40]

Another crisis occurred in October 1857. It appears to have been precipitated by a crisis in the US, which provoked a series of failures among British firms with large American investments. The Bank responded by steadily increasing Bank rate and lending extensively, but its reserve fell sharply. By the evening of 12 November, its reserve had fallen to only £384,144. With bankers' balance alone of over £5 million, the governor afterwards acknowledged that 'the Bank could not have kept its doors open an hour [more]' (MacLeod (1896), p. 161). With 'universal ruin ... at last impending', the government sent a letter to the Bank indicating that it was prepared to present a Bill of Indemnity to release the Bank from the note restrictions of the Bank Charter Act, with the relaxation to operate for as long as the discount rate was at least 10 per cent (MacLeod (1896), p. 160). As in 1847, 'the public alarm was at once abated', but this time there continued to be a high demand for discounts for more than a fortnight (Andreades (1909), p. 349). Unlike 1847, the Bank Charter Act was actually breached, and the Bank issued an additional £2 million of notes in excess of the 1844 limit, although the amount of these notes in circulation never reached £1 million.[41]

A third crisis occurred in 1866. A series of failures in early 1866 had produced an atmosphere of mounting alarm. Then on Wednesday, 9 May, a judgment was delivered to the effect that certain bills held by the great broking firm of Overend-Gurney were worthless. There was already considerable public concern about Overends, and the firm did not have the resources to withstand a major run. The firm therefore appealed to the Bank for assistance, but the loan was refused because Overends could not meet the Bank's demands for security, and the firm suspended business at the end of the next day (10 May). The market opened on Friday to complete panic: there was a wild rush to sell virtually anything for notes, and asset prices plummeted. As Powell later wrote, that was a day 'of tragic memory, even at the distance of half a century' (Powell (1915), p. 401). That evening the Chancellor announced to Parliament that, following the earlier precedents, the government would bring in a Bill to indemnify the Bank if the Bank thought it proper to exceed the note limits specified by the 1844 Act.[42]

The Chancellor's announcement had 'such an effect that the next day the crisis seemed to be at an end' (Andreades (1909), p. 359). Once again, the knowledge that the Bank had the power to issue the extra notes was sufficient to abate the panic, and in the event no additional notes needed to be issued. Nonetheless the demand for discounts continued to be considerable (the Bank made over £12 million in discounts over the next week), a number of failures occurred the week after Black Friday, and Bank rate remained at 10 per cent until early August. After that, the markets returned to normal and the crisis was followed by a comparatively long period of calm.[43]

It is highly significant that each of the last three panics was cured by a promise to relax the note restrictions of the Bank Charter Act. Each panic was a panic for notes – an excess demand, in other words, to convert one form of bank liability into another – and the panic abated as soon as it became clear that the notes could be obtained. At no point was the gold standard itself in danger – the danger was always that the Banking Department would default while the Issue Department remained full of gold which it could neither lend out nor issue notes against. It is therefore difficult to avoid the conclusion that whatever the shocks that triggered off the panics, it was the note restrictions that converted those shocks into major crises. The situation was somewhat different in 1825, but even then the main demand was to get rid of country bank notes, and most of those who wanted to do so would have been happy to take Bank of England notes if they could have got them. As in the crises of 1847, 1857 and 1866, it was the unwillingness to meet the demand for Bank notes that really fed the panic, and the panic subsided once people became convinced that Bank notes could be obtained. There is much truth in MacLeod's assessment: 'Monetary panics, in this country at least, have been invariably produced by bad banking legislation, or by bad management of the Bank of England, sometimes by both. Monetary panics are therefore ... avoidable' (1896, p. 95)

BAGEHOT AND HANKEY

The 1866 crises led to renewed controversy over the role of the Bank in financial crises. On 22 September Walter Bagehot published an article in *The Economist* in which he wrote that the Bank had used its reserves well to support the market, and that in a recent speech the governor, David Salomons, had to all intents and purposes admitted the Bank's responsibility towards the market.[44] The view that the Bank should support the market by lending freely in a crisis was accepted opinion in the City,[45] had the support of a number of leading economists,[46] and had considerable support even in the Court of the Bank itself.[47]

The following year one of the Bank directors, Thomson Hankey, published a stinging attack on Bagehot's views in his book *The Principles of Banking*. He denounced the Bagehot view that the Bank had a responsibility to support the market in a crisis as 'the most mischievous [doctrine] ever broached', and he saw no hope for sound banking till it was 'repudiated' (quoted in Clapham (1944, p. 284). He claimed to be reiterating the opinion of the framers of the 1844 Act, and suggested that Peel's statement that the Banking Department be 'governed on precisely the same principles as would regulate any other body dealing with Bank of England Notes' could only be interpreted in this light. Hankey was supported by another bank director, George Warde Norman, who supported him because he wished to make the other banks hold greater reserves.

Hankey's argument can be summarized as follows:

1 The Bank's only responsibility was to its shareholders.
2 In a crisis, the Bank should bear its full share of the pressure – Timberlake (1978, p. 218) calls this the 'fair share' doctrine – but it had no responsibility to support the market as a whole.
3 The admission by the Bank of a responsibility to support the market would create a moral hazard problem – the other banks would reduce their reserves in the knowledge that they could obtain support from the Bank of England – and thereby increase the pressure on the Bank to provide that support in a crisis.
4 A policy to support the market would require someone with the discretion to authorize its use, and a clearly recognizable signal for taking action.

Bagehot countered in *The Economist*, and then in *Lombard Street* (1873). In principle, he felt that the best system – the 'natural' one – was one of multiple reserve banks, of not altogether unequal size, but he felt that it would be pointless to propose such a system in the circumstances of his day. He therefore set himself the task of making the existing system work as well as it could, and that meant giving the Bank suitable guidelines to follow.

Bagehot recommended that in normal times (i.e. outside of a panic), the Bank should seek to protect its reserve and, if necessary, augment it. More specifically, he suggested that the Bank aim to prevent its reserve from ever falling below £11–11½ million, and should take measures to protect its reserve whenever it fell below an 'apprehension minimum' of £15 million. This recommendation implied a significant increase in the Bank's reserve[48] and, therefore, a reduction in its profits.

During a panic, however, the Bank should pursue an expansionary policy:

1   The reserve should be advanced freely and promptly, but at a high interest rate. This penalty rate would encourage gold imports, reduce precautionary balances, 'operate as a heavy fine on unreasonably timidity', and ration the scarce gold reserve. The penalty rate would also provide a test of the soundness of distressed borrowers, and provided it was kept above the market rate, it would make them go to the market before they went to Bank.

   To stop the panic, 'it is necessary ... to diffuse the impression that though money may be dear, still money is to be had'. If people could be persuaded that they could get money, though at a price, then they would cease to demand money in such a mad way. The policy of lending freely was recommended not because it would guarantee the safety of the Bank and the rest of the monetary system, but because it gave them the best chance to survive it: 'The only safe plan for the Bank is the brave plan ... This policy may not save the Bank; but if it does not, nothing will save it' (1906, pp. 220–1).

2   In lending, the Bank should make advances on securities that would be considered good under normal conditions.

3   The Bank should support the market, but not specific institutions as such. Individual institutions – even large ones – should be allowed to fail.

4   The Bank's support policy ought to be clearly announced in advance. To make loans otherwise was 'to incur the evil of making them without obtaining the advantage', since people would be inclined to run if they were in any doubt about whether the Bank

would support the market. A problem with the Bank, wrote Bagehot, was that it 'has never laid down any clearly sound policy on the subject ... The public is never sure what policy will be adopted at the most important moment; it is not sure what amount of advance will be made, or on what security it will be made ... until we have on this point a clear understanding with the Bank of England, both our liability for crises and our terror at crises will always be greater than they otherwise would be' (1962, p. 101). Bagehot went on to criticize Hankey who 'leaves us in doubt altogether as to what will be the policy of the Bank of England in the next panic, and as to what amount of aid the public may then expect from it' (1906, p. 175).

Though it came to be widely accepted, there are a number of serious problems with Bagehot's analysis. First, there was an obvious conflict between the advice to protect the reserve and the advice to lend freely.[49] Bagehot tried to resolve it by suggesting that the Bank protect the reserve in normal times, and lend in a panic, but this advice requires that the Bank be able to distinguish in practice between cases of genuine panic and cases of mere market apprenhension. As Rockoff (1986) observed, Bagehot's schema makes everything depend on the Bank's psychoanalysis of the market, but he gave the Bank no advice to enable it to distinguish between the two cases. This policy gave rise to twin dangers: on the one hand, the Bank might mistake market apprehension for real panic and lend freely, in which case its falling reserve might increase market apprenhension and either provoke a panic or leave the Bank in a weakened position to deal with a panic if one should break out; on the other hand, if the Bank mistook a real panic for mere apprehension and did nothing to counter it, the panic could well intensify, and possibly get out of control.

Second, it was also far from clear that Bagehot's advice would have helped in some past crises. Rockoff (1986, pp. 169–72) plausibly suggests that the Bank had no way of knowing when apprehension turned to real panic in 1839 and 1847, and points out that the Bank's attempts in 1857 to lend freely on Bagehot's lines were not enough to stem the panic. He goes on to suggest that only the panic of 1866 seems to fit at all easily into Bagehot's schema: 'one cannot help thinking that his theory was essentially a generalisation of this experience', and that 'despite Bagehot's jamming and pushing not all of [the earlier crises] can be made to fit into the 1866 mould' (1986, p. 172).

Third, a common criticism of Bagehot is that the lender of last resort function he proposed would create a problem of moral hazard. If the banks can count on the support of the Bank in a crisis, they will rationally take more risks and hold fewer reserves than they would otherwise have chosen to do. This point was raised by Hankey, of course, and Bagehot did little to answer it beyond claiming that the other banks were already counting on the Bank's support anyway.

A fourth criticism is that Bagehot really had no solution to the problem of the Bank's inadequate reserves beyond telling the Bank that it ought to hold more.[50] He also failed to appreciate the extent to which the problem of the reserve and the problem of discount rate policy were really different aspects of the same problem (see next section), and he failed to anticipate the ultimate solution adopted by the Bank: 'a powerful Bank Rate weapon within a "thin film of gold"' (Sayers (1958), p. 18).[51]

THE DEVELOPMENT OF BANK RATE POLICY

One cannot understand the development of the Bank's reserve and lender of last resort policies without also examining the more or less concurrent development of Bank rate policy. These policies were intimately linked. As Sayers (1958, p. 10) observed:

> Oddly enough, arguments about the need for a stronger Bank Rate policy and about the need for a bigger reserve run parallel in many of the discussions throughout this period, and there seems to have been little realization that the two lines of attack were alternatives, in the sense that a bigger reserve implied less need for a flexible Bank Rate, and more effective use of Bank Rate made a big reserve less necessary.

The policy of using discount rate to manipulate the Bank's gold reserves can be traced to the provision of the 1833 Bank Charter Act which freed the Bank from the impact of the usury laws.[52] A high Bank rate worked by attracting gold to London from abroad and from domestic circulation, and a higher Bank rate was used to protect (and augment) the Bank's reserve when it was running low. The typical scenario was where a shortage of notes would lead to country and foreign bankers drawing on their London correspondents, who in turn would draw on the discount houses in London. The discount houses would then withdraw (or borrow) from the Banking Department of the Bank, whose reserve would fall. At some point the Bank would stop and then reverse the fall in its reserve by raising its discount rate. When 'the Bank did act firmly, it got quick results because the gold reserve was in this period extremely responsive to changes in market rate' (Sayers, (1958), p. 13). Sayers goes on to suggest three reasons for this responsiveness: (1) high rates would draw gold from the country banks, an effect which was particularly strong in the third quarter of the century; (2) London's foreign lending was large and very interest-sensitive; and (3) the world's stock of gold was rising for much of this period, and London was well-placed to tap it.

Bank rate was first actively used in 1839,[53] when it was raised to protect the Bank's dwindling reserve. After 1844 it was used more often, and more vigorously, but even then it was usually used with a certain reluctance. Apart from exposing the Bank to sometimes severe public criticism, the use of Bank rate was also expensive. The cost arose because the Bank sometimes felt obliged to engage in open market operations to make its Bank rate policy effective.[54] These costs arose not just because the execution of these policies used up resources (e.g. the Bank had to pay interest on funds it borrowed), but also because they created opportunities for arbitrage profits at the Bank's expense.[55] As a consequence, when the Bank's responsibility 'clearly called for' such operations, the Bank 'did bear the expense, but it did grudgingly' (Sayers (1958), p. 12), and as 'the situation was often not clear . . . doubts in diagnosis too often provided the excuse for delay in action' (*loc. cit.*). Losses also arose because for a long time the Bank insisted on discounting for its regular customers at Bank rate, and as this was almost always above market rate, the consequence was a steady loss of its regular discount business.[56] Because of these costs, the use of Bank rate policy and open market operations was kept to a minimum, and in normal times Bank rate tended to follow the market rate rather than the other way round (Sayers, (1958)).

An additional influence on the Bank's discount policy was its concern that the joint stock banks – its commercial rivals – were able to cut down their reserves by relying on the discount houses (and indirectly on the Bank) to provide them with funds if they needed them. This created a moral hazard problem and meant that the Bank was indirectly subsidizing its commercial competitors. The Bank responded to these problems by adopting the '1858 rule', by which it retreated from day-to-day operations in the discount market. In doing so, the Bank effectively served notice to the discount market that it must stand on its own feet. The 1858 rule was an indication of the Bank's willingness (sometimes, at least) to sacrifice its own profits to secure other ends – in this case, to force the joint stock banks to be more prudent. It therefore marks an important step along the Bank's development from a profit-making 'private' bank to a 'central bank' that was less concerned with its own profits and more concerned with 'broader' objectives relating to the banking system generally. The rule was subsequently modified in 1878 and 1883 before being abolished in June 1890.[57] By then, of course, the transition to 'central bank' was much more complete.

The history of Bank rate policy in this period can be considered as a series

> of alternating periods of stringency and ease, each usually extend-
> ing over some years. In a period of stringency recurrent applica-
> tions of dear money are needed to correct a persistent tendency of
> the reserve to fall below the prudent limit ... At last the corner is
> turned, possibly at the cost of a financial crisis. There follows a
> period of ease, when the reserve grows bigger and bigger in spite of
> cheap money. Presently currency begins to pass into circulation
> again, but cheap money continues with little interruption so long as
> the reserve, though falling, remains above the prudent level
> (Hawtrey (1938), p. 46).

The reserve eventually falls below the prudent level, dear money is needed again, and the cycle repeats itself.

In 1878 the Bank announced that it would discount for its regular customers at market rate, irrespective of Bank rate, and that it would always be willing to lend on approved security at penal rate to everyone else. The effect was to put the Bank's customers on the same level as the rest of the market, and protect the Bank from a further loss of business. The readiness of the Bank to borrow in the market meant that the market would never get too independent of the Bank (and vice versa), but the market could now rely on the Bank's assistance (at the penal rate) at any time.

> The technique had thus attained a textbook simplicity: Bank Rate
> was a penal rate, not applicable to the Bank's ordinary customers;
> [and] the market's knowledge that the Bank would ordinarily

operate at this penal rate made it ready to operate on a pretty narrow margin of funds, so that the position of the penal rate was ordinarily a matter of daily concern and therefore influential over market rate itself (Sayers (1958), pp. 16–17).[58]

THE CONSOLIDATION OF BANK POWER

One of the most interesting and least discussed banking issues in the late nineteenth century was how the Bank's influence over the monetary system seemed to increase, and this despite the fact that the growth of the big joint stock banks meant that the Bank's relative financial strength – as measured by its share of the discount business, or its size relative to the big joint stock banks – was diminishing. Even if it had contributed to it in the past, its relative financial strength was no longer particularly important to the Bank's power over the monetary system. The source of that power, as discussed earlier, was the Bank's control over the banks' redemption media, and that control was well-established by the time the bank resumed specie payments in 1821. In addition, however, the Bank had to be ready to use that power, and in practice that meant it had to be willing to sacrifice its profits (e.g. by engaging in open market operations and using Bank rate). As time went by, its doubts about making those sacrifices seemed to diminish, and its influence in the market increased.

It is important to stress that the Bank's influence did not rest on any legislation which specifically compelled the other banks to use Bank liabilities as their reserves. Legislation had established the basis of the Bank's power by granting the Bank its earlier privileges, but its hegemony then evolved in the environment that the legislation did so much to create. In my earlier discussion, I specifically mentioned the restrictions which weakened the banking system and prevented it protecting itself against crises. I also mentioned the role played in the Restriction period by legal tender, the Bank's power to intimidate other banks, and the depreciation of Bank notes which called Gresham's law into operation to drive the 'good money' – i.e. gold – out of banks' reserves. The return to gold in 1821 put some gold back into banks' reserves, but it did not restore the *status quo ante bellum*. The question then arises: given that they were under no legal obligation to use Bank liabilities as reserves, why did individual banks continue to use them when the price, in effect, was their own independence?

The banks appear to have accepted the Bank's supremacy for several reasons. One was the extreme difficulty of finding an alternative redemption medium to the Bank's notes that the public would be willing to accept. The Bank note had the twin advantages that it was familiar and that it was issued by the most secure bank in the land. It would have been very difficult to match these advantages while Bank notes were still available, and the only way to remove them from circulation would have been to destroy the Bank itself (e.g. by organizing a collective withdrawal of deposits in the hope of making the Bank default). An attempt to do that would have risked a major crisis, however, and even if it succeeded in causing the Bank difficulties, it was more than likely that the government would have intervened to support it. In addition, as Fetter (1965, p. 270) observed,

> it would have been necessary for the London bankers to present a united front. That would have meant civil war in the City, and even those who thought that rebellion would succeed might still question whether the fruits of victory would equal the costs ... Leaders of threatened revolts rarely advertise their intentions openly, and one might expect this to be particularly true with gentlemen of the City of London. Only a little appeared in print, but what did would indicate that at various times the problem had been raised in private discussions.

The leader of a prospective coup would have faced an awesome task establishing a united front, and the very considerable danger that the Bank would find out what was afoot and make an example out of him by launching a pre-emptive attack before he was ready. In any case, the primary responsibility of the other banks was to their shareholders, and that responsibility would have given them relatively little leeway to engage in dubious attempts to stir up a revolution. One must also bear in mind that many managements would have felt some degree of goodwill towards the Bank for supporting them in past crises, and the Bank itself hardly seemed like an overbearing tyrant. There was therefore never any real possibility of a serious challenge to the Bank.

THE BARING CRISIS[59]

In 1890 there occurred the most significant crisis since Overend-

Gurney. There had been a great deal of speculative British investment in Argentina, but the situation there deteriorated and gave rise
to mounting anxiety about the soundness of some of the British
finance houses that were involved. Against this background, on 8
November, 'the appalling intelligence was made known to the
governor ... that [the] great house [of Baring Brothers] was in the
extremest danger of stopping payment ... and that the most ener-
getic measures must be taken without a moment's delay to avert the
catastrophe' (MacLeod (1896), p. 167). The governor's response was
swift and effective: he called a meeting of the managers of the leading
banks and City firms, and 'persuaded' them to participate in a fund to
guarantee Baring's liabilities. The Bank itself would provide for the
firm's immediate obligations, and arranged for credits from Russia
and France. The settlement was publicly announced and the market
instantly calmed down.

The Baring affair was remarkable in a number of respects. Unlike
earlier crises, it was very localized and it was resolved almost before
the market knew that there was anything going on. The governor
broke with precedent by refusing to raise Bank rate beyond 6 per
cent, and he refused the offer of a suspension of the Bank Charter
Act. He also broke with Bagehot by arranging a rescue package for a
specific institution, and came up with a solution – a collective
guarantee, with the other parties cajoled into participating – that
Bagehot had not foreseen. In effect, he abandoned all precedent –
and Bagehot's advice – by arranging an intervention package to pre-
empt the crisis, and he entirely succeeded. The crisis was averted,
and the contributors to the guarantee fund lost nothing in the end.

The Baring episode is also very interesting in that it revealed the
extent of the Bank's influence over the rest of the financial system,
and the governor's readiness to use it:

> There is a City tradition that one of the joint-stock banks ...
> endeavoured to evade its share in the agreement to refrain from
> calling in its loans ... The matter was brought to the attention of
> [the governor] Mr. Lidderdale, who, with characteristic decision,
> sent for the manager and informed him that if the bank did not
> adhere loyally to the agreement he would close its account at the
> Bank of England and announce the fact in the evening newspapers.
> He is said to have given the manager an hour to make up his mind.
> It would be superfluous to add what the manager's decision was
> (Powell (1915), pp. 526–7).

CONCLUSION: BRITISH CENTRAL BANKING IN THE 1890s

By 1890 a distinctive system of central banking had evolved in Britain. Its origins went back to earlier centuries, but some of its key features had evolved only more recently. The developments of the previous 80 years can be summarized in the following three principles:

1   The Bank had a responsibility to support the market, and this responsibility was by now accepted at the Bank itself.[60] In addition, a tradition[61] had grown up on the question of how the Bank should discharge that responsibility.
2   There was no longer any doubt about the Bank's hegemony over the banking system, and the other banks had accommodated themselves to it.
3   It was more or less understood that the Bank's private interests (i.e. its profits) now had to take second place to its broader responsibilities to the monetary system.[62] Though it was never made explicit, this was the price the Bank had to pay for its supremacy.

In these respects the British system of central banking in 1890 was not that dissimilar to what it is 100 years later. However, two other principles also underlay the post-Baring régime, and make that regime quite different from English central banking in the late twentieth century – the commitment to the gold standard, and the freedom of deposit banking from regulation. There is a strong case that it was these principles that made the British banking system then more stable than it is today,[63] but this is not the place to pursue that particular theme. In any case, how those principles were abandoned and what happened when they were is another long story – the story of central banking in the twentieth century.

Notes

I would like to thank Larry White and, most especially, Leslie Pressnell for detailed comments, which have improved this chapter considerably. The usual caveat applies.

1.   An example is Goodhart (1988), who emphasizes that central banking to a large extent simply evolved, but the critical issue is not the evolution *per se*, but the role that the state played in that evolution.

2. The work of Rolnick and Weber, among others, indicates that US 'free banking' before the Civil War was considerably more successful than had earlier been appreciated. Dowd (1989, ch. 5) provides an assessment of this experience. White (1984) indicates that something close to free banking worked very well in Scotland until 1845, and the work of Schuler (1988), Selgin (1988a) and Jonung (1985) indicates the competitive note issue was successful in Canada, China, and Sweden. Selgin (1988b, pp. 5–15) and Schuler (1989) provide overviews of these and other experiences of free banking.

3. There were instances where the Bank acted as lender of last resort even in the late eighteenth century. For more on these episodes, see Lovell (1957) and Ashton (1950).

4. Indeed, since the Bank had the responsibility for managing an inconvertible currency, it was more like a modern central bank during the Restriction period than it was even in 1890.

5. The precise date at which the other banks abandoned their issues is not entirely clear. Most writers suggest the 1780s, but MacLeod (1896, p. 103) reports an example of a London bank note dated April 1793.

6. The Bank apparently had a policy of refusing accommodation to those who issued their own notes, or who used other notes than those issued by the Bank. In the 1840s, for example, it granted some country banks accommodation favours in return for their using its notes instead of their own (Powell, (1915, p. 344)).

7. It is interesting to note that Hawtrey (1962, p. 131) saw the source of the central bank's power not in its being a bank of issue, but in its being a lender of last resort (and therefore, by implication, in its control of base money). He went on to say: 'If the essential character-istic of a central bank is its function as the lender of last resort rather than its privilege of note issue, that does not mean that the evolution of the former function has not been intimately associated with that of the latter. It is obvious that a bank which can create currency in an emergency out of nothing has a great advantage, in facing the responsibilities of the lender of last resort, over one which runs the risk of stopping payment.'

8. The outbreak of war in 1793 gave rise to a financial crisis. The Bank first tried to accommodate the crisis, but the directors' 'nerves could not stand the daily demand for guineas; and, for the purpose of checking the demand, they curtailed their discounts to a point never before experienced', and in the process gave the market an 'electric shock' which greatly aggravated the panic (MacLeod (1896), p. 100). The government then intervened to issue £5 million in exchequer bills, and the crisis abated. (MacLeod (1896), pp. 98–101 has a good discussion of the crisis.) This episode was highly influential in promot-ing the doctrine, put forward shortly after by Sir Francis Baring and Henry Thornton, and later by Bagehot, than an expansionary policy was the best way to handle a financial panic.

9. 'The enormous abuses which might be perpetrated by an unscrupulous government, and the dangerous power which so potent an engine as the Bank of England would confer upon them ... had inspired ... a

well-founded jealousy' and led to 'stringent precautions' in the 1694 Act against unauthorized lending to the government (MacLeod (1896), p. 104).

10.   It would be wrong, however, to blame Pitt alone for the suspension. The Bank's earlier policies also contributed to its crisis. As MacLeod (1896, p. 115) wrote: 'Never was there a more unfortunate example of monopolizing selfishness. It [the Bank] would neither establish branches of its own in the country, nor would it permit any other private company, of power and solidity, to do so, whose credit might have interposed and aided in sustaining its own. Moreover, when a failure of confidence was felt in the country notes, it refused to issue notes of its own to supply their place. The power of issuing . . . was absolutely forbidden to powerful and wealthy companies, and left in unbounded freedom to private persons – a vast number of them nothing but small shopkeepers, with no adequate capital or property to support their issues, and whose credit vanished like a puff of smoke in any public danger. The bank consequently was left alone to bear the whole brunt of the crisis, solitary and unsupported, and finally succumbed'.

11.   Bank notes were treated as if they were legal tender until their depreciation provoked Lord King in 1811 to insist on payment of his rents in gold (as he had every right to do). The response was Stanhope's Act (1811) which made Bank paper legal tender, though the government went through contortions to avoid using that term, since it reminded too many people of the assignats (Clapham (1944), pp. 31–2).

12.   The Bank started to issue £5 notes in 1795, and it began to issue £1 and £2 notes at about the time it suspended. Previously, notes of less than £5 had been banned by Act of Parliament in 1777. The reasons normally given for banning them were: (a) that they were inflationary, and (b) that the poor should be protected against losses in the event that a bank failed. The first argument does not apply to a specie standard, and the second implies that the poor cannot discriminate between 'good' and 'bad' banks. It also ignores the consideration that banning small notes effectively deprived the poor of many of the benefits of banking – a curious way to help them. One suspects that the real reason for banning small notes was to create an entry barrier against smaller banks. The extent of the government's concern for the poor can perhaps be gauged from the fact that the old objections to small notes were 'thrown to the winds' when it was realized that the issue of small notes would enable the Bank to lend more money to the government (Smith (1936), p. 12).

13.   No banker would rationally redeem his liabilities with gold when he had the legal right to give out Bank notes of the same nominal value which sold at a discount against gold. The depreciation of the Bank's notes and their legal tender thus combined to call Gresham's law into operation and drive out the 'good' (i.e. undepreciated) money from other banks' reserves.

14.   To some extent, however, their ennunciation of the 'real bills' doctrine

can be considered as an attempt to intellectualize the discount practices of the Bank which had some degree of soundness. The practice, therefore, was perhaps sounder than what the directors claimed to be doing. I am grateful to Leslie Pressnell and Bill Allen (in his discussant's comments) for pointing this out.

15. Thornton in many ways anticipated Bagehot's analysis of the lender of last resort issue, but his work tended to be forgotten and had comparatively little influence on the monetary debates later in the century. For more on Thornton, see Hayek (1939) and Hetzel (1987). Humphrey and Keleher (1984, pp. 303–5) provide a good comparison of the views of Thornton and Bagehot.

16. I would suggest two possible reasons why some of the theory of the Restriction period was later overlooked. Much of it was concerned with managing an inconvertible currency, and therefore had no relevance to monetary experience later in the century. A second, more tentative, reason, and one that applies particularly to Thornton, is that it gave too much scope for central bank 'discretion' for later economists' tastes. This would especially be the case with economists of the currency school, who devoted much of their effort to imposing 'rules' on the Bank of England.

17. Bank notes were now used by the public throughout England and Wales. In the eighteenth century, with the solitary exception of Lancashire, Bank notes did not circulate very much beyond a 60-mile radius of Charing Cross (Richards (1934), p. 195).

18. They could defy their shareholders to a certain extent by dividing them or depriving them of information. As Dodwell (1934, p. 57) notes, 'The Directors gave no statement of accounts to the Proprietors till 1832, though suits were brought by some malcontents in the attempt to compel them to do so'. For a long time the management appeared to hide behind the ancient Bank custom of secrecy to prevent shareholders obtaining information that could be used against them.

19. The relationship between the Bank and the government was never particularly clear. Their relationship was complicated further by the government's insistence that the issue of notes was a state prerogative because it trespassed on the state's 'sovereign right' to issue money. Yet at the same time as it insisted on the right to control the note issue, it acknowledged that it had no right to regulate deposits: 'The more firmly the Government stated the principle of the absolute right of the State over the note issue, the more completely it seemed to abdicate any claim to regulate, or even to ask for information about, deposits' (Fetter (1965), p. 224)).

20. Many observers blamed the crisis on 'excessive issues' by the country banks, and this view was widely accepted afterwards. However, as our earlier discussion indicates – and Wood (1939, ch. 1) confirms – the country banks had comparatively little scope to pursue policies independent of the Bank of England. One might also note that the Bank itself was under considerable pressure from the government to engage in 'cheap money' policies during the period 1822–4, and it went along with these policies only with some reluctance.

21. 'The extent to which the distress had reached was melacholy to the last degree. Persons of undoubted wealth were seen walking about the streets of London, not knowing whether they should be able to meet their engagements for the next day' (MacLeod (1896), pp. 122–3).

22. MacLeod (1896, p. 124) quotes an eminent country banker as saying: 'when the panic came country bank paper was brought in for Bank of England paper, and therefore all that was immediately wanted was an exchange of paper'. This strongly suggests that the main demand was for notes, not for gold as such, and therefore that the crisis could have been averted or ameliorated by a more expansionary note issue on the part of the Bank.

23. An old and forgotten box of £1 notes had been utilized the previous day with government approval, and the Bank had run out of £5 and £10 notes by Saturday evening (Clapham (1944), p. 100). MacLeod (1896, p. 123) appears to be mistaken when he suggests that the box of £1 notes was opened the next week.

24. There is a legend that the Bank at one point in the crisis actually did suspend, by refusing to cash £16,000 presented to it by a City banker (Powell (1915), p. 330). This story is difficult to substantiate, but even Clapham (1944, p. 101) freely admits that 'As between continued cash payments and a brief actual, if not statutory, suspension it was, as the Duke said of Waterloo, "a damned nice thing – the nearest run thing you ever saw in your life" '.

25. The government's determination to legislate was ominous for the Bank. The government had already modified the monopoly of the Bank of Ireland in 1821 in the aftermath of an Irish crisis the previous year, and this despite the opposition of the Bank of England. For more on the Irish banking reform, see Ollerenshaw (1987, p. 10) and Bodenhorn (1989). The Bank of England's privileges had also come under attack at home. In 1821, Thomas Joplin had published an influential critique of the Bank's joint-stock monopoly, and both the Prime Minister (Lord Liverpool) and the Chancellor (Robinson) were unsympathetic to the Bank's privileges. As they wrote to the Bank, 'Such privileges are out of fashion, and what expectation can they have that theirs will be renewed?' (quoted in White (1984), p. 61). In retrospect, the Bank did well in 1826.

26. The Act actually said that 'to prevent any Doubts' about the lawfulness of such action, the Bank was formally authorized to 'empower agents to carry on banking business in any place in England' (quoted in Clapham (1944), p. 107). There was nothing to stop the Bank setting up branches earlier except its own reluctance to do so. See also note 10.

27. The feeling in the country seems to have been against the extension of the Bank's charter, but the government struck a deal with the Bank and steered the Bill through Parliament. For more on this episode, see White (1984, pp. 65–8) and Dowd (1989, ch. 5).

28. What remained of the usury restrictions was finally swept away in 1854 (Clapham (1944), p. 224).

29. The Resumption Act of 1819 required the weekly average of notes in

circulation to be provided to the Privy Council, and a quarterly figure to be published in the *London Gazette*. Later on, the 1844 Act required the Bank to publish weekly returns as well (Dodwell (1934), p. 58).

30. One must bear in mind the respect in those days in which private commercial information was held. As Dodwell (1934, p. 57) observes, the Bank 'was not willing to give more than a minimum of information about its affairs even to Parliamentary Committees; this attitude was considered correct, and the committees were not inclined to force the Bank to make unwilling disclosures'. The compelling of the Bank to provide such information is therefore difficult to accont for unless one accepts that it indicated a recognition of a public responsibility by the Bank.

31. I am grateful to Leslie Pressnell for straightening out my thinking on the Palmer rule. For more on the subject, see the discussion on it in the 1832 Parliamentary Report, reprinted in T. E. Gregory (ed.) (1929, pp. 3–6) and Matthews (1954, pp. 165–76, and p. 166, n. 1). I am grateful to Pressnell for these references as well.

32. The Bank was only beginning to learn how to use Bank rate to control the levels of its reserves – see the discussion of Bank rate policy below – and it could not easily control its liabilities because they were demand-determined.

33. Horsefield (1953, p. 114) saw the Palmer rule as the Bank's attempt to put into practice Ricardo's (1817) theory that a 'currency which acted in all respects like gold, whether it consisted of coins, paper, or both together' would prevent commercial crises. Previous to that, the Bank directors had believed that the right rule was the real bills fallacy. Horsefield saw these attempts to condense 'their proper policy . . . into a simple and automatic rule' as a long-running 'delusion', resulting from their desire to 'escape from the unwanted burden of monetary management' (p. 115).

34. The Bank would have been acutely aware of this danger: recall how close the Bank came to not getting its charter extended in 1833 (see note 25).

35. The roots of the currency principle can be traced to Ricardo (1817) (see note 33) and even further back to Hume (1752). Its origins are discussed in Sayers' introductory essay in Sayers (ed.) (1963) and Robbins (1958). Its fallacies are explained in MacLeod (1896) and Andreades (1909, pp. 275–7).

36. Exactly why the Bank management suggested these provisions is something of a mystery, since the 100 per cent reserve requirement considerably reduced the Bank's profit from note-issuing. Some idea of the loss to the Bank can be gained from the figures on its note circulation. In September 1844 its note issue was £28,351,295 (Andreades (1909), p. 290). Its fiduciary issue was £14 million, so the Bank had to hold the difference between these two figures in gold at the Banking Department. This difference – £14,351,295 – overstates the cost to the Bank in so far as the Bank would have held some gold against the note issue, but it takes no account of the likelihood that the Bank's note issue would have increased over time. It is therefore not

unreasonable to consider it as a ballpark figure for the cost of the reserve requirement to the Bank. To give it some perspective, it is not far off the size of the Banking Department's average reserve. Against this cost, the 1844 Act also gave the Bank the note privileges it had been hankering for, and consolidated its position as the Government's bank. It therefore seems probable that the Bank embraced the currency school because it gave the Bank an excuse to push for the privileges that the bank really wanted, and the reserve requirement was simply the price that the Bank had to pay to get it.

One might add that Peel would have liked to abolish the 'private' note issues there and then, but he allowed them to continue to avoid the political consequences of taking on the bankers' lobby. Nevertheless, clause 25 of the Act envisaged private note issues continuing only until 1856. The bankers' clung to their local note privileges even after 1856, however, and the last English private note issue (Fox, Fowler and Co., of Wellington in Somerset) did not disappear until 1921. I would like to thank Professor Pressnell for this information.

37.   In the 1820s, Peel was convinced that 'the root of the evil [of crises] lay in the monopoly of the Bank of England' (MacLeod (1896), p. 128), but by this time he had come round to the views of the currency school. He was influenced both by the arguments put foward by the currency school and by the lessons he drew from the failure of issuing banks (such as the Bath Bank in 1841). His main argument against free banking was that competition would undermine the quality of the currency. He had apparently abandoned his own earlier arguments about the superiority of the Scottish system of banking. Peel's arguments are summarized in MacLeod (1896, pp. 128–9) and Andreades (1909, pp. 285–8).

38.   In the event that any note-issuing bank gave up its right to issue, the Bank was allowed to increase its own fiduciary (i.e. unbacked) issue by up to two-thirds of the amount of the lapsed note issue.

39.   Note, however, that the 1844 Act did not remove the ambiguity about the Bank's responsibility, and there were some who believed that the Bank still had a public responsiblity, even though it was not defined by legislation. The House Committee on Commercial Distress (1847–8) 'clearly asserted that the Bank had a special public responsibility in the conduct of its banking business' (Dodwell (1934), p. 63). It went on to say that the Bank's unique circumstances – including its 'special and exclusive privileges' and its 'peculiar relation to the Government' – imposed on it the 'duty of a consideration of the public interest, not indeed enacted or defined by law, but which Parliament . . . has always recognised and which the Bank has never disclaimed' (quoted in Dodwell, *loc. cit.*).

40.   For more on this panic, see Andreades (1909, pp. 331–42) or Powell (1915, pp. 343–63).

41.   For more on this episode, see Andreades (1909, pp. 343–52); MacLeod (1896, pp. 156–61); Powell (1915, pp. 364–94).

42.   Again, subject to the proviso that it keep Bank rate at no less than 10 per cent.

43. This period lasted till the Baring crisis, and it was disturbed only by the comparatively minor crisis occasioned by the failure of the City of Glasgow Bank in 1878. For more on the 1866 crisis, see Andreades (1909, pp. 353–61); MacLeod (1890, pp. 162–6), or Powell (1915, pp. 395–410).

44. He also suggested that the Bank Charter Act be amended with an expansive clause to allow the Bank to issue additional emergency currency without having to rely on the government to offer it a Bill of Indemnity.

45. Note, for instance, the comment of Andreades (1909, p. 326): 'the bankers have always refused to [hold more reserves], being convinced that in case of need the Government would always intervene to save the Bank of England'.

46. Apart from Sir Francis Baring and Thornton who originated the doctrine at the end of the eighteenth century, it was also supported by John Stuart Mill and was consistent with the views of the Banking School, whose leader Tooke consistently advocated that the Bank should hold a bigger reserve, and denied that it was just a joint stock bank like any other.

47. One reason for the support of this view within the Court would have been the argument that lending expansively in a crisis gave the Bank the best chances of surviving it. A second reason would have been that financial panics gave the Bank the opportunity to make 'arbitrage profits' by buying up assets at bargain-basement prices. Both these reasons are based on the Bank's own self-interest. A third reason, mentioned earlier, is that the members of the Court would have had personal interests in ensuring that the Bank led support to the firms they worked for or did business with.

48. Pressnell argues in correspondence that Bagehot had something of a fixation about the level of reserves. Bagehot tended to overlook that a significant part of bankers' balances at the Bank was for clearing purposes, and was therefore unlikely to be removed. As far as the Bank was concerned, the serious withdrawal risk attached only to 'hot money' balances, which were only part of the deposits held at the Bank. I agree with this, though subject to the potential qualifications discussed in note 58. Professor Pressnell also points out that 2 years after *Lombard Street*, Bagehot retreated somewhat from his earlier position on reserves in his evidence to the Select Committee on Banks of Issue (see Pressnell (1968) and St. John-Stevas (ed.) (1979, pp. 104–55)).

49. Bagehot himself was aware of the problem, even if he did not provide a convincing resolution to it: 'It is with serious difficulty that the same bank which keeps the ultimate reserve should also have the duty of lending in the last resort. The two functions are, in practice, inconsistent – one prescribes keeping money, and the other prescribes parting with it' (*The Economist*, 1 September 1866).

50. He also failed to appreciate that any reserve rule the Bank adopted (e.g. a working minimum of £15 million) might itself create problems as the reserve fell to the target minimum.

51. Had he appreciated the link between Bank rate policy and the reserve, Sayers suggests he 'could scarcely have worried quite so much about the size of the reserve' (1958, p. 15).

52. The idea originated with Thornton's evidence to the Lords' Committee on the Bank Restriction in 1797. The theory of bank rate was explained by Palmer to the 1832 Parliamentary Committee, and Hawtrey was of the opinion that the theory of Bank rate he put forward there was substantially the same as that propounded by the Cunliffe Committe in 1918.

53. In fact, Bank rate had been used earlier, in 1822, when the Bank was criticized for keeping it too high. This had led to open disagreement between the Bank and the government, but the Bank eventually gave in and lowered its discount rate.

54. Wood (1939, p. 86) and Clapham (1944) have made it clear that the Bank did engage in open market operations, though disguised ones, and writers earlier than them – and also Hawtrey – have tended to misunderstand the Bank's *modus operandi*.

55. In the exceptional cases where Bank rate fell below market rate (e.g. in November 1838, see Andreades (1909, p. 267)), the Bank faced considerable additional losses, as it would have attracted all the market demand for discounts.

56. An interesting question is why the Bank retained any discount business. While an ordinary market operator would not usually wish to deal with the Bank on such terms, the Bank always had at least a potential market with the discount houses. See also the discussion of the 1858 rule in the text.

57. I should like to thank Leslie Pressnell for this information on the 1858 rule. Note, however, that the 1858 rule only reduced the Bank's moral hazard problem and it did not eliminate it.

58. A problem that was never satisfactorily solved was the vulnerability of the British banking system to the danger of large – and especially politically motivated – withdrawals of gold from abroad. Bagehot had worried about it but had no solution. The problem was aggravated by the Bank's small reserve. In the 1860s, for instance, the Bank's reserve varied between £12 million and £24 million – considerably less than the reserves of such foreign central banks as the Bank of France and later the Reichsbank, and very small compared to the value of the Bank's demand liabilities (Hawtrey, (1938), p. 41). An ill-disposed foreign government would have had little difficulty in mounting a very serious threat to the basis of English credit: 'the inferiority of England in this respect [i.e. its low reserves] was dangerous owing to the difficulty of rapidly attracting gold; gold could always be obtained, but time was necessary . . . [given how easy conspiracies could be formed] an attack on the English stock of bullion would be a most simple matter' (Andreades (1909), p. 372).

59. The Baring crisis is discussed in more detail in Pressnell (1968) and Ziegler (1988).

60. 'There was no formal acceptance of Bagehot's views by the Bank, and both in and out of the Bank there were those who did not like them . . .

Increasingly this [opposition to Bagehot] was a minority view. From the middle 1870's the principle was no longer in doubt, although there might, as in 1890 or 1907, be a question as to how that principle was to be put into effect. The Bank of England as a lender of last resort was ... accepted as the foundation of monetary and banking orthodoxy' (Fetter (1965), pp. 274–5).

61. That tradition was much more complex than the simple acceptance of any 'Bagehot principle' as Fetter seems to suggest. What was accepted was the need for central bank support, but as the Baring crisis indicates, the kind of support the Bank gave went beyond Bagehot and contradicted him in significant ways. The widespread idea that central banks simply accepted Bagehot's advice is a myth.

62. There seems to have been considerably less concern about the Bank's profits in the later part of the nineteenth century. As the Bank's profits did not significantly increase, one can only suppose that this represented resignation on the part of the Bank and its shareholders that their profits now had to take second place.

63. At least if one judges stability on the basis of inflation or interest rate volatility. For more on the destabilizing effects of twentieth-century central banking, see Dowd (1989, ch. 6).

References

ALLEN, W. A. (1989) 'Discussant's Comments' on this paper, appearing in F. CAPIE and G. E. WOOD (eds) (1990) *Unregulated Banking: Chaos or Order?* (London: Macmillan).

ANDREADES, A. (1909) *History of the Bank of England, 1640 to 1903*, 4th edition reprinted in 1966, with an introduction by P. Einzig (London: Frank Cass and Co.).

ASHTON, T. S. (1959) *Economic Fluctuations in England, 1700–1800*, (Oxford: The Clarendon Press).

BAGEHOT, W. (1873) *Lombard Street: A Description of the Money Market*, revised editions, 1906 and 1962 (London: Kegan Paul, Trench, Troubner and Co.; and Homewood, Ill.: Dow Jones-C. Irwin 1962, respectively).

BODENHORN, H. (1989) 'Irish Free Banking', unpublished ms, Rutgers University, NJ; forthcoming in K. Dowd (ed.) (1991) *The Experience of Free Banking* (London: Routledge).

CLAPHAM, Sir J. (1944) *The Bank of England: A History*, Vol. II: *1797–1914* (Cambridge: Cambridge University Press).

DODWELL, D. W. (1934) *Treasuries and Central Banks, Especially in England and the United States* (London: P. S. King and Son).

DOWD, K (1989) *The State and the Monetary System* (Oxford: Philip Allan).

THE ECONOMIST (1866), 'Editorials', 1 and 22 September.

FETTER, F. W. (1965) *Development of British Monetary Orthodoxy, 1797–1875* (Cambridge, Mass.: Harvard University Press).

GOODHART, C. A. E. (1988) *The Evolution of Central Banks* (Cambridge, Mass. and London: MIT Press).

GREGORY, Sir T. E. (ed.) (1929) *Select Statutes, Documents, and Reports Relating to British Banking, 1832–1928* (Oxford: Oxford University Press).

HANKEY, T. (1867) *The Principles of Banking* (London).

HAWTREY, R. G. (1938) *A Century of Bank Rate* (London: Longman, Green and Co.).

HAWTREY, R. G. (1962) *The Art of Central Banking*, 2nd edition (London: Frank Cass and Co).

HAYEK, F. A. (1939) 'Introduction' to F. A. Hayek (ed.) *An Enquiry into the Nature and Effects of the Paper Credit of Great Britain [1802] by H. Thornton* (New York: Rinehart and Co.).

HETZEL, R. L. (1987) 'Henry Thornton: Seminal Monetary Theorist and Father of the Modern Central Bank', Federal Reserve Bank of Richmond, *Economic Review* (July–August), pp. 3–16.

HORSEFIELD, J. K. (1944) 'The Origins of the Bank Charter Act, 1844', in T. S. Ashton and R. S. Sayers (eds) (1953) *Papers in English Monetary History* (Oxford: Clarendon Press; reprinted from *Economica*).

HUME, D. (1752) 'Of Money', incorporated D. Hume (1758) *Essays, Moral, Political and Literary* (London: Oxford University Press, 1962 reprint).

HUMPHREY, T. M. and R. E. KELEHER (1984) 'The Lender of Last Resort: A Historical Perspective', *Cato Journal*, Vol. 4, no. 1, pp. 275–318.

JONUNG, L. (1985) 'The Economics of Private Money: The Experience of Private Notes in Sweden, 1831–1902', paper presented to the Monetary History Group Meeting, London (September).

JOPLIN, T. (1822) *An Essay on the General Principles and Present Practice of Banking, in England and Scotland* (Newcastle: Edward Walker).

KINDLEBERGER, C. P. (1978) *Manias, Panics, and Crashes: A History of Financial Crises* (New York: Basic Books).

LOVELL, M. C. (1957) 'The Role of the Bank of England as Lender of Last Resort in the Crises of the Eighteenth Century', *Explorations in Entrepreneurial History*, 11 (October), pp. 8–21.

LOYD, S. (1837) *Further Reflections on the State of the Currency and the Action of the Bank of England* (London: Pelham Richardson).

MACLEOD, H. D. (1896) 'A History of Banking in Great Britain; With a Historic Analysis of the Principles Governing Banking, Currency, and Credit', in W. G. Sumner (ed.) (1896) *A History of Banking in All the Leading Nations*, Vol. II (New York: Augustus M. Kelley, 1971 reprint).

MATTHEWS, R. C. O. (1954) *A Study in Trade-Cycle Theory: Economic Fluctuation in Great Britain, 1833–1842* (Cambridge: Cambridge University Press).

OLLERENSHAW, P. (1987) *Banking in Nineteenth Century Ireland* (Manchester: Manchester University Press).

POWELL, E. T. (1915 and 1966) *The Evolution of the Money Market, 1385–1915* (London: Frank Cass and Co.).

PRESSNELL, L. S. (1956) *Country Banking in the Industrial Revolution* (Oxford: Clarendon Press).

PRESSNELL, L. S. (1968) 'Gold Reserves, Banking Reserves, and the Baring Crisis of 1890', in C. R. Whittlesey and J. S. G. Wilson (eds) *Essays in Money and Banking* (Oxford: Clarendon Press).

RICARDO, D. (1817) *Proposals for an Economical and Secure Currency* (London).

RICHARDS, R. D. (1929) *The Early History of Banking in England* (London: P. S. King and Son).

ROBBINS, L. C. (1958) *Robert Torrens and the Evolution of Classical Economics* (London: Macmillan).

ROCKOFF, H. (1986) 'Walter Bagehot and the Theory of Central Banking', in F. Capie and G. E. Wood (eds) *Financial Crises and the World Banking System* (London: Macmillan).

ST. JOHN STEVAS, N. (ed.) (1978) *The Collected Works of Walter Bagehot*, Vol. 11 (London: The Economist).

SAYERS, R. S. (1958) 'The Development of Central Banking After Bagehot', in R. S. Sayers, *Central Banking after Bagehot* (Oxford: Clarendon Press).

SAYERS, R. S. (ed.) (1963) *Economic Writings of James Pennington* (London: London School of Economics and Political Science).

SCHULER, K. (1988) *The Evolution of Canadian Banking, 1867–1914*, unpublished manuscript, University of Georgia, Athens, GA.

SCHULER, K. (1989) 'The World History of Free Banking', unpublished manuscript, University of Georgia, Athens, GA.

SELGIN, G. A. (1988a) 'Free Banking in China, 1800–1935', unpublished manuscript, University of Hong Kong.

SELGIN, G. A. (1988b) *The Theory of Free Banking: Money Supply Under Competitive Note Issue* (Totowa, NJ: Rowman and Littlefield; Washington: Cato Institute).

SMITH, V. C. (1936) *The Rationale of Central Banking* (London: P. S. King and Son).

THORNTON, H. (1802) *An Enquiry into the Nature and Effects of the Paper Credit of Great Britain*, edited with an introduction by F. A. Hayek (1939) (New York: Rinehart and Co.).

TIMBERLAKE, R. H., JR. (1978) *The Origins of Central Banking in the United States* (Cambridge, Mass. and London: Harvard University Press).

VINER, J. (1937) *Studies in the Theory of International Trade* (London: George Allen and Unwin).

WHITE, L. H. (1984) *Free Banking in Britain: Theory, Experience, and Debate, 1800–1845* (Cambridge: Cambridge University Press).

WOOD, E. (1939) *English Theories of Central Banking Control, 1819–1858, With Some Account of Contemporary Procedure* (Cambridge, Mass.: Harvard University Press).

ZIEGLER, P. (1988) *The Sixth Great Power: Barings, 1762–1929* (London: Collins).

Comment on Chapter 5
W. A. Allen

Dr Dowd's review of the development of central banking in England in the nineteenth century is prefaced by some more general remarks to the effect that 'unregulated' banking systems of the past – i.e. systems without a central bank – had a better record of stability than those which did have a central bank. With this as his starting point, it is natural for him to wonder why central banking developed, and that is the main theme of the paper.

If I understand it correctly, Dr Dowd's analysis of developments in the nineteenth century is that the special privileges enjoyed by the Bank of England were so extensive and important that they put other banks into an unnaturally weak competitive position. As a result, other banks were prone to crises of confidence, manifested in 'runs on the bank', and, moreover, when such crises occurred, they were not so well able to handle them by themselves than they otherwise would have been. I would like to examine the credibility of this thesis.

Two main privileges are adduced in this connection: the restriction on other banks in England and Wales to partnerships of no more than six with unlimited liability; and the restrictions on other banks' note issues. The partnership restriction, however, became much less significant with the advent of joint stock banks after 1826, but the crises did not come to an end, and for that reason I find it hard to see it as a complete answer to questions about the source of instability in the banking system in the nineteenth century as a whole.

The restrictions on other banks' note issues were permanent, and it is interesting to read that their tightening in 1826 after a crisis 'reflected a widespread opinion that the issue of small notes had been a major contributory factor to the commercial crisis'. In other words, contemporary observers plainly did not share Dr Dowd's view of the consequences of note issue restrictions; I think it is imprudent to attach no weight to their opinion.

Nevertheless, it is not incredible to suggest that, in the long-term, restrictions on commercial banks' note issue, by limiting their access to an important source of funding, had the effect of inducing them to make higher-yielding and higher-risk loans than they otherwise would have done. If they mispriced the risks they were taking on, then they would have made themselves vulnerable to loss of confidence among their creditors. Moreover, it is also possible to argue that if commercial banks had been able to have larger note issues, assuming that notes were a more stable source of funds than deposits, then they might have been more easily able to ride out crises of confidence. A possible analogue in our own times is Continental Illinois, which is said to have suffered from its inability to develop a stable deposit base because of the restrictions on bank branching imposed by Illinois state legislation. It is, however, not credible that banks struggling with the consequences of a loss of confidence among their depositors could in those circumstances have issued additional notes to replace lost deposits, because the root of the problem would not have been a surge in demand for notes at the expense of deposits, but rather a surge in demand for the liabilities of banks perceived as safe – in particular the Bank of England – at the expense of liabilities of other banks.

To summarize the argument, it is not impossible to believe that restrictions on banks' note issues made the banking system somewhat less robust than it might otherwise have been. However, it requires a considerable leap in logic to get from this proposition to the quite different, and to me implausible, proposition that without the note restriction there would have been no crises at all, or very many fewer crises.

Moreover, if crises there were to be, the history of the times suggests that it was quite useful to have a central bank around. Indeed, the conventional wisdom is that it was precisely because there was an evident need for a central bank that the Bank of England developed into one. Dr Dowd appears at one point to suggest that banking panics were fuelled by the Bank of England's unwillingness to provide notes to meet demand. But while it was subject to the provisions of the 1844 Bank Charter Act, the Bank had no choice in the matter; Dr Dowd's criticism should therefore be directed at the inflexibility of the Act. It is interesting to note that that inflexibility created an essential operational role for the government in the period after 1844, because it was the government which in times of crisis released the Bank from the provisions of the Bank Charter Act, thereby enabling the Bank to make more of its own notes available to satisfy the surge in demand arising from what would now be called a 'flight to quality'.

Dr Dowd's narrative covers ground which has of course been well-trodden by economic historians. I had some difficulty with the suggestion that during the Napoleonic wars the Bank had the power to manipulate the reserves of the banking system as it pleased, because in reality it could hardly have refused requests from the Government for advances. Indeed Dr Dowd acknowledges as much elsewhere in the paper, though in speculating about the Bank's motives for acquiescing in government requests, he neglects to mention the most obvious one, namely the desire not to obstruct the prosecution of the war.

Dr Dowd also refers to the 'real bills doctrine', which has had a generally bad press. If the real bills doctrine is interpreted as a kind of cure-all prescription for central bankers – i.e., if it is suggested that all central bankers needed to do to maintain the value of the currency was to observe the real bills doctrine – then, of course, its bad press is amply deserved. But it can be interpreted in a much more modest way. On this interpretation it simply says that, other things being equal, bills are a safer investment for banks the shorter the pay-off period of the project they are financing, and that banks with liquid liabilities ought to be wary of financing projects which do not promise a pay-off in the near future. In this less objectionable form, what has been called the real bills doctrine is no more than a piece of horse sense for commercial bankers. Which interpretation is the right one is a matter for historians of economic literature. But at a time when the Bank of England had not yet fully assumed or had publicly thrust upon it the mantle of a central bank, it is perhaps not surprising that it explained its operations in public in the same terms as those which might have been used by the management of a prudently run commercial bank.[1]

On the larger questions raised by Dr Dowd, my own conclusion from the evidence would be that the conventional wisdom about the development of central banking in this country in the nineteenth century, namely that it was a gradual and, on the whole, well-directed response to a real problem, stands up well, and that the contrary case – that central banking was a destabilizing influence – is far from proven.

Note

1. See J. A. Schumpeter, *History of Economic Analysis* (George Allen and Unwin), p. 696.

Comment on Chapter 5

Michael Collins

I have been impressed with Dr Dowd's survey of 100 years or more of English central banking. On the whole this is efficiently done, with most of the main milestones well illuminated, although I believe more perhaps could have been made of the City's international role and how this affected the Bank of England's position. Generally, though, I have few disputes with his brief portrayal of the historical facts.

But there are problems over interpretation, for I believe his eagerness to advocate a free-banking case cannot be derived from the historical record of this period, at least as he has presented it. In places in the paper I found his arguments a bit confusing and his evidence contradictory – at the minimum, the case for non-regulation is unproven and the case for greater regulation is equally strong. It is essentially a judgemental, subjective intepretation that he presents.

Before looking at Dr Dowd's contentions in a little detail, I should like to raise a general, maybe banal, question: namely, what do we mean by a 'central bank'? In his paper Dr Dowd adopts a minimalist approach. He accepts that he is dealing with the institution that acts as lender of last resort to the financial system and with that institution which is responsible for maintaining the value of the domestic currency. But we know, of course, that a central bank can be much more than this – it may (as in the case of the Bank of England) have important additional functions regarding the servicing of public sector debt, or (as has been the case in twentieth-century Europe) it may be an integral part of the state's economic policy-making machinery (with broad responsibilities, say, for stimulating industrial development or for facilitating the monetary changes necessary to accommodate a full-employment budget).[1] Obviously questions of regulation and deregulation for such a creature are wholly different from the ones dealt with in Dr Dowd's paper. It is obvious, but too easily forgotten, that English central-bank experience was in many respects exceptional.

But, to return to this limiting case of England in the nineteenth century, Dr Dowd asserts that the evidence supports his two main hypotheses. Namely:

1   That central banking in England did not evolve to counter market instability.
2   That legislative restrictions were major contributing factors in the liquidity crises of the mid-nineteenth century.

Now I would agree that there is some truth in both these contentions but, left as they are, they are highly selective interpretations which I believe detract from our understanding of what really happened.

Let us consider the first hypothesis that central banking in England did *not* evolve to counter market instability.

I wholeheartedly agree with Dr Dowd that a critical part of the story of the Bank's evolution as a central bank arose from the early privileges conferred on it by the state. These secured high esteem and ensured the safety and acceptability of its liabilities. But it was only part of the story. Another critical part was the response of the government and legislature to market instability. On occasions this intervention imposed more regulations on money market institutions (including the Bank of England); on other occasions, though, it reduced regulatory controls. In addition, whereas it sometimes favoured the Bank, at other times it damaged the Bank's interests. There is little need to go into detail because Dr Dowd recalls all the main interventionist measures in his paper, but what he does not acknowledge is that many were responses to instability either as immediate measures or (more commonly) after a period of more considered public and parliamentary debate. Among the most important of those bearing on the Bank of England's development as a central bank were:

1   The restoration of gold convertibility after a period of price and exchange rate instability during the Restriction Period.
2   The abolition of notes of under £5 denomination in 1826 (effective in 1829).
3   The encouragement given to the Bank in 1826 to open provincial branches (and, thus, facilitate its note issuing and tax-collecting functions).
4   The establishment of Bank of England notes as legal tender in 1833.
5   The 1844 restriction on rival note issues and the completion of the gold standard legislation with the passing of the Bank Charter Act.

All were – to some degree – attempts to instil greater stability into the system (as, indeed, were the attacks on the Bank's joint-stock monopoly in 1826 and 1833).[2] In the real, historical world there was market instability and this did provoke political response; and it did affect how the Bank of England developed as a central bank.

Now for the second hypothesis, that legislative restrictions were probably the major contributory factor to the monetary crises of 1826, 1847, 1857 and 1866.

Two main types of restrictions are stressed by Dr Dowd. The first was the restriction to six on the maximum number of partners permitted in English and Welsh banks, which was not removed until 1826 for provincial banks and not until 1833 for banks operating in London. This was undoubtedly an unnecessary restriction on the supply of proprietors' capital available to banks, and the undue small scale of English banks probably added to the 'domino effect' of bank failures during the crisis of 1826.

Even so, a number of caveats are in order. Apart from this restriction and that on the issue of small notes, the system in the early 1820s was exceptionally free from regulation. For instance, there were no regulations regarding minimum capitalization, nor official rules governing liquidity or the general composition of portfolios. In a different world perhaps the debacle of 1826 might have led to demands for more regulation, not less. The second caveat is that removal of the limitation on the number of partners did not induce an immediate transformation. Private banking remained an important sector in England and Wales for a very long time. There were 327 private banks in 1850 and 236 in 1875 – still accounting for some two-thirds of the total number at the later date and responsible for operating about one-third of the banking offices in England and Wales – although, throughout, they were losing ground to the new joint stock banks.[3] Moreover, crises did not disappear once the restriction on partners was removed; the 'reform' was no magic wand.

The second was the restriction on private sector note issuing. Dr Dowd, of course, has an explanation of why crises did not disappear, he points to the state's error in imposing new restrictions, those on the note-issue. In particular, he is keen to argue that in the liquidity crises of 1847, 1857 and 1866 the imposition of these restrictions was a – perhaps *the* – major factor in provoking the crises. Now, the operation of the 1844 Bank Charter Act was a factor – how could it fail to be? – but only in a similar way that the dockers' strike of 1967 was a factor in the devaluation of that year. It was part of the story but not a critical part.

Dr Dowd emphasizes that in a liquidity crisis the banking sector cannot meet the public's demand for bank liabilities. It is important to acknowledge, of course, that this is not an argument in favour of removing restrictions on non-Bank of England notes. Typically in a crisis it seems that the demand for the liabilities of the generality of deposit banks fell, as the public switched to currency (including Bank of England liabilities). Notes issues by banks other than the Bank of England attracted some opprobrium in such circumstances – instead, the public preferred to hold more coin and Bank of England notes (and, in fact, the banking sector as a whole also built up balances at the Bank).[4] Indeed, one argument of some of the so-called 'reformers' – or 'interventionists', if you like – of the early nineteenth century was that monopolization of the note issue, whether in the hands of the Bank of England or not, might reduce public anxieties in future crises.[5]

So, to the extent that Dr Dowd's argument is valid it is not an argument in favour of an unrestricted note issue *per se*.

But even when we come to consider restrictions on Bank of England notes, it is possible to put a completely different interpretation on events. Dr Dowd argues that if the restrictions had not been in place, then the crises would have been less severe. Maybe, maybe not. Before 1844 the restrictions were not in force, of course, but there were still bank runs in 1826, 1837 and 1839. Just as significant, there were liquidity crises after 1866 when the Bank Charter Act did not have to be suspended and the impact of its stipulations is not considered to have been important. In particular, during the severe crisis of 1878 the Bank found itself able to meet the demand for legal tender because of the effectiveness of Bank rate changes and because it was able to tap into the world's supply of monetary gold (in this instance, partly from the coffers of the Bank of France).[6]

The point I am making, then, is this. History shows that crises arose, subsided or were avoided during this period irrespective of whether the regulations of the 1844 Bank Charter Act were in operation. The critical factor, as Dr Dowd rightly says, was the ability and willingness of the central bank to act as lender of last resort. To me, the fact that the Bank of England came unstuck on occasions is at least as much an argument for greater regulation as it is for less. Would the problem not have been eased if, say, the state had taken a monopoly of the supply of legal tender, had established a national bank and had stipulated that it hold a gold reserve adequate to meet all contingencies?

But we did not get this, of course. Instead the nineteenth-century evolution of central banking took place in a largely unregulated environment – one in which a laissez-faire, non-interventionist philosophy dominated. In these circumstances (and, of course, within the constraint of gold convertibility), it was left to the market to determine the adequacy of the reserves, to sort out the proportion to be held by the various private sector institutions, to arrange the means by which the institutions could gain access to currency in an emergency, to develop the means by which to accommodate international pressures on the reserves, so on. It was a largely unregulated system. So, criticisms from 'free banking' advocates seem somewhat misplaced and run some danger of being turned into arguments in favour of more state involvement, not less.

Notes

1. Gianni Toniolo (ed.) (1988) *Central Banks' Independence in Historical Perspective* (Berlin and New York: Walter de Gruyte).
2. The various Parliamentary enquiries of the period clearly reveal contemporary concerns. These anxieties are fully discussed in Frank Whitson Fetter (1965) *Development of British Monetary Orthodoxy, 1797–1875* (Cambridge, Mass.: Harvard University Press), where detailed bibliographical notes are given.
3. Michael Collins (1988) *Money and Banking in the UK. A History*, p. 52 (London: Croom Helm).
4. Michael Collins (1988) 'English Banks and the Mid-Nineteenth Century Business Cycle', in P. L. Cottrell and D. E. Moggridge (eds) (1988) *Money and Power*, pp. 1–39 (Macmillan).
5. Among a mixed group of commentators see Robert Torrens (1837) *A Letter to the Right Honourable Lord Viscount Melbourne*; J. Horsley Palmer (1837) *The Causes and Consequences of the Pressure upon the Money Market* (1837); Samson Ricardo (1837) *Observation on the Recent Pamphlet of J. Horsley Palmer* (1837) and *A National Bank the Remedy for the Evils Attendant upon our Present System of Paper Currency* (1838); George Wade Norman (1838) *Remarks upon Some Prevalent Errors, with Respect to Currency and Banking.*
6. Michael Collins (1989) 'The Banking Crisis of 1878', *Economic History Review*, XLII, pp. 504–27.

6 Does Bank Regulation Produce Stability? Lessons from the United States

George J. Benston

Two aspects of stability should be distinguished: systemic stability and the stability of individual banks. The effect of the failure of individual banks on the stability of the financial system is considered first. This leads to the conclusion that the central bank alone can maintain systemic stability. Although individual bank failures may set off runs that result in multiple bank failures, this outcome can be prevented by central-bank actions, even when very large banks fail. The role of the Federal Reserve in preventing systemic collapse is then analysed and found wanting. Payments system risk also is considered; regulations that restrict branching have given the Fed a monopoly over nationwide check clearance, which has exacerbated the risk.

Regulation affects individual bank stability in four main ways: constraints on diversification, effects on profitability, limits on opportunities for and incentives of bank owners and managers toward risk-taking or avoidance, and interventions through monitoring, supervising, and preventing fraud and grossly incompetent management. Each of these influences is discussed. The general conclusion is that regulation tends to be destabilizing because diversification is restricted, profitability is reduced, and risk-taking is encouraged (as a consequence primarily of deposit insurance). While supervision is necessary, it generally has not been adequate.

Finally, alternative explanations for regulation are considered.

INDIVIDUAL BANK FAILURES AS CAUSES OF SYSTEMIC FAILURE

The failure of individual banks can affect systemic stability and economic well-being in two principal ways – reduction of the money supply and constraints on credit. The more important is the effect of bank failure on the money supply. As is well known, a fractional reserve banking system is particularly subject to exogenous changes in high-powered money. When banks fail, deposits against which fractional reserves are held may be converted to currency, which is 100 per cent reserve money. When the United States was on the gold standard, specie could be exported or hoarded, with a resulting decrease in bank reserves and in the money supply. This could have occurred, for example, in 1890, when the London banking firm of Baring Brothers, which specialized in financing US enterprises, failed. Its European creditors demanded that Americans pay their debts in gold. The outflow of gold resulted in a liquidity squeeze, but prompt action was taken by the New York Clearing House, which issued certificates to banks experiencing runs, thereby preventing a panic from spreading (Schwartz, 1986, p. 18). However, the failure of the Erie Railroad and fears that silver advocates would force the United States off the gold standard led to the removal of reserves from New York banks, the panic of 1893, and the suspension of 491 commercial banks (*op. cit.*, p. 19). Another example is the failure in 1907 of the Knickerbocker Trust Company of New York City, when it was unable to meet nervous customers' demands for gold. The bank suspended operations (until 1908) and other trust companies experienced runs.[1] When the New York Clearing House was tardy in issuing certificates, the result was the Panic of 1907 (*op. cit.*, p. 20).

The failure of one or more banks thus can result in a run on other solvent banks. The attempt by these banks to sell assets to meet their depositors' demands could result in lower 'fire sale' asset prices. The losses incurred could be sufficient to drive these banks into insolvency. However, if the withdrawn funds are redeposited in other banks, and if the average bank-desired reserve ratio did not change, the money supply would not be affected. There is reason to believe, though, that desired reserves would increase as bankers who survived runs kept resources on hand (e.g. gold and currency in the vault) to demonstrate that they could meet depositors' demands. When low interest rates accompany financial distress (as often occurs), the opportunity cost of this strategy is small. Indeed, such was the situation in the United States in the early 1930s. As Friedman and Schwartz (1963, pp. 511–34) discuss, banks held reserves considerably in excess of requirements. They show that when the Federal Reserve increased reserve requirements in 1936–7 to 'mop up' what it believed were excess reserves that might fuel inflation, individual banks responded by increasing reserves, thereby pulling down the money supply and causing a sharp recession.

The failure of banks also may result in a reduction in credit availability, as the failed institutions are no longer available as sources of loans. As Bernanke (1983) points out, the failure of many banks in rural areas and small towns, where there were few alternative sources of credit, apparently restricted economic activity and increased the holding of currency.[2] However, very few towns and no cities were deprived of banking services in the 1930s. Where branch banking is permitted there has been almost no serious disruption in banking services (Benston and Kaufman, 1988, pp. 18–20).

It should be noted that the prevention of bank runs and failures may increase financial instability. The possibility of runs gives bank owners incentives to control risks and hold higher levels of capital so as to obviate or meet depositors' demands for funds. Similarly, were the possibility of failures eliminated, bank owners would be foolish to forgo risk-taking activities, as they would gain the benefits but not fully incur the losses that might result.

THE ROLE OF THE FEDERAL RESERVE AS A REGULATOR

The Federal Reserve was established to prevent systemic failures. It can produce as much high-powered money as is necessary to offset any desires of the public to hoard or export base money. Further, by means of its role as lender of last resort, the Fed can delay the legal insolvency of any institution and prevent fire sales losses. However, in exercising this power, it runs the risk of expanding the money supply beyond the growth of the economy, thus causing inflation, with an attendant redistribution (and waste) of resources as people restructure relationships to deal with unexpected changes in the value of contracts. The Fed also has (or acts as if it believes it has) control over interest rates, which followers of Keynes (and others) say importantly affects the economy.

The essential role of the Fed

It is clear that financial system collapse can be prevented by the central bank. Short of nuclear war, which relegates concern for financial instability to insignificance, financial collapse cannot occur if the Fed takes the appropriate action. In support of this strong assertion, consider the US banking equivalent of a nuclear war – the default by countries such as Mexico on their debts, with the results that several banks, large and small, become insolvent. In the first instance, the stockholders and possibly the *de facto* uninsured creditors of these banks lose some or all of the wealth they have invested. In the United States, losses also probably would be incurred by the Federal Deposit Insurance Corporation (FDIC). In effect, there would be a shift of wealth from these persons and organizations to the taxpayers and public officials of the defaulting countries, to the extent that the defaults were not anticipated.[3] Second, if banks were closed rather than reorganized, there probably would be a loss of wealth as banking relationships were disrupted – in particular, funds would not be available to the failed banks' customers as expected, and some customers would have to establish new banking connections. Third, some additional wealth would be lost as lawyers were diverted from more productive pursuits, such as suing doctors and airlines, to suing auditors and bank directors, and as bank examiners and supervisors were shifted from preventing frauds to sorting out the mess. Fourth, there might be some foreign policy effects. But there is no reason to expect a systemic collapse.

Loss of consumer confidence

Those fearful of a systemic collapse have argued that there would be a loss of consumer confidence in the banking system should major or many banks fail. Depositors might fear that other banks were similarly subject to failure. However, this fear, even if contagious, should not result in a systemic collapse, as shown by the following description of what people who fear other failures might do.

First, consider the options available to holders of large deposit balances. They can either shift their balances to presumably safe banks or use the balances to purchase securities or other assets they believe to be safe from default. Keeping the funds in currency is not an option, except for those few who have large, secure vaults. Even then, these former depositors not only lose the use of their funds for transactions purposes (which, presumably, is the reason they were holding the balances), but also they lose interest earnings that, say, US government bills could yield. If the funds were deposited in other banks, there would be no decline in the money supply and no systemic liquidity problem (though transactions costs to the banking system would be greater). If safe securities were purchased, it seems clear that the sellers of the securities would deposit the funds in some bank, thus returning the funds to the banking system. (If they did not trust any bank, they would not have sold the securities for cash.) This is not to say that there would be no effects on the financial system – interest rates would increase somewhat and costs would be incurred as securities were traded and bank acounts were changed. Velocity might change, but the Federal Reserve can offset such changes with appropriate open market operations.

Second, consider the possible actions of holders of small deposits. Given deposit insurance, they have no reason to remove their funds unless they fear the bankruptcy of the deposit insurance agency. In this event, they may convert their deposits into currency that is held in safes or mattresses; or, as seems to have occurred during the Great Depression in the United States, gold could be hoarded, which could be a problem if gold were a part of the monetary base.[4] Unless the central bank took offsetting actions, there could be a decline in the money supply, such as occurred before and during the Great Depression. But, even if the Fed does not do its job, as post-federal deposit insurance experience indicates, there is little reason now to expect such conversions of fractional-reserve to one-hundred-percent-reserve money. Even though the Federal Savings and Loan Insurance Corporation (FSLIC) clearly is massively insolvent, there have been no runs on insured institutions.

The failure of very large banks

A similar analysis could be conducted for the effects of the failure of a large bank, such as the Continental Illinois Bank. Indeed, Continental Illinois did fail – its shareholders lost most of their investments and the officers lost their jobs (if not their pensions). But the bank went on. Had the interests of the depositors and other creditors not been protected, these persons would have lost some or all of their funds to the benefit of the FDIC. There also might have been runs on some other banks. Had this occurred, these banks would have had to sell assets and/or borrow funds in the market or from the Fed. Some might have been found to be or would have become insolvent. (However, the cost of fire sale losses could, and should, be reduced to minor proportions if the Fed operates effectively as the lender of last resort.) As a result, their shareholders would have lost wealth and, possibly, their officers would have lost their jobs. There would have been some disruption in financial and employment relationships, perhaps a costly disruption to those effected, but the financial system would not have collapsed.

It should be noted that the insolvency even of a bank that cannot be merged with another bank, sold, or transferred to creditors (such as a giant bank or one in a unit banking state that prohibits holding company acquisitions) need not be resolved by its dissolution. Instead, the FDIC could impose a modified trusteeship in which the claims of the shareholders are eliminated and a 'haircut' is applied to the claims of uninsured depositors and other creditors equal to the expected loss plus a cushion for estimation error. The balance of their funds could be freely transferred. From past experience, the amount impounded might be about 10 to 25 per cent of their claims, except in cases of fraud or massive mismanagement. The disruption in commerce, then, should not be very serious, even for those depositors who suffer losses.

Some concerned observers might argue that foreigners, nevertheless, would fear a collapse of the US banking system. The result might be a run from the dollar. But unless foreigners feared the failure of *all* banks, they simply would redeposit their funds in banks they considered to be safe. Even if foreign (or domestic) depositors distrusted all domestic banks, base money could not decline if the funds were redeposited in a foreign bank, since the funds would have to return to the US banking system by way of the central bank. It is only if foreigners feared that the Federal Reserve would not maintain the level of base money that there would be a change in the relative value of the dollar. In this event, though, the fault would lie in the failure of the central bank to act appropriately, rather than in the failure of the banking system.

Finally, some might argue that there would be a chilling psychological effect on bankers and investors. Bankers might become overly cautious in making loans, and investors might take fewer chances and/or demand higher expected rates of return. Against this possibility one should consider the expectation that bankers and investors would make excessively risky loans and investments on the assumption that no bank would be permitted to become insolvent. I believe that the recent record of banking operations and losses provides some evidence that excessive rather than insufficient risk-taking is the more important concern.

Thus systemic collapse is not a problem, assuming that the central bank does not sharply reduce base money. Before considering the effect on regulation to prevent the failure of individual financial institutions and/or to mitigate the effect of failures, I analyse the record of the central bank in the United States with respect to system stability.

The record of Federal Reserve regulation

It is not clear whether the Fed has, on balance, reduced or exacerbated financial instability. In its attempt to reduce what was believed to be a destabilizing inflation of stock market prices, the Fed allowed and possibly caused the money supply to decline in the early 1930s. As people converted their deposits to currency and gold, the Fed could have used open market operations and/or a reduction in reserve requirements to replace the high-powered money removed from the system. In part because it was legally constrained by its limited holdings of gold and the legal requirement for a gold reserve against Federal Reserve notes, and in part because it misjudged the situation and was more fearful of inflation than depression, it did not perform well during this period. Indeed, there is reason to believe that the Fed was, itself, the primary cause of the reduction in reserves as it constrained banks' borrowings from it (Friedman and Schwartz, 1963, ch. 7). In any event, the money supply declined by over a third from 1929 to 1933. As an important consequence, over 9,000 banks failed. (Another, perhaps as important, cause of the large number of failures was the banks' inadequate diversification, imposed by state-enacted anti-branching laws and other laws and regulations. This is discussed further below.)

Until the late 1970s, the US experienced a very low rate of financial institution failure, in part because the Federal Reserve did not allow or create large decreases in base money. Regulations limiting entry also played an important role by increasing the value of bank charters, and hence of bank capital, thereby increasing bankers' incentives towards avoiding risks that might reduce the value of their charters. However, the Fed's 1979 shift from a policy of stabilizing and restraining nominal interest rates to one of allowing these rates to increase as the supply of money increased may have resulted in an unexpectedly sharp increase in market rates. An alternative explanation is that inflation induced by the increase in the money supply in the mid-1970s resulted in an expected inflation-driven increase in nominal interest rates. In either event, as a result of the higher interest rates either caused or permitted by the Fed, the market (present) values of fixed-rate obligations decreased sharply.

Thrift institutions were particularly hard hit, because they specialized in fixed-rate mortgages while holding essentially short-term liabilities (Benston, 1985, ch. 1). Between January 1981 and August 1986 over 230 savings and loans associations (S&Ls) officially failed, 6.0 per cent of the number operating at the beginning of the period. Over 300 more were merged by arrangement of the authorities to avoid their being closed. As of 31 December 1988, 364 S&Ls were insolvent according to generally accepted accounting principles, 500 were insolvent when intangible assets are excluded, and the number probably would be greater were the net worth to be measured on a market value basis. These economically insolvent institutions have been permitted to remain open by the authorities. Once savings and loans' economic capital was made negative or close to negative, their managers and owners had considerable incentives to make very risky loans and other investments on the rational expectation that they would be saved and possibly enriched were the investments successful, and could be no worse off were the loans and other investments disasters. The consequences of these events are that the United States taxpayers are subject to a bill of at least $150 billion.

It is possible that unexpected nominal interest rates could have gone up as much in the absence of central bank regulation over banking and interest rates (although, I believe, not in the absence of central bank control over the money supply). However, the Fed did keep interest rates very stable during most of the years following the Great Depression, for which it has claimed credit. It therefore must accept blame when interest rates go up, particularly in the absence of some natural disaster. Interestingly, it may be that the interest-rate stability the Fed imposed before 1979 was responsible for thrift associations and legislators believing that the thrifts could safely hold duration-unbalanced portfolios, even though these were subject to interest-rate risk, because the risk was slight. Thus, the regulation of interest rates may have created the climate that led to the present debacle. (Other regulatory factors, though, also played a role, as is discussed below.)

PAYMENTS SYSTEM RISK

Another aspect of a system-wide collapse is the risk of a payments system failure. Former and present Federal Reserve officials (Chairman Volcker and NY Federal Reserve President Corrigan) have emphasized that banks are special because they offer payments services to consumers and have access to the payments system and the Federal Reserve's discount window. In this regard, these officials demand both too little and too much regulation. If it is true that the failure of a bank could disrupt the payments system, the Fed should deny access to the system by all banks that do not meet stringent equity tests. It has not done so. But, the Fed should not justify regulation by reference to the presumed 'special nature' of commercial banks. An institution that specializes in loans rather than in bonds, equities, real estate, or other sets or combinations of assets is not, for that reason, less likely to fail suddenly (which characterizes the risk to the payments system). Indeed, the history of sudden bank failures is dominated by the failure of lending institutions that were too highly specialized or were subjected to loan-related fraud by top management rather than by banks with other types of asset-value problems.

It should be noted, though, that the payments system in the United States is particularly prone to disruption because it is a monopoly of the central bank. As a result of this monopoly (discussed further below), which is a result of regulation that prevents banks from conducting nationwide depository activities, alternative systems have not developed. Nor has there been development of procedures that tend to impose costs on banks that operate opportunistically so as to subject the payments system to excessive risks. As Flannery (1988) points out, banks have incentives to set up remote disbursements and to use daylight overdrafts so as to borrow funds at zero interest rates from the Federal Reserve. While the Fed has attempted to prevent these moves, it is constrained by its monolithic position as the virtually sole operator of a nationwide payments system.

INDIVIDUAL BANK STABILITY

Regulation affects the stability of individual banks by (1) constraining banks from diversifying efficiently, (2) enhancing or reducing the profitability of regulated institutions, (3) limiting opportunities for and incentives of owners and managers towards risk-taking or avoidance, and (4) monitoring, supervising, and preventing fraud and grossly incompetent management. Each of these effects of regulation are discussed briefly.

DIVERSIFICATION

It is not possible for people to predict events perfectly. Hence, diversification of assets, liabilities, and operations generally is recognized as an important means of ensuring financial stability. Regulations in the United States imposed by both state and federal governments have tended to reduce the opportunities of banks to diversify; indeed, these regulations often encourage specialization that has resulted in considerable instability. Among these regulations are those limiting branching and limiting the assets and liabilities that banks can hold.

Regulations restricting branching

Among the more important government regulations constraining institutions from diversifying efficiently are restrictions on branching. Although it is not required by the US Constitution, the states have had sovereign rights over the chartering of banks with three major exceptions. One is the First and Second Banks of the United States, each of which received 20-year charters. Opposition by state-chartered banks, which objected to competition from the branches of the federally chartered banks and their restraints on state banks' note expansion, kept the federal charters from being renewed. The second is the establishment of the National Banking System in 1864. A tax on notes issued by state-chartered banks was designed to supplant the state banks as a means of supporting finance of the Civil War (national banks had to back their notes with US securities). The result, however, was the rapid development of deposit banking. When the National Banking Act was interpreted as limiting national banks to a single office, the power to restrict branching was ceded to the states. Only recently have groups of states (with some exceptions) permitted regional holding company banking. Third is the federal savings and loan system (the Federal Home Loan Bank Board, FHLBB, since 1985 the Office of Thrift Supervision), which can allow savings and loans (which now have depository powers similar to those allowed commercial banks) to branch without limit.

The insolvency of many banks that served agricultural and natural resource producers in the 1920s and the 1980s was due, in large measure, to restrictions on branching. Smaller banks in the United States tend to serve a geographically determined set of customers, who, as a consequence, often are relatively homogeneous with respect to economic impacts. Thus, banks located exclusively in single-industry towns, such as steel producers, or in rural areas tend to suffer and fail when these industries decline or fail. This occurred at a rate of about 600 banks a year in the 1920s. In the 1930s, over 90 per cent of the failures were banks with less than $2 million in assets; all except a few were unit banks.[5] Bank failures in the 1980s have been dominated by banks that served specific industries and regions that were hit by economic downturns.

Restrictions on assets and liabilities

Tax laws encouraged and regulations required thrifts (savings and loans and savings banks) to specialize in fixed-rate mortgages that were funded by short-term liabilities, thus subjecting them to interest rate risk. Before 1980, most thrifts were not permitted to make consumer or business loans except those related to real estate or education. Federally-chartered and most state-chartered thrifts were not permitted to make variable-rate mortgages until 1981. Rather, they were limited to fixed-interest-rate mortgages. Furthermore, long-term mortgages were encouraged by Federal Housing Administration (FHA) credit guarantees and the development of subsidized secondary markets by the Federal National Mortgage Association (Fanny Mae) and Government National Mortgage Association (Ginny Mae). When the Federal Home Loan Bank Board decided that variable-rate mortgages were *the* means for S&Ls to reduce interest-rate risk, investments in these assets was very strongly encouraged. To overcome consumer resistance, S&Ls offered below-market introductory ('teaser') rates. It is now becoming apparent that these mortgages have subjected S&Ls to considerable credit risk, as borrowers are unable to meet the higher payments required when the interest rates increase. Furthermore, earlier regulations which limited thrifts to making mortgages on properties within 100 miles or so of their home office subjected them to area-related credit risk. Banks' mortgage-making powers also were limited by regulation, which tended to concentrate these loans in the specialized S&Ls.

Other asset restrictions include direct investments, which are restricted to 3 per cent of assets for federally chartered S&Ls and, when permitted by states for S&Ls they charter, have been federally limited. Commercial banks are prohibited from holding corporate securities and direct investments.

The liabilities of financial institutions were constrained by ceilings on the interest that could be paid on deposits. Regulation Q limits on time deposit interest on deposits below $100,000 encouraged institutions to shift to larger deposits, which made them more subject to rapid outflows of funds. The prohibition of explicit interest payments on demand deposits also distorts bank portfolios, encouraging disintermediation and making funds more sensitive to interest-rate changes.

The consequences of these regulatory constraints have ranged from unfortunate to disastrous. As mentioned above, the interest-rate risk to which thrifts were subject became a reality in the 1980s, at a cost of over $150 billion. Commercial banks, which could hold much better duration-balanced portfolios, suffered relatively little from the sharp increase in nominal interest rates. It is not clear how much the statutory and regulatory restraints on commercial bank assets has increased their susceptibility to interest-rate and other risks.

REGULATED INSTITUTIONS' PROFITS

Interest rate controls have both enhanced and reduced the profits of regulated institutions. The prohibition of interest on demand deposits initially enhanced profits, because commercial banks had a monopoly on third-party transactions accounts. However, as the opportunity value of unregulated substitutes (e.g. cash management by corporate treasurers and cash management accounts offered by brokerage firms) increased with increases in nominal interest rates and improvements in technology, this advantage was eroded severely. Thus, it is doubtful that many business depositors do not receive explicit interest payments in the form of 'free' services, such as checking charges that depend on average balances and low- or no-fee credit-line commitments. Although banks may have been able to take advantage of the cost to depositors with smaller balances of switching their funds to investments that paid market rates of interest, since the early 1980s banks have been permitted to pay interest on consumer checking accounts. They now actively compete for these accounts.

Regulation Q ceilings on time deposits benefited institutions initially. But then the ceilings, when they became binding, served to divert competition to the provision of 'free' services and convenience. An important consequence was construction of local branch offices, where these were permitted. When disintermediation forced removal of interest rate ceilings, banks were left with higher operating costs that could not readily be reduced. Another related consequence appears to have been a fatal delay (for many thrifts, at least) in adapting their operations to changing market conditions. Thus, it does not appear that, on balance, Reg Q benefited depository institutions.

The Glass-Steagall Act (Banking Act of 1933) prohibition against most non-government security transactions and holdings appears to have been detrimental to banks' profits. On the other hand, constraints on entry into banking benefited banks. However, technology now has allowed securities broker-dealers to enter the bankers' markets, while Glass-Steagall still constrains bankers from competing with securities firms.

Banks also have been subject to a special and often onerous tax in the form of required non-interest-bearing reserves held at Federal Reserve banks. The forgone revenue that could have been earned on these assets was offset, somewhat, by 'free' services (e.g., security safekeeping, currency on demand, and check clearance) provided by the Federal Reserve banks. However, since 1980, the Fed has been required to charge for its services. Although the required reserve ratios have declined somewhat, the revenue forgone on funds deposited with the Fed represents a tax on deposit money. While this tax is now imposed on all banks within broad size groupings, it is not imposed on suppliers of alternatives to bank money. Hence, this form of regulation puts regulated banks at a competitive disadvantage.

Finally, regulation imposes considerable administrative costs on banks. They must provide regulators with many reports, be subject to supervisory inquiries and field examinations, and become expert in dealing with regulators' and legislators' demands. (Such demands include demonstrating that the banks' local communties have been well served, with the extent of service often defined by self-proclaimed community representatives.)

OPPORTUNITIES FOR AND INCENTIVES TOWARDS RISK-TAKING OR AVOIDANCE

Restraints on investments and activities as a means of reducing opportunities towards risk-taking

In the United States, commercial banks are not permitted to invest directly in equities or firms or undertake various activities, because these limitations are believed to constrain their ability to engage in excessive risk-taking. In particular, the Glass-Steagall Act prohibits commercial banks from offering full-service securities activities, particularly underwriting non-government obligations. Commercial banks also may not engage in many finance-related activities, such as offering or underwriting insurance, or engage in activities considered not to be directly related to banking.

The assumption underlying these limitations, with respect to stability concerns, that excessive risk-taking thereby will be limited, is not consistent either with reasoning or evidence. The activities permitted to banks allow them a very wide range of risk-taking alternatives. For example, commercial banks and thrifts can make loans with almost any degree of risk, taking payment in fees and points if they want to avoid recording a very high nominal rate of interest. They also can invest in long-term fixed-interest government bonds and gamble that interest rates will fall. Before 1990, thrifts could buy high yield/high risk (junk) bonds. Both types of institutions can purchase and sell futures and options contracts. Thrifts can make direct investments and equity-kicker loans. Long-term fixed-interest liabilities can be sold. Off-balance sheet guarantees can be sold. These (and other) products can be held and sold so as to give risk-seeking managers as much exposure as they want. It is doubtful that giving them additional powers (such as securities underwriting) could offer them opportunities to take risks that bring them beyond where they now want to be.

Empirical evidence supports the conclusions from reasoning. Most bank failures not due to fraud and self-dealing have been the result of loan losses and losses resulting from unexpected interest-rate changes. As noted above, these losses resulted in failures when banks were insufficiently diversified and capitalized to absorb the losses. Furthermore, the experience of the United States in the period before the Glass-Steagall Act separated commercial and investment banking, and the experience of countries, such as Germany, that permitted universal banking, shows that banks engaging in a wider-range of activities experienced very few failures.[6]

Additionally, empirical studies indicate that the removal of restraints on activities has not resulted in greater risk-taking, *ceteris paribus*. For example, in the early 1980s several states permitted state-chartered S&Ls to make direct investments (where the S&L owned the investment rather than only had an equity participation in a loan). I studied the record of these investments over the three years ended June 1984, and found little evidence of excessive risk-taking

(Benston, 1985, ch. II). Almost all S&Ls with more than small amounts of direct investments earned significantly positive net profits (often sufficiently great to offset losses on other operations), and virtually none of the failures were associated with direct investments. Higher net worth was associated with greater proportions of direct investments, indicating that direct investments increased net worth and/or that stronger S&Ls tended to make direct investments. The key variable with respect to failures and successful direct investments and growth appears to be 'net worth'. (I would feel more secure about drawing conclusions, however, if net worth were measured in terms of market rather than accounting values.) In addition, commercial (non-real-estate business) and consumer loans, which S&Ls also were permitted to make in 1982, were not associated with failures. An additional study of California S&Ls using stock market data indicated that higher risk was associated with direct investments only at S&Ls with low levels of capital (Benston and Koehn, 1989). Thus, these studies do not support the belief that failures were the consequence of deregulation of thrifts' investment powers.

However, it should be noted that deregulation of entry into banking has the effect of reducing bank capital. An important asset held by banks in markets in which entry is restrained is the present value of their franchises. As regulations on entry are relaxed or removed, competition increases and the value of bank charters declines. In recent years, though, deregulation of entry has not been the principal means by which competition has increased. Rather, advances in computer technology have reduced the cost of entry by non-chartered firms who can offer cost-effective alternatives to bank money. In fact, regulation of interest rates has encouraged entry by such firms as securities brokers and money market management funds. These firms have acquired billions of dollars in funds by offering consumers bank-like deposits (such as Merrill Lynch's money management accounts) paying market rates of interest. In the absence of ceilings on deposit interest, banks could have competed with these alternative suppliers. While the value of their franchises would have been eroded as a result of this competition, the reduction would have been smaller and more gradual.

Deposit insurance

Government-provided deposit insurance that is not priced according to risk introduces a very serious problem of moral hazard, which gives banks with insured deposits incentives towards excessive risk-taking. Moral hazard results from depositors having little reason to be concerned with how an insured institution operates (as long as the deposit insurance fund is considered to be adequate). In the United States, depositors with under $100,000 in an account are covered by federal insurance. After the FDIC bailed out *all* Continental Illinois' creditors in 1984, all depositors (and perhaps all creditors) of similarly large banks appear to have little reason to be concerned with losing their funds because of the way their banks were operated. Furthermore, as long as the authorities are slow in closing an insolvent institution, all uninsured depositors need to do is monitor rumours rather than analyse banks' portfolios and operations.

Deposit insurance also gives bank owners incentives to reduce the amount of their investment so as to maximize the return from underpriced insurance (the premiums on which are not related directly to the risks imposed on the insurance funds). As Orgler and Taggart's (1983) model (among others) and Peltzman's (1970) and Mingo's (1975) data show, bank capital in the United States declined as deposit insurance coverage increased.

It is important to recall that deposit insurance in the US was raised from $40,000 to $100,000 per account in 1980. It does not appear to be a coincidence that thrift and bank failures followed shortly thereafter. Deregulation of interest rates also played a role by allowing risk-seeking owners and managers to offer higher rates of interest on federally insured funds. Hence, they could obtain large amounts of funds, either through brokers or directly, which could be placed at risk according to the banking rule of riches – 'heads I win, tails the FDIC (or the FSLIC, which, before 1990, insured depositors in S&Ls) loses'.

However, although deposit insurance was increased for almost all banks, not all of them failed or engaged in excessive risk-taking. Thus, all the failures should not be blamed on the moral hazard of deposit insurance. Even with a complete pay-off of creditors by the FDIC and FSLIC, owners and managers (who, in mutual thrifts, really are the owners) lose their investments and positions. Deposit insurance, though, does remove the incentive for depositors to monitor risk-taking by banks and, with interest-rate controls removed, allows risk-seeking bankers to obtain the funds required for their gambles.

Capital

Given government-provided deposit insurance, the important constraint on excessive risk-taking is capital invested by bank owners,
including debentures that are subordinated to deposits. When bank
owners (or investors in any enterprise) have their assets at stake, they
have reason to balance expected returns and losses. The evidence on
failures supports this conclusion. In particular, the major determinant
of excessive risk-taking and failure among S&Ls is the level of
capital. Although the situation resulting in a loss to US taxpayers of
more than $150 billion has not been sufficiently analysed as yet, it
appears that the S&Ls taking high risks were those with very low or
negative capital (Benston, 1985; and Benston and Koehn, 1989).
The record with respect to commercial banks is not as clear, although
it appears likely that most failures would not have occurred if the
banks had had capital to asset ratios of the magnitudes common
before the advent of federal deposit insurance.

Regulation has played a conflicting role with respect to capital. As
noted above, restrictions on entry tend to increase capital by
increasing the bank's charter value. Also noted above are the effects
of high nominal interest rates and improvements in computer technology in eroding the legal entry restrictions. With respect to S&Ls, the
regulatory agency (the Federal Home Loan Bank Board) severely
reduced the capital required of the institutions they supervised as
these instututions' economic capital was sharply reduced because of
interest-rates increases. The agencies regulating commercial banks
also relaxed their requirements as banks' capital declined because of
losses on farm-related loans. Thus, the regulatory agencies acted to
reduce the legal necessity of their having to close banks with low
capital, which tended to increase the incentive for these banks to take
excessive risks.[7]

For reasons that are unclear to me, the regulatory authorities
also have not fully counted subordinated debenture as capital.
Subordinated debentures not only would protect the deposit insurance agencies from loss, as would equity capital, but also would be
preferable to equity capital, as long as the debentures could not be
redeemed by the bank for a period long enough for the authorities to
force its reorganization and recapitalization when it is in danger of
becoming insolvent. Marketable debentures would provide the authorities with market evidence of the risks taken by a bank, as these

would be reflected in the price at which the debentures traded. The ease or difficulty with which a bank refinanced its debentures as they came due also would provide the authorities with market evidence about risks. Hence, it would be desirable for subordinate debentures to have staggered maturities, such that a bank would be continually forced to go to the market for a reaffirmation of its risk profile (see Benston *et al.*, 1986, ch. 7, especially pp. 192–5, for a further elaboration).

It also should be recognized that subordinated debentures simply are explicitly uninsured time-dated deposits. Thus, the only cost to a bank of issuing such liabilities is that it is forced to give up some or all of the deposit insurance subsidy it receives from the government in the form of underpriced insurance by having to pay a rate for funds that includes the cost of risk.

MONITORING, SUPERVISING, AND PREVENTING FRAUD AND GROSSLY INCOMPETENT MANAGEMENT

Although higher capital requirements can considerably reduce the incentive for banks to take excessive risks, such requirements cannot entirely eliminate this incentive as long as government-provided deposit insurance is not priced to offset fully the benefits from risk-taking. Thus, a large part of the regulation and supervision of financial institutions is and should be related to preventing fraud and excessively risky behaviour. Aside from losses resulting from poor diversification and grossly inadequte capital, the largest losses incurred by the FDIC and the FSLIC are the result of fraudulent and self-serving acts that were not detected or stopped sufficiently quickly by the authorities. Because these government agencies bear much of the cost of fraud and gross mismanagement, they have a legitimate interest in preventing or reducing it.

Fraud is difficult to identify and stop because the perpetrators know that what they are doing is illegal. Hence, they have incentives and opportunities to alter the records to make detection difficult. Unfortunately, there are no simple regulatory answers. Almost any asset or liability is subject to a fraud, so that limiting a financial institution's operations to a specified subset will not be successful. Indeed, mechanical supervision by regulation often makes frauds easier to perpetrate. Rather, evaluation of the quality of management (including a complete check on the managers' personal records in fiduciary capacities), testing banks' internal control systems, and careful monitoring of institutions, particularly those with low levels of economic capital, are required. Gross mismanagement can be more easily discovered from analysis of financial statements and trends. While high rates of growth, overall and in particular areas, do not prove gross mismanagement, they often are associated with a breakdown of controls and with poor investment practices.

The record of the supervisory authorities in preventing fraud has not been very good. A review of bank examination reports in the United States indicates that, during the period January 1959 through April 1971, 59 per cent of the fifty-six banks that failed were rated as 'no problem' in the examination prior to failure (Benston, 1973, p. 43). Models that predict failures using only publicly available data have proven as good and often better than examiners in forecasting which banks would fail (see studies reviewed in Benston (1984)). The bank examiners who learned that Penn Square Bank of Oklahoma City was selling bad loans to Continental Bank did not inform the supervisory authorities responsible for Continental of that fact. The FHLBB failed to close down or seriously restrain S&Ls for years after they became economically insolvent. Indeed, as noted above, the FHLBB changed the accounting rules to allow S&Ls to defer losses and reduce the amount of capital required for legal solvency. Allowing these insolvent or close-to-insolvent institutions to continue and greatly to expand their operations has apparently lead to massive losses.

SUMMARY AND CONCLUSIONS

Banking system failure

Regulation of the money supply is sufficient but perhaps not necessary for systemic financial stability. The central bank could offset runs to currency and other declines in base money so as to prevent the banking system from experiencing a liquidity crisis. This conclusion is strengthened by the presence of credible deposit insurance and holds for the failure of very large as well as smaller banks. As lender of last resort, the central bank also can provide a solvent bank with resources to keep it from incurring 'fire sale' losses. There is no reason to believe that regulation of bank assets, liabilities, and activities has any role to play in this process.

However, the record in the United States indicates that the Federal

Reserve has not done its job well. The money supply was allowed to decline and banks were allowed to fail during the Great Depression. The Fed also may be responsible for the greatest loss of resources in US (perhaps, world) banking history – the $150 billion or more losses incurred by thrifts (S&Ls and savings banks). Had the Fed not allowed the money supply to grow during the 1970s and/or not permitted interest rates to increase sharply in 1979–80, the thrifts (which were well known to be subject to interest-rate risk) would not have experienced massive capital losses.

Furthermore, evidence from the United Kingdom (White, 1984) indicates that a banking system without a central bank (Scotland) appears to have been considerably more stable than one with a central bank (England). I am not aware of a similar careful comparative study of the stability of the United States' financial system before and after the establishment of the Federal Reserve in 1913. However, a casual review of the cost of inflations and depressions before and after that date does not seem to support the belief that the Fed represents a net improvement.

Payments system risk similarly is exacerbated by the position of the Fed as a monopoly supplier of nationwide payments facilities. This position is the consequence of a banking regulation that prevents nationwide branching in the United States.

Individual bank stability

Regulation has played an important role in the United States for making banking significantly less stable by constraining banks from diversifying efficiently. The principal regulation in this regard is the restriction on branching, both within states and nationwide. It seems clear that branching restrictions are responsible for most of the commercial bank failures during the 1920s and 1930s, and also in the 1980s. Laws and regulations that subsidized and prevented thrift associations from diversifying their portfolios so as to eliminate largely interest-rate risk are responsible initially for the massive loss that now must be paid by US taxpayers. Other laws (in particular, the Glass-Steagall Act separation of commercial and investment banking) restrict banks from efficiently diversifying their assets.

The profitability of regulated institutions also is reduced by regulation. As noted, the Glass-Steagall Act prevents some banks from serving their customers effectively. Laws which prevented thrifts from offering checking accounts, business loans, and consumer cash loans similarly restrained their profitabilty. Required reserves represent a tax on bank money paid only by regulated depositories. Supervision, examinations, and 'consumer protection' regulations impose considerable administrative costs on banks.

Opportunities for and incentives of owners and managers towards risk-taking or avoidance have been affected by regulations restricting the assets banks can hold and services they can provide, by deposit insurance, and by capital requirements. Because banks can take almost any level of desired risk, it is unlikely that restraints on their activities will be effective in reducing risk-taking. In fact, evidence supports this conclusion. Deposit insurance, on the other hand, gives banks incentives to take risks, which they have done. Capital requirements (preferably including subordinated debentures), though, are an effective means of restraining risk-taking. Given the expectation that deposit insurance serves to reduce banks' desired levels of capital, imposition of capital requirements is necessary (see Benston and Kaufman, 1988, for a specific proposal).

Fraud and grossly incompetent management have been important causes of bank failures. Hence, monitoring, supervising, and examining banks appear to be desirable aspects of regulation. It does not appear, though, that this aspect of regulation has been conducted as well as it could.

Finally, it should be noted that the US experience with relatively unregulated banking (the 'free banking era' – 1837 through 1865) has been found to be more stable than was previously assumed. Rockoff (1974) and Rolnick and Weber (1983) report that while bad banking practices had some effect, the principal cause of instability and failure was state-imposed requirements. In particular, the states required banks to hold their state bonds as security for bank notes, which provided these banks with undiversified portfolios. As Rolnick and Weber (1984) show, exogenous declines in the value of state bonds often were disastrous.[8]

In sum, I must conclude that regulation has overwhelmingly tended to make the banking system and individual banks less stable. Central bank control of the money supply and of supervisory monitoring of bank activities to reduce fraud and gross mismanagement are notable possible exceptions. Given the existence of governmentally-provided deposit insurance (*de facto* or *de jure*), capital requirements are necessary. Other regulations of banks' portfolios and activities have been detrimental to the goal of enhancing financial stability.

BANKING REGULATION FOR REASONS OTHER THAN PROMOTING FINANCIAL STABILITY

Enhancing financial stability cannot be the primary reason for regulating banks, as bank regulation predated concerns for financial stability by hundreds of years. Banks have been regulated almost since the dawn of national commerce. Furthermore, as the analysis presented above indicates, regulation has tended to exacerbate rather than promote stability.

The principal reason for bank regulation, I believe, is taxation by government authorities of seigniorage.[9] Because governments tended to debase the money they produced to maximize siegniorage in the short run, bank-produced money often came to dominate state-produced money. Those in power could increase the tax they could impose on bank money (for example, via low- or no-interest-rate loans to the state and to powerful persons) by limiting entry into banking, thereby maximizing banks' profits and the amount that could be taxed. Hence, bank regulation was almost exclusively limited to restrictions on entry. In the United States, taxation often took the form of sale of bank charters (via contributions to legislators) and requiring banks to back their notes with government securities. At present, non-interest-bearing required reserves now serve the purpose. If this still is a reason for regulating banks, the tax would be enhanced by reducing restrictions on entry and assets, as this would increase the public demand for reservable bank money.

Enhancement of productive efficiency is mentioned as another reason for regulation. If there were significant economies of scale, these might be achieved by restricting the number of banks that could operate. However, empirical studies do not find such economies, except perhaps among giant banks.[10] Furthermore, banking is a worldwide market, in which entry by giant banks into national markets cannot be restrained successfully.

A contemporary reason for regulating banks is support of ethical precepts. These include requirements that banks provide 'life line' services to the poor. Checking services often are mentioned, as are mortgage loans even though those who can own houses should not be classified as 'poor'. While it is unlikely that a lack of banking services ranks high in poor persons' lists of deprivations, improvements are more likely to be achieved by increasing competition among suppliers of banking services and by direct subsidization of the poor. For this purpose, a removal of regulation would be desirable. Importantly, it should be recognized that regulations restricting the amount of interest that could be paid to depositors with smaller account balances, even when these reduce costs to home-buyers (which, in fact, does not appear to be the case), are detrimental to the interests of the less wealthy.

Some of the more administratively expensive regulations imposed on banks in the United States are those presumably designed to prevent invidious discrimination against persons and to require banks to lend to borrowers in their local market areas. The record on invidious discrimination by banks against such persons as blacks and women has been studied. While anecdotal evidence indicates such discrimination in the past, formal studies (reviewed in Benston, 1983) do not support such allegations. The evidence on banks' discrimination against local borrowers (often called 'redlining') does not support the allegations. Rather, this form of regulation appears to be costly without a redeeming social benefit.

Finally and, I suggest, most importantly, regulation is imposed to redistribute wealth to those with political power. These regulations include those that restrict entry into markets or confer subsidies. Restrictions on branching enhance the market power and the sale price of banks established in markets. The separation of commercial and investment banking protects the markets of securities underwriters and brokers. Prohibitions against banks selling insurance, travel services, and other products protect the markets of current suppliers of those products. Limiting the corporate ownership of banks to a sub-set of banking firms protects the positions of bank managers. Thus, whatever its benefits to some parties, bank regulation tends to disadvantage consumers.

Notes

1. The successful prior campaign of the Secretary of the Treasury to stabilize interest rates set up the panic, for two reasons. First, banks were induced to hold lower levels of reserves. Second, the goal was accomplished with a stabilization fund of gold acquired with a Treasury-provided import subsidy. The Bank of England retaliated in 1906 by raising its discount rate and by asking British banks not to renew American finance bills (Cleveland and Huertas, 1985, ch. 3, pp. 27–8).
2. The failure of individual banks also affects the lives of their employees and owners, which has some macroeconomic effect. However, it should

be noted that the failure of banks is less disrupting to employees than is the failure of most other enterprises, as banks are relatively homogeneous producers. Hence, most bank employees have industry- rather than firm-specific skills and are less disadvantaged when their employer fails than are the employees of many other firms.

3. The citizens of the defaulting countries also are likely to experience costs, such as severe restrictions on credit, restraints on trade, and seizure of goods. The expectation of these and other costs may explain the fact that the debtor countries have not, as yet, defaulted on their obligations.
4. See Wigmore (1987) for some evidence.
5. See White (1983) for an excellent analysis and Benston (1973) for data on failures in the 1920s and early 1930s.
6. See White (1986) and Benston (1990, chs 3 and 10) for evidence supporting this conclusion.
7. See Kane (1988) for an analysis of why regulators act in this manner.
8. See Rockoff (1986) and Rolnick and Weber (1986) for valuable discussions and references to additional literature.
9. A fairly complete list of other reasons are explored at length in Benston, 1983.
10. See Benston, Hanweck, and Humphrey (1982) and Hunter and Timme (1986).

References

BENSTON, GEORGE J. (1973) 'Bank Examination', *The Bulletin* (now Monograph Series in Finance and Economics), New York University Institute of Finance, Nos. 89–90 (May).

BENSTON, GEORGE J. (1983) 'Federal Regulation of Banking: Analysis and Policy Recommendations', *Journal of Bank Research*, 13 (Winter), pp. 216–44. Also reprinted, with small changes in George G. Kaufman and Roger C. Kormendi (eds) (1986) *Deregulating Financial Services: Public Policy in Flux* (NY: Ballinger Press), as 'Federal Regulation of Banking: Historical Overview', pp. 1–47.

BENSTON, GEORGE J. (1984) 'Financial Disclosure and Bank Failures', *Economic Review* Federal Reserve Bank of Atlanta (March), pp. 5–12.

BENSTON, GEORGE J. (1985) *An Analysis of the Causes of Savings and Loan Association Failures*, Monograph Series in Finance and Economics No. 4/5 (New York: Salomon Brothers Center for the Study of Financial Institutions, New York University).

BENSTON, GEORGE J. (1990). *The Separation of Commercial and Investment Banking: The Glass-Steagall Act Revisited and Reconsidered* (London: Macmillan; New York: Oxford University Press).

BENSTON, GEORGE J., ROBERT A. EISENBEIS, PAUL M. HORVITZ, EDWARD J. KANE, and GEORGE G. KAUFMAN (1986) *Perspectives on Safe & Sound Banking, Past, Present and Future.* (Cambridge, MA: MIT Press).

BENSTON, GEORGE J., GERALD A. HANWECK and DAVID B. HUMPHREY (1982) 'Scale Economies in Banking: A Restructuring and Reassessment', *Journal of Money, Credit, and Banking*, XIV (November, part 1), pp. 435–56.

BENSTON, GEORGE J. and GEORGE G. KAUFMAN (1988) *Risk and Solvency Regulation of Depository Institutions: Past Policies and Current Options*, Monograph Series in Finance and Economics (New York: Salomon Brothers Center, New York University).

BENSTON, GEORGE J. and MICHAEL F. KOEHN (1989) 'Capital Dissipation, Deregulation, and the Insolvency of Thrifts', working paper No. 89–02, Shadow Financial Regulatory Committee (revised June 1989).

BERNANKE, BEN S. (1983) 'Non-monetary Effects of the Financial Crisis in the Propagation of the Great Depression', *American Economic Review*, 73 (June), pp. 257–76.

CLEVELAND, HAROLD VAN B. and THOMAS F. HUERTAS (1985) *Citibank, 1912–1970* (Cambridge, MA: Harvard University Press).

FLANNERY, MARK J. (1988) 'Payments System Risk and Public Policy', in *Restructuring Banking and Financial Services in America*, William S. Haraf and Rose Marie Kushmeider (eds) (Washington, DC: American Enterprise Institute for Public Policy Research), pp. 261–87.

FRIEDMAN, MILTON and ANNA J. SCHWARTZ (1963) *A Monetary History of the United States*, National Bureau of Economic Research (Princeton, NJ: Princeton University Press).

HUNTER, WILLIAM C. and STEPHEN G. TIMME (1986) 'Technical Change, Oranizational Form and the Structure of Banking Production', *Journal of Money, Credit and Banking*, 18 (2), pp. 162–6.

KANE, EDWARD J. (1988) 'How Market Forces Influence the Structure of Financial Regulation', in *Restructuring Banking and Financial Services in America*, William S. Haraf and Rose Marie Kushmeider (eds) (Washington, DC: American Enterprise Institute for Public Policy Research), pp. 343–82.

MINGO, JOHN J. (1975) 'Regulatory Influence on Bank Capital Investment', *Journal of Finance*, 30 (September), pp. 1111–21.

ORGLER, YAIR E. and ROBERT A. TAGGART, JR. (1983) 'Regulatory Influence on Bank Capital Investment', *Journal of Money, Credit and Banking*, 15 (May), pp. 212–21.

PELTZMAN, SAMUEL (1970) 'Capital Investment in Commercial Banking and Its Relationship to Portfolio Regulation', *Journal of Political Economy*, 78 (January), pp. 1–26.

ROCKOFF, HUGH (1974) 'The Free Banking Era: A Re-Examination', *Journal of Money, Credit and Banking*, 6 (May), pp. 141–67.

ROCKOFF, HUGH (1986) 'Institutional Requirements for Stable Free Banking', *Cato Journal*, 6 (Fall), pp. 617–34.

ROLNICK, ARTHUR J. and WARREN E. WEBER (1983) 'New Evidence on the Free Banking Era', *American Economic Review*, 73 (December), pp. 1080–91.

ROLNICK, ARTHUR J. and WARREN E. WEBER (1986) 'Inherent Instability in Banking: The Free Banking Experience', *Cato Journal*, 5 (Winter), pp. 877–90.

SCHWARTZ, ANNA J. (1986) 'Real and Pseudo-financial Crises', in Forest Capie and Geoffrey E. Wood (eds) *Financial Crises and the World Banking System* (London: Macmillan), pp. 11–31.

WHITE, EUGENE N. (1983) *The Regulation and Reform of the American Banking System* (Princeton, NJ: Princeton University Press).

WHITE, EUGENE N. (1986) 'Before the Glass-Steagall Act: Analysis of the Investment Banking Activities of National Banks', *Explorations in Economic History*, 23, pp. 33–55.

WHITE, LAWRENCE H. (1984) *Free Banking in Britain: Theory, Experience, and Debate, 1800–1845* (Cambridge: Cambridge University Press).

WIGMORE, BARRIE A. (1987) 'Was the Bank Holiday of 1933 a Run on the Dollar Rather than on the Banks?', *Journal of Economic History* (September), pp. 739–55.

Comment on Chapter 6

Michael D. Bordo

George Benston provides some evidence from the US experience to answer the question whether regulation of the banking system promoted stability.

According to Benston, regulation is supposed to promote stability in two ways: (a) by improving the stability of the banking system; (b) by enhancing the stability of individual banks. Stability of the banking system would be provided by some monetary authority serving as a lender of last resort and providing high powered money to the monetary system in the face of a banking panic. Also through judicious use of the tools of monetary policy it would provide a stable monetary environment.

Regulation affects the stability of individual banks by: (a) influencing their ability to efficiently diversify their portfolios; (b) by enhancing or reducing their profits; (c) by limiting the risk taking opportunities of bank managers; (d) by monitoring, supervising and preventing fraud and grossly incompetent management.

Although effective provision of a LLR presumably obviates the need for any regulation of individual banks to preserve macro stability (Goodfriend and King 1988), an environment not characterized by frequent bank failures and runs would lessen the likelihood of the LLR making a mistake.

Benston's survey of the American experience ends up with the conclusion that regulation has led to a less rather than more stable financial system. With respect to system-wide regulation, monetary authorities (the Treasury) did not prevent major panics on numerous occasions in the nineteenth century, and the Federal Reserve System, established in 1914 primarily for this purpose, failed miserably during the Great Depression 1930–33. Also in the 1970s and 1980s Fed induced rapid inflation and then disinflation are credited, in combination with individual bank regulations, with producing the current spate of bank and S and L failures.

With respect to individual banks, instability was enhanced by regulation in several ways: by laws preventing portfolio diversification through branching; by laws restricting the assets banks can hold in their portfolios; by laws separating commercial from investment

233

banking (Glass-Steagall); by interest rate ceilings; by inadequate supervision; by insufficient capital requirements; and finally by the provision of government provided deposit insurance.

The last regulation, designed to prevent bank panics from starting in the first place, enhanced stability for forty years. That it has recently backfired, according to Benston, may have something to do with raising coverage from $40 000 to $100 000 and hence removing any effective oversight from uninsured depositors.

The conclusion that comes from this survey is that regulation failed to improve the stability of the financial system in the US. Three questions come to mind: (1) Was the US experience unique among advanced countries or have regulations designed to enhance stability had similar effects elsewhere?; (2) If the US experience was unique what made it so special?; (3) Are there regulations which can improve stability?

History and current experience tells us that most other countries have had less financial instability than the U.S. Without getting into details of other countries regulations and experience this suggests that the US among other countries is unique.

An answer to the question as to why the US experience is so unique requires going back into history. The US financial system, though spawned from origins similar to the British system evolved differently. The primary reason for this was a strong fear of concentration of economic power in individual banks and the banking system. This motive was responsible for many of the features of the US banking system in the nineteenth century including: the absence of a central bank (with two brief exceptions and in each case the central bank was dissolved because of fear of its power); the absence of interstate banking; unit banking and the dual (federal, state) banking system. The resultant fragmented system was characterized by large numbers of undercapitalized, undiversified financial institutions.

The Fed was established to overcome the problems of seasonal and cyclical inelasticity of high powered money which characterized the nineteenth century system and to serve as lender of last resort (LLR) in the face of banking panics. The Fed succeeded in the first goal in its first two decades but not in the second. The disaster of the massive bank failures in the 1930s involved two elements: the failure of the Fed to use its policy tools to expand the money supply in the face of banking panics and the legacy of a weak dual unit banking system unable to withstand the shocks buffeting the world economy.

In response to the bank failures of the 1930s, the federal government set up a safety net designed to prevent a recurrence. Key elements of the safety net include: the Fed to act as LLR; federal deposit insurance; and regulations on bank structure, bank assets and interest rates to prevent risky behaviour.

As Schwartz (1988) has pointed out, as long as the price level remained stable in the ensuing forty years the system worked. However in the face of inflation in the 1970s, disinflation in the 1980s and partial deregulation (especially the removal of interest rate ceilings), many financial institutions (especially S and L's with mismatched portfolios) failed. The problem has been exacerbated by the moral hazard induced by inapropriately priced and overly extended deposit insurance and by the Fed's policy of bailing out insolvent banks.

What emerges from this sad tale is not that regulation *per se* has created the current mess in the US but that the type and mix of regulation is the culprit.

As Benston cogently points out here, and in many other places, a package encompassing features which have worked successfully elsewhere would go a long way in producing a stable financial system. This package would include: no restrictions on banks' abilities to diversify their portfolios; adequate capital requirements; market value accounting; enhanced supervision against fraud and gross mismanagement; market priced deposit insurance with co-insurance; and above all a central bank acting as a proper LLR and providing a stable monetary environment.

References

GOODFRIEND, M. and R. A. KING, (1988) 'Financial Deregulation, Monetary Policy, and Central Banking' in W. S. Haraf and R. M. Kushmeider (eds) *Restructuring Banking and Financial Services in America* (Washington D.C., American Enterprise Institution).
SCHWARTZ, A. J. (1988) 'Financial Stability and the Federal Safety Net' in W. S. Haraf and R. M. Kushmeider (eds) *Restructuring Banking and Financial Services in America* (Washington D.C., American Enterprise Institution).

Comment on Chapter 6

Sir Peter Middleton

I found this paper quite fascinating. Inevitably, from my background, I look at things in terms of the pressures one sees for regulation. In this area, they seem to be overwhelming. If regulation of banks is destabilizing or generally undesirable, the public and legislators do not perceive it that way. So I ask myself, does Benston's paper – which certainly shows some dreadful consequences from regulation as it has operated in practice in the USA – amount to a criticism of banking regulation in general, or is it just a criticism of bad regulation?

FAILURES OF REGULATION IN THE US

Benston argues that, in the United States, banking regulation has tended to make the banking system and individual banks less rather than more stable. The main examples of instances where regulation has actually reduced stability are restrictions on branching; deposit insurance; and regulations on thrifts, which effectively place them in positions of high interest rate risk. He is also critical of the ways in which the US authorities have set and monitored capital requirements during the 1980s. In each of these cases, the US regulatory approach has been somewhat different from that in the UK and in other European countries, and the United States may have something to learn in studyng the experience of others.

BRANCHING RESTRICTIONS

Branching restrictions are very much an American peculiarity. As Benston observes, the individual states have traditionally had sovereign rights over the chartering of banks, with very limited exceptions. If branching restrictions are regarded as making a negative contribution towards banking stability, yet the states are unwilling to cede their rights to charter banks to a federal authority, then one way forward might be to follow the EC example. Under the second banking directive the individual member states will continue to license and regulate their own banks. But any bank so licensed will be free to operate in any other member state, without having to apply afresh for a further licence.

DEPOSIT INSURANCE

Deposit insurance poses a serious problem of moral hazard, which Benston believes has been an important contributory factor in encouraging excessive risk-taking by US banks. But he accepts the case for government-provided deposit insurance as a means of preventing individual bank failures turning into disastrous runs on other banks which would otherwise be perfectly solvent, and generally leading to systemic failure. It may be worth considering the merits of the UK bank deposit insurance scheme, whereby only 75 per cent of deposits are insured – thus ensuring that the depositor bears some residual risk. The ceiling in the UK scheme, at £20,000, is also well below that in the US – $100,000. This is admittedly a compromise between wishing to avoid the moral hazard involved with 100 per cent deposit insurance and the strong public demand for some sort of assurance scheme to protect depositors.

CAPITAL ADEQUACY REQUIREMENTS

Given government-provided deposit insurance, capital requirements are, as Benston observes, an essential tool for preventing individual banks from indulging in excessive risk. Benston is very critical of the behaviour of the United States authorities on capital requirements during the 1980s. In particular, he cites their failure to 'fully count subordinated debenture as capital'; and he alleges that the regulators have reacted to situations in which a number of banks were getting into difficulties with capital requirements by reducing those requirements – whereas they should have been enforcing them. The implication is that the US authorities were downgrading capital requirements just at the time when their enforcement was becoming more important, because of the need to prevent bank failures through excessive risk-taking.

If true, then this is both surprising and frightening. The rest of the world has been paying rather more attention of late to capital requirements than it had previously done. Indeed, the BIS has been responsible for developing the risk asset ratio system as the norm for capital adequacy monitoring throughout the developed world. The US Federal Reserve took an active part in the consultations between bank supervisors.

THRIFTS

It is by now generally accepted that regulation of the thrifts in the United States has seen some serious mistakes. In particular, a system which effectively set up a group of institutions with fixed-rate assets but floating-rate liabilities was creating a massive exposure to interest-rate risk. And the moral hazard implications of 100 per cent insurance encouraged them to continue to lend when existing loans were at a discount.

Here again, other countries do things differently. In the UK, mortgage lending – whether by the building societies or by other financial institutions, including the banks – has generally been at variable (administered) rates. Indeed, the building societies only consider it prudent to do fixed-rate lending to the extent that it is financed by fixed-rate funding. They also hedge against prepayment. In some other European countries, e.g. West Germany and Denmark, fixed-rate mortgage lending is the norm. But in these countries mortgages are normally securitized. The United States has now gone down both these routes, with adjustable rate mortgages now permitted and widespread, and a fairly rapid development of securization, backed by government agencies (Freddie Mac and Fannie Mae).

THRIFTS AND MONETARY POLICY

As Benston points out, the thrifts might have been able to manage despite their fixed-rate assets if interest rates had not risen sharply in the 1980s. Does that mean that the Fed was wrong to tighten monetary policy to the extent that it did – as the paper half suggests? The operation of monetary policy obviously has to take into account the current circumstances of the financial system – and the wider world. But the control of inflation is of such overwhelming importance that monetary policy cannot in the end be hamstrung by worries about the financial system. Any constraints should operate the other way round; financial regulations must be designed to promote the stability of the system in such a way that monetary policy is still free to do its job. That is the real lesson of the crisis of the thrifts.

BENSTON'S ACCOUNT – NOT AN ARGUMENT FOR UNREGULATED BANKING

Benston's indictment of US bank regulation thus amounts primarily to a critique of how the US regulators have carried out their job. Unless all regulation is bound to be bad regulation, this does not constitute a case against banking regulation in principle, and in favour of unregulated banking.

Benston accepts the need for a central bank in order to enhance the stability of the banking system through control of the money supply and its function as lender of last resort. He also accepts the necessity of some regulation of individual banks in the form of capital requirements – and of monitoring and supervision aimed at preventing fraud and grossly incompetent management.

This is the nub of the case for banking regulation. Although the central bank stands ready to act as lender of last resort, it is better that the last resort never be reached. This is where good banking regulation comes in.

The regulator's functions in my view are twofold: to protect investors from 'fraud and grossly incompetent management', and to protect the banking system from the knock-on effects of individual bank failures. It is clearly possible to over-regulate. There is generally no need for bank regulators to operate direct controls on interest rates and on lending, though many have done so at times. But there is a need to monitor the adequacy of banks' capital backing, in the light of their liabilities and the riskiness of their assets; and moral hazard notwithstanding, it may be desirable to provide some kind of deposit insurance for small investors – for systemic reasons (to prevent bank runs) as much as for individual investor protection.

When individual banks fail, otherwise healthy banks can catch a cold. The central bank then administers a cure, through acting as lender of last resort. But, as we all know, prevention is better than cure. Prevention is what good banking regulation is all about.

Index